Macmillan's Magazine, 1859–1907

T0373667

Macmillan's Magazine, 1859–1907

'No Flippancy or Abuse Allowed'

GEORGE J. WORTH

Routledge
Taylor & Francis Group

LONDON AND NEW YORK

First published 2003 by Ashgate Publishing

2 Park Square, Milton Park, Abingdon, Oxfordshire OX14 4RN
52 Vanderbilt Avenue, New York, NY 10017

Routledge is an imprint of the Taylor & Francis Group, an informa business

First issued in paperback 2019

British Library Cataloguing in Publication Data

Worth, George J. (George John), 1929–
    Macmillan's Magazine, 1859–1907: 'no flippancy or abuse
    allowed'. – (The nineteenth century series)
    1. Macmillan's magazine 2. English literature–19th century
    –History and criticism 3. English literature–periodicals
    –History
    I. Title
    820.9'008

Library of Congress Cataloging-in-Publication Data

Worth, George J. (George John), 1929–
    Macmillan's magazine, 1859–1907: no flippancy or abuse allowed/George J.
    Worth.
        p. cm. – (The Nineteenth century series)
    Includes bibliographical references.
    1. Macmillan's magazine. I. Macmillan's magazine. II. Title. III. Nineteenth
    century
    (Aldershot, England).
    PN5130. M33 W67 2002
    052'0942' 09034–dc21   2002018516

ISBN 13: 978-0-7546-0986-5 (hbk)
ISBN 13: 978-0-367-88775-9 (pbk)

Contents

The Nineteenth Century Series
General Editors' Preface

The aim of the series is to reflect, develop and extend the great burgeoning of interest in the nineteenth century that has been an inevitable feature of recent years, as that former epoch has come more sharply into focus as a locus for our understanding not only of the past but of the contours of our modernity. It centres primarily upon major authors and subjects within Romantic and Victorian literature. It also includes studies of other British writers and issues, where these are matters of current debate: for example, biography and autobiography, journalism, periodical literature, travel writing, book production, gender, non-canonical writing. We are dedicated principally to publishing original monographs and symposia; our policy is to embrace a broad scope in chronology, approach and range of concern, and both to recognize and cut innovatively across such parameters as those suggested by the designations 'Romantic' and 'Victorian'. We welcome new ideas and theories, while valuing traditional scholarship. It is hoped that the world which predates yet so forcibly predicts and engages our own will emerge in parts, in the wider sweep, and in the lively streams of disputation and change that are so manifest an aspect of its intellectual, artistic and social landscape.

Vincent Newey
Joanne Shattock

University of Leicester

Introduction

My acquaintance with *Macmillan's Magazine* began during the early 1980s while I was writing a book on Thomas Hughes, one of its founders, who produced some of his best work for it. I soon became intrigued by what I was learning inductively about the *Magazine* through that project: about its contributors' responsiveness to significant public events during an exciting and often troubled age, their sense of mission, their intellectual curiosity, and (in most cases) their literary expertise – all pervaded by vintage mid-Victorian earnestness. In quest of further information about *Macmillan's*, I turned for help to the first volume of the *Wellesley Index to Victorian Periodicals* (1966), where I found – in addition to a long list identifying most of those who contributed fictional and nonfictional prose to *Macmillan's* between November 1859 and December 1900 – the flat statement that 'There is no study of *Macmillan's Magazine*.' This was corroborated in the next standard source I consulted, the MLA-sponsored *Victorian Periodicals: A Guide to Research* (1978): in their chapter on 'Histories and Studies of Individual Periodicals', Lionel Madden and Diana Dixon included *Macmillan's* in a roster of significant nineteenth-century magazines that 'have received no detailed study'.

It soon occurred to me that I might be the one to undertake such a study, envisioning it in those early days as a thoroughgoing history of the *Magazine* from its beginning to its end in 1907. However, I was dissuaded from this grandiose idea by the realization that that kind of book, devoted to that kind of subject, would be unwriteable in what was left of my scholarly lifetime; if by some miracle written, it would, I feared, also be quite unreadable. Moreover, as time passed, work on *Macmillan's* was published by other hands – work that I saw little sense in duplicating.

Even before 1966, as the *Macmillan's* section of the *Wellesley Index* pointed out, the *Magazine* had been discussed in Charles Morgan's *The House of Macmillan, 1843–1943* (1944), in Charles L. Graves's *Life and Letters of Alexander Macmillan* (1910) and *Life & Letters of Sir George Grove* (1903), and in the second volume of F.W. Hirst's *Early Life & Letters of John Morley* (1927), as well as in a 1910 *Notes and Queries* piece by John Collins Francis. There is valuable material in each of these texts, and I draw on all of them in the body of this book, but their treatments of *Macmillan's Magazine* are necessarily brief and scrappy. More useful is a historical and evaluative survey by A.J. Gurr in the *Review of English Literature* (1965), not mentioned in the first volume of

Wellesley, which presumably went to press before Gurr's article came out. However it too is short, and a similar, later effort, Keith Wilson's essay on *Macmillan's* in the *Victorian and Edwardian Age* volume of *British Literary Magazines*, edited by Alvin Sullivan (1983), is even shorter.

Two other scholars, Alan Hertz and Ann Parry, were working on *Macmillan's* at about the time that I got started. Hertz's major contribution, an excellent 1982 Cambridge dissertation called '*Macmillan's Magazine* under David Masson: 1859–1867', has unfortunately not been published; two offshoots of his research – '*Macmillan's Magazine*: A New Source and Further Attributions' (1981) and 'The Broad Church Militant and Newman's Humiliation of Charles Kingsley' (1986) – are more readily available, but quite restricted in their scope. Ann Parry's three publications dealing with *Macmillan's* – 'The Grove Years 1868–1883: A "New Look" for *Macmillan's Magazine*?' (1986); 'The Intellectuals and the Middle Class Periodical Press: Theory, Method, and Case Study' (1988) and 'Theories of Formation: *Macmillan's Magazine*: Vol. 1, November 1859[.] Monthly. 1/0'(1993) – are also narrowly focused as well as methodologically questionable.

In addition to the work done by Hertz and Parry on *Macmillan's Magazine*, the 1980s also witnessed the beginning of a new interest in Victorian periodicals generally. Among the publications dating from the last two decades of the twentieth century that I found most useful were *The Victorian Press: Samples and Soundings*, edited by Joanne Shattock and Michael Wolff (1982), especially for Walter Houghton's 'Periodical Literature and the Articulate Classes'; the special issue on theory of the *Victorian Periodicals Review* (Fall 1989), especially for Margaret Beetham's 'Open and Closed: The Periodical as a Publishing Genre' and Lyn Pykett's 'Reading the Periodical Press: Text and Context', both of which reappeared the following year in *Investigating Periodical Journalism*, edited by Laurel Brake, Aled Jones and Lionel Madden (the former essay thoroughly revised as 'Towards a Theory of the Periodical as a Publishing Genre'); *Serials and Their Readers*, edited by Robin Myers and Michael Harris (1993), especially for Laurel Brake's '"The Trepidation of the Spheres": The Serial and the Book in the 19th Century'; Brake's *Subjugated Knowledges: Journalism, Gender and Literature in the Nineteenth Century* (1994); *Literature in the Marketplace: Nineteenth-Century British Publishing and Reading Practices*, edited by John O. Jordan and Robert L. Patten (1995), especially for Kelly J. Mays's 'The Disease of Reading and Victorian Periodicals' and Laurel Brake's 'The "Wicked *Westminster*", the *Fortnightly*, and Walter Pater's *The Renaissance*'; and *Writing and Victorianism*, edited by J.B. Bullen (1997), especially for Laurel Brake's 'Writing, Cultural Production, and the Periodical Press in the Nineteenth Century'.

With the notable exception of Houghton's magisterial essay, most of those publications tried to bring Victorian periodicals under the umbrella of recent critical theory, in ways that I found stimulating but of only limited relevance to my own more traditional, more empirical approach to *Macmillan's Magazine*; some of them, too, argued from premises that struck me as quite remote from the facts that I was unearthing.

As I continued my own research, much of which resulted in published articles and in conference papers delivered throughout the 1990s, and especially after I had two extended opportunities to burrow in the treasure trove that is the British Library's huge Macmillan Archive, it became clear to me that there were several important issues regarding my subject that had not yet received adequate attention. First, where did *Macmillan's* come from, in 1859 of all years – not sooner, not later? Second, exactly how did Alexander Macmillan, the head of Macmillan and Co. and the *Magazine's* guiding spirit during its formative early years, put his distinctive stamp on its editorial philosophy and its contents? Third, to what extent did *Macmillan's* during that same period reflect the broad range of concerns associated with the Christian Socialist movement in general and Frederick Denison Maurice, its acknowledged leader, in particular? Fourth, how did the *Magazine* and its parent firm deal with authors and juggle their periodical work and the related books they often produced? (In addressing that complicated question, I thought it best to concentrate on one writer, Margaret Oliphant, unique but also in a number of ways representative, whose association with both the *Magazine* and the publishing house endured for four busy decades.) Finally, what accounted for the palpable decline in the quality and fiscal health of *Macmillan's* during the last 25 years of its life and, ultimately, for its death? Each of the five chapters of this book treats one of these questions in some depth. There are of course important interrelationships among them; none of the chapters, therefore, can quite satisfactorily stand by itself.

I do not claim to have arrived at any definitive answers to the five questions that have determined the structure of this book. Indeed, the longer I worked on this study the more persuaded I became that all of them are in some sense – to use a fashionable, ugly, but useful word 'undecidable'. Although the investigator of the *Magazine's* history has access to an almost overwhelming amount of factual material, it is not always feasible to transmute those data into sure knowledge. There is much about *Macmillan's* that we can never know, not only because there are gaps and contradictions in the surviving records but also, and especially, because written documents, which are all we have to go on, do not unfailingly teach us what we may want to learn about the complexities and ambiguities of human motivations, human achievements and human failings. One is, of course, obliged to reach the best conclusions possible under the circumstances, but also, I would argue, to refrain as much as possible from imposing one's ideological or theoretical preconceptions on the available materials.

What follows, then, is not a coherent narrative tracing the development and decline of *Macmillan's*. I tread lightly through the editorships of David Masson and George Grove, because they have already been dealt with, by Hertz and Parry respectively, and in the case of Grove's in an excellent chapter called 'The Editor's Chair' in Percy M. Young's *George Grove 1820–1900: A Biography* (1980). Besides, as will become apparent, I take the view that it was really Alexander Macmillan rather than Masson or Grove who was in charge of the *Magazine* during those first two editors' terms of office. Unlike their predecessors, however, the last two men who held that position, John Morley and especially Mowbray Morris, enjoyed considerable autonomy – really a kind of benign neglect by the second generation of the Macmillan family and their associates at Macmillan and Co. – and their work as editors has generally been disregarded by my forerunners. My last chapter is intended to render them some sort of belated justice. Although they were not without their shortcomings, neither Morley nor Morris can fairly be blamed for the *Magazine's* decline and demise: they did their best to keep the ship afloat during a quarter-century when it became increasingly obvious that the aging vessel had outlived its moment, particularly when Alexander Macmillan was no longer on the bridge.

I do not attempt to recount all the stories worth telling about *Macmillan's* – for example, the famous one about Harriet Beecher Stowe's exposure of Byron's alleged incestuous relationship with his half-sister and Alexander Macmillan's reasons for printing it in the September 1869 number, which is told by Charles L. Graves in his 1910 biography of Macmillan, repeated by A.J. Gurr in his 1965 article, and again by Richard Davenport-Hines in his 1992 *The Macmillans*. Nor do I, except when it is unavoidable, go over ground already covered in such valuable histories of Macmillan and Co. as Charles Morgan's or Rosemary VanArsdel's account in Volume 106 of the *Dictionary of Literary Biography* (1991); my subject, after all, is the *Magazine* and not the publishing house, although there are obviously important connections between them.

In referring to correspondence relevant to the *Magazine*, I have whenever possible used primary texts in the Macmillan Archive (and, in a very few cases, in the Berg Collection of the New York Public Library), but I have occasionally had to resort to previously published material in the *Letters of Alexander Macmillan*, edited by his son George (1908), and in *Letters to Macmillan*, edited by Simon Nowell-Smith (1967), fully realizing the fallibility of such secondary sources. There are already in print book-length studies of the correspondence between Macmillan and Co. and such authors as the Rossettis (edited by Lona Mosk Packer, 1963), Lewis Carroll (edited by Morton N. Cohen and Anita Gandolfo, 1987), Henry James (edited by Rayburn S. Moore, 1993) and Walter Pater (edited by Robert M. Seiler, 1999); these have little to say about *Macmillan's Magazine*, but do give some sense of the ambience in which its authors did their work and the ways in which they were treated by its proprietors.

Finally, when I required information about the publication of books that originated as contributions to the *Magazine*, I frequently resorted to the remarkable *Bibliographical Catalogue of Macmillan and Co.'s Publications from 1843 to 1889* (1891), which achieves a level of accuracy and reader-friendliness seldom reached in our age of computer-generated texts of that kind. After wrestling for some time with the question of how to cite my numerous sources, primary and secondary, I abandoned the idea of using parenthetical documentation, which struck me as unacceptably intrusive in a project of this kind. I have, instead, fallen back on the more traditional endnotes, which the reader is of course free to ignore but which are there after each chapter for the information of those who may want to consult them. Many of these notes refer to manuscript material: the designation 'Add MSS' is the conventional shorthand for the 'additional manuscripts' held by the British Library, followed in each case by the appropriate volume number and folio number(s). Where appropriate, I have combined such references when these occur in the same paragraph of my text. (A confession: I was not always able to resist the temptation to indulge in discursive endnotes when I thought they might be of interest. These too may be skipped.)

At the end of these introductory remarks, I supply three lists: of the secondary works I have been mentioning, a number of which are followed by keywords in bold type that will recur in the endnotes of my chapters so as to avoid repeating sometimes rather cumbersome citations; of the standard abbreviations for the relatively few titles of scholarly serials to which I refer in those notes, in a further effort to save a little space; and of six names – five of them of members of the Macmillan family – that I hope will be helpful in sorting out 'Who Was Who at Macmillan and Co.' during the period dealt with in this book.

Secondary works mentioned

Beetham, Margaret. 'Open and Closed: The Periodical as a Publishing Genre'. *Victorian Periodicals Review* 22 (1989): 96–100.

A Bibliographical Catalogue of Macmillan and Co.'s Publications from 1843 to 1889. London: Macmillan, 1891.

Brake, Laurel. '"The Trepidation of the Spheres": The Serial and the Book in the 19th Century'. *Serials and Their Readers*. Ed. Robin Myers and Michael Harris. Winchester: St Paul's Bibliographies, 1993. 83–101. (Cited as **Brake 1993**.)

Brake, Laurel. *Subjugated Knowledges: Journalism, Gender and Literature in the Nineteenth Century*. New York: New York University Press, 1994. (Cited as **Brake 1994**.)

Brake, Laurel. 'The "Wicked *Westminster*", the *Fortnightly*, and Walter Pater's *The Renaissance*'. *Literature in the Marketplace: Nineteenth-Century British Publishing and Reading Practices*. Ed. John O. Jordan and Robert L. Patten. Cambridge: Cambridge University Press, 1995. 289–305.

Brake, Laurel. 'Writing, Cultural Production, and the Periodical Press in the Nineteenth Century'. *Writing and Victorianism*. Ed. J.B. Bullen. London: Longman, 1997. 54–72.

Cohen, Morton N. and Anita Gandolfo, eds. *Lewis Carroll and the House of Macmillan*. Cambridge: Cambridge University Press, 1987.

Davenport-Hines, Richard. *The Macmillans*. London: Heinemann, 1992.

Francis, John Collins. '"Macmillan's Magazine"'. *Notes and Queries* 11th ser. 1 (1910): 141–2. (Cited as **Francis**.)

Graves, Charles L. *Life and Letters of Sir George Grove, CB*. London: Macmillan, 1903.

Graves, Charles L. *Life and Letters of Alexander Macmillan*. London: Macmillan, 1910. (Cited as **Graves**.)

Gurr, A.J. '"Macmillan's Magazine"'. *Review of English Literature* 6.1 (1965): 39–55. (Cited as **Gurr**.)

Hertz, Alan. "*Macmillan's Magazine*: A New Source and Further Attributions'. *Victorian Periodicals Review* 14 (1981): 119–21. (Cited as **Hertz 1981**.)

Hertz, Alan. '*Macmillan's Magazine* under David Masson: 1859–1867'. Dissertation Cambridge University, 1982. (Cited as **Hertz 1982**.)

Hertz, Alan. 'The Broad Church Militant and Newman's Humiliation of Charles Kingsley'. *Victorian Periodicals Review* 19 (1986): 141–9. (Cited as **Hertz 1986**.)

Hirst, F.W. *Early Life & Letters of John Morley*. 2 vols. London: Macmillan, 1927. (Cited as **Hirst**.)

Houghton, Walter F., ed. *The Wellesley Index to Victorian Periodicals*.

Vol. 1. Toronto: University of Toronto Press, 1966. (Cited as **Wellesley 1.**)

Houghton, Walter E. 'Periodical Literature and the Articulate Classes'. *The Victorian Periodical Press: Samples and Soundings*. Ed. Joanne Shattock and Michael Wolff. Leicester: Leicester University Press; Toronto: Toronto University Press, 1982. 3–27. (Cited as **Houghton.**)

Macmillan, George A., ed. *Letters of Alexander Macmillan*. Glasgow: privately printed, 1908. (Cited as **G.A. Macmillan.**)

Madden, Lionel and Diana Dixon. 'Histories and Studies of Individual Periodicals'. *Victorian Periodicals: A Guide to Research*. Ed. J. Don Vann and Rosemary T. VanArsdel. New York: MLA, 1978. 99–122.

Mays, Kelly J. 'The Disease of Reading and Victorian Periodicals'. *Literature in the Marketplace: Nineteenth-Century British Publishing and Reading Practices*. Ed. John O. Jordan and Robert L. Patten. Cambridge: Cambridge University Press, 1995. 165–94. (Cited as **Mays.**)

Moore, Rayburn S., ed. *The Correspondence of Henry James and the House of Macmillan, 1877–1914*. Baton Rouge: Louisiana State University Press, 1993. (Cited as **Moore.**)

Morgan, Charles. *The House of Macmillan, 1843–1943*. New York: Macmillan, 1944. (Cited as **Morgan.**)

Nowell-Smith, Simon, ed. *Letters to Macmillan*. London: Macmillan, 1967. (Cited as **Nowell-Smith.**)

Packer, Lona Mosk, ed. *The Rossetti–Macmillan Letters*. Berkeley: University of California Press, 1963.

Parry, Ann. 'The Grove Years 1868–1883: A "New Look" for *Macmillan's Magazine?*' *Victorian Periodicals Review* 19 (1986): 149–57. (Cited as **Parry 1986.**)

Parry, Ann. 'The Intellectuals and the Middle Class Periodical Press: Theory, Method and Case Study'. *Journal of Newspaper and Periodical History* 4.3 (1988): 18–32. (Cited as **Parry 1988.**)

Parry, Ann. 'Theories of Formation: *Macmillan's Magazine*: Vol. 1, November 1859 [.] Monthly. 1/0'. *Victorian Periodicals Review* 26 (1993): 100–104. (Cited as **Parry 1993.**)

Pykett, Lyn. 'Reading the Periodical Press: Text and Context'. *Victorian Periodicals Review* 22 (1989): 100–108.

Seiler, Robert M., ed. *The Book Beautiful: Walter Pater and the House of Macmillan*. London: Athlone Press, 1999. (Cited as **Seiler.**)

VanArsdel, Rosemary T. 'Macmillan and Company …'. *Dictionary of Literary Biography*. Vol. 106. Ed. Patricia J. Anderson and Jonathan Rose. Detroit: Gale Research, 1991. 178–95.

Wilson, Keith. 'Macmillan's Magazine'. *British Literary Magazines: The Victorian and Edwardian Age, 1837–1913*. Ed. Alvin Sullivan. Westport, CT: Greenwood Press, 1983. 215–19.

Young, Percy M. *George Grove 1820–1900: A Biography*. London: Macmillan, 1980.

Abbreviations

NCF   *Nineteenth-Century Fiction*
SB   *Studies in Bibliography*
VPN   *Victorian Periodicals Newsletter*
VPR   *Victorian Periodicals Review*
VS   *Victorian Studies*
YES   *Yearbook of English Studies*

Who was who at Macmillan and Co.

Daniel Macmillan (1813–57)
Alexander Macmillan (1818–96), Daniel Macmillan's brother
George Lillie Craik (1837–1905), Alexander Macmillan's partner and 'finance minister' from 1865
Frederick Macmillan (1851–1936), Daniel Macmillan's elder son
Maurice Macmillan (1853–1936), Daniel Macmillan's younger son
George A. Macmillan (1855–1936), Alexander Macmillan's younger son (his elder brother, **Malcolm Macmillan** [1853–89], took little part in the affairs of the family firm)

Acknowledgments

Like most of its predecessors, this book could not have been written without financial support from the University of Kansas, my academic home for four decades. A grant from its General Research Fund, a fellowship from the Hall Center for the Humanities and the last of my sabbatical leaves enabled me to get off to a running start, more years ago than I care to admit. For these and other boons I am deeply grateful to the University.

Among the Kansas colleagues to whom I owe thanks for their help with my *Macmillan's* project are Rob Melton, the long-time bibliographer for English-language and comparative literature, and others in Watson Library, who came to my rescue on many occasions. In our research library, two successive Spencer Librarians, Alexandra Mason and William Crowe, have also done much for me – not least in allowing me the use of a tranquil study in that fine building.

Away from Kansas I benefited enormously from the kindness of the staff of the Manuscript Students' Room at the British Library, who patiently put up with what must have seemed my importunate demands for ever more volumes of the Macmillan Archive. I thank the British Library and the Henry W. and Albert A. Berg Collection of English and American Literature at the New York Public Library (Astor, Lenox and Tilden Foundations) for permission to quote from manuscript material in their collections.

Over the years I have had many opportunities to discuss my work with fellow-members of the Research Society for Victorian Periodicals. I am grateful to them all for their helpful suggestions, but I want to single out for special commendation D.J. Trela, whose generous readiness to share with me the results of his own labors on Margaret Oliphant was little short of heroic.

Portions of my first three chapters have been previously published, in severely truncated form, in the *Victorian Periodicals Review* during the editorships of Barbara Quinn Schmidt and Richard Fulton, and I am pleased to have an opportunity to repeat myself at greater length – with improvements, variations and embellishments – in what I hope will be this more meaningful context. A much-abbreviated version of Chapter 4, the outgrowth of one of my conference papers, appeared in *Macmillan: A Publishing Tradition*, edited by Elizabeth James (Palgrave, 2002).

CHAPTER ONE

The Beginning

1859, before and beyond

The first number of *Macmillan's Magazine* appeared at the end of October 1859. Its 80 closely printed double-columned pages, unrelieved by illustrations, contained eight pieces: a sober account of 'Politics of the Present, Foreign and Domestic'; the first installment of a new novel by Thomas Hughes, the author of *Tom Brown's School Days*, a best-seller of two years earlier; two meditative essays – 'Paper, Pen, and Ink: An Excursus in Technology' and 'Cheap Art'; a poem based on Cobbett's *Rural Rides*, preceded by a prose introduction; an article about the ongoing Italian struggle against Louis Napoleon; and a half-serious, half-convivial 'Colloquy of the Round Table', in which a varied group of men discuss matters of current and perennial concern, drink, smoke and listen to one of their number sing a song about the bibulous 'Old Sir Simon the King', 'son to Old King Cole'.[1]

There is nothing here, surely, to set our pulses racing today. Yet *Macmillan's* immediately achieved the solid if unspectacular success for which its backers had been hoping,[2] going on to become what one scholar has called 'the most respectable and respected magazine of "serious" literature and comment of its time'.[3] We shall never understand fully why the early *Macmillan's* prospered as it did, but it is possible to point to certain features of the mid-nineteenth-century scene that will help us to reach an explanation. As we attempt to do so, we should not be excessively beguiled by the well-known textbook fact that 1859, the year of the *Magazine*'s birth, was an *annus mirabilis* in the history of English literature – the year of George Eliot's first novel (*Adam Bede*) and George Meredith's first successful one (*The Ordeal of Richard Feverel*), Dickens's *A Tale of Two Cities* and Thackeray's *The Virginians*, FitzGerald's *The Rubáiyát of Omar Khayám* and Tennyson's first four *Idylls of the King*, Darwin's *The Origin of Species* and Mill's *On Liberty*.[4] More directly to the point of this discussion is the related fact that 1859 was a landmark year in the history of periodical journalism, as the founding of *Macmillan's*, generally regarded as the first shilling monthly magazine,[5] was both an outgrowth of the same potent trends that had brought about this spate of memorable imaginative and intellectual writing and an important factor in the continuing extension and definition of an audience for such work.

The nineteenth century in England was not only an age of rapidly increasing population but also one during which the rate of literacy and the demand for suitable reading increased strikingly.[6] Helping to create and feed that demand were significant changes in government policy, such as the piecemeal abolition of the 'taxes on knowledge' and the gradual provision of support for education, as well as dramatic changes in technology: new methods of production and distribution resulted in the placement of more printed materials into the hands of more people more cheaply and more rapidly, and new domestic conveniences permitted more leisure time for reading in more comfort. The ascent of the bourgeoisie, the primary beneficiaries of such changes, was accelerating. So was their need to define their place, and that of their class, in the world – a need that was met largely by the new books and periodicals that were becoming so abundantly available to them. The publishers of many of these books and periodicals were themselves emerging as a much more visible component of the professional middle class, while their trade continued to evolve from a small-time offshoot of bookselling into something approaching modern big business; authors too were achieving a measurably heightened sense of their own professionalism.[7]

Richard Altick has singled out the 1850s as the first decade in which there was 'a mass [reading] public in anything like modern terms' in the British Isles.[8] Yet a growing portion of that public, which Q.D. Leavis was one of the earliest to label 'middlebrow',[9] was not being served adequately by most of the periodicals, old and new, that were rolling off the presses in rapidly increasing numbers – certainly not by the august and relatively expensive quarterlies or by the modest penny weeklies addressed to a working-class audience as eager for instruction as for diversion. Clearly, there was a widening breach between those whom Leavis called 'the minority' and 'the people':[10] those who perused the *Edinburgh Review* and the *Quarterly Review*, established early in the century, and those who devoured such recently founded periodicals as *Cassell's Illustrated Family Paper*, the *London Journal, Reynolds' Miscellany*, the *Home Magazine*, the *Family Herald* and the *Welcome Guest*.[11] It was probably a sign of the times rather than a coincidence that attention was being insistently called to the existence of this gap just before *Macmillan's* came on the market.[12]

In August 1858, both Margaret Oliphant in *Blackwood's* and Wilkie Collins in *Household Words* described these newer penny weeklies and their readership in fascinated detail – apprehensively in her case, hopefully in his. A writer in the *British Quarterly Review* for April 1859 took much the same line, although he or she sounded more like Oliphant than Collins in making dismayed reference to that flood of Cheap Literature which, like the modern Babylon itself, no living man has ever been able to traverse, which has sprung up, and continues to spring up, with the mysterious fecundity of certain fungi, and which cannot be accounted for in its volume, variety, and universality by any ordinary laws of production.[13]

All three of these writers insisted that quantity and availability were no substitutes for quality and solidity, indirectly pointing to a need that was very soon to be met by *Macmillan's* and its successors.

Others perceived, or rather misperceived, that same need. The publisher Richard Bentley, whose monthly *Bentley's Miscellany* had anticipated some of the features of *Macmillan's* two decades earlier, launched *Bentley's Quarterly Review* in April 1859, but his usually shrewd appraisal of the public taste failed him on this occasion. Although Bentley had given much thought to the question of what sort of new periodical would sell, the magazine turned out to be a financial disaster and lasted for only four numbers. As the historian of the House of Bentley has written, '1859 was the time not for a six-shilling review but a one-shilling magazine: that much is clear from the brilliant success of the *Cornhill Magazine* [whose first number appeared in January 1860] and *Macmillan's Magazine*.'[14]

The publisher of the *Cornhill*, George Smith, saw things differently from Richard Bentley. Reminiscing about the origin of that monthly more than four decades later, he wrote: 'Early in 1859 I conceived the idea of founding a new magazine. ... The existing magazines were few, and when not high-priced were narrow in literary range.' Smith believed 'that a shilling magazine' containing, 'in addition to other first-class literary matter', a serial by an established novelist 'must command a large sale'.[15] Smith was right and Bentley wrong. That the age was ready and waiting for periodicals like *Macmillan's* and the *Cornhill* was proved by the creation of numerous others within the next few years in what Walter Houghton called a veritable 'outburst of shilling magazines':[16] *Good Words* and *Temple Bar* later in 1860, the *St James* in 1861, the *Victoria* in 1863, the *Argosy* in 1865, *Belgravia* in 1866 and *Tinsleys'*, *Saint Pauls* and *Broadway* in 1867.

None of these new arrivals, however, was able to seize and hold a lion's share of the market; even the circulation of the *Cornhill*, whose first number had sold the 'astounding total ... of 120,000 copies',[17] soon declined after its novelty had worn off. There were simply too many shilling monthlies in competition with one another – 'more magazines in the wretched field than there were blades of grass to support them', as yet another publisher, William Tinsley, complained. He wrote in his memoirs that 'there was a rage amongst publishers for shilling magazines' when he started *Tinsleys'*, and he ruefully styled himself 'one of the foolish sheep who rushed into the next field, and did not find the food so plentiful as it was in the field I had left'.[18] He estimated his loss on the first 12 numbers of *Tinsleys'* at £3000.

Financial ledgers by no means told the whole story, however. Edmund Downey, who worked for Tinsley at his Catherine Street establishment, remarked that, although *Tinsleys'* may have cost its proprietor some money (never more, according to Downey, than £25 a month, 'and this was recouped by profits from his Christmas and Summer Annuals'), the magazine brought his firm less tangible but nevertheless real benefits. Downey quotes Tinsley as often saying to him: 'What cheaper advertisement can I have for twenty-five pounds a month? It advertises my name and publications and it keeps my authors together.'[19]

The point here is not whether we ought to believe Tinsley or Downey, whose figures disagree; it is, in any case, prudent not to place too much trust in the circumstantial recollections of garrulous late-Victorian autobiographers. Rather, the remark Downey attributed to Tinsley serves as a useful reminder that firms like Tinsley Brothers, Macmillan and Co. and Smith, Elder used their magazines to attract and nurture authors and to promote their much more lucrative trade in books, especially novels. John Sutherland has put it as follows:

> These journals after the initial and considerable expense of founding them, earned revenue for the publisher, displayed his wares and enabled him to test the market to see how a novel 'pulled' with the public. The advantages even went so far as to outweigh the occasional unprofitability of the venture from a purely book-keeping point of view.[20]

In making his case that the 'development ... of periodical literature' was arguably the most 'distinctive and characteristic ... single feature of the English literary history of the nineteenth century', George Saintsbury went beyond its effect on prose fiction and the market for it:

> Very large numbers of the best as well as of the worst novels ... have originally appeared in periodicals; not a very small proportion of the most noteworthy nineteenth century poetry has had the same origin; it may almost be said that all the best work in essay, whether critical, meditative, or miscellaneous, has thus been ushered into the world. Even the severer and more academic muses – history, philosophy, theology, and their sisters, have condescended to avail themselves of this means of obtaining a public audience; and though there is still a certain conventional decency in apologising for reprints from periodicals, it is quite certain that, had such reprints not taken place, more than half of the most valuable books of the age in some departments, and a considerable minority of the most valuable in others, would never have appeared as books at all.[21]

To say about the post-1859 era, as Michael Wolff did, that 'Everybody wrote for the magazines',[22] may be an exaggeration, but not by very much. Certainly the multiplication of magazines did not go unremarked by intelligent readers. 'Do you see how the publishing world is going mad on periodicals?' George Eliot asked Charles Bray in a letter written in November 1859, less than four weeks after the appearance of the first number of *Macmillan's*.[23] Some other members of the reading public who also happened to be writers were worried about this phenomenon of the age. 'Reading magazines breaks one's mind all to bits', Tennyson grumbled in 1880.[24] Twelve years later, in the history of *The Victorian Age of Literature* that Margaret Oliphant wrote with the help of her son Francis, there was a similar lament, which sounds at least as apt today as it must have been over a century ago:

> It is a common thing to hear said in our day that people read nothing but magazines. There has indeed been such an extraordinary increase in our own time of periodical publications that we can imagine the conscientious student of the literature of the day hardly finding time to work his way through all the latest numbers in the space of a month, while a margin of leisure for looking at books would be to such a person a complete impossibility. It has, indeed, always been a standing mystery to us where the constantly increasing recruits of this noble army find any readers at all, and we have sometimes thought that the real cause of the constant multiplication might be that nobody in the present day feels called upon to read, while every one attempts to write, and desires to see him or herself in print.[25]

We have moved ahead rapidly from 1859 to nearly the end of the Victorian period, which also takes us close to the demise of *Macmillan's Magazine* in 1907. It is time to move back, even before 1859, and, as we revert from glancing at the consumption of Victorian periodicals in general to examining the production of the particular one with which we are concerned here, to look more closely at the origins of *Macmillan's*. It will not be enough to consider the position of Macmillan and Co. at the time of the *Magazine*'s founding, although we shall begin with that; it is also necessary to inquire into the ideology that animated the firm in its early days, clarified and amplified through its close connection with the so-called Christian Socialist movement of the mid-nineteenth century, and to come to some conclusions about the man who did more than anyone else to shape both the company and the *Magazine* into the 1880s.

Publishers and periodicals

The business that was to grow into Macmillan and Co. began its life in February 1843 as a modest bookshop at 57 Aldersgate Street in the City of London. A few months later, the two remarkable young Scotsmen who ran it, Daniel Macmillan (born in 1813) and his brother Alexander (born in 1818), decided to move to more suitable quarters in Cambridge, at 17 Trinity Street. Soon, in 1845, they relocated again, to 1 Trinity Street (later the premises of the well-known bookseller Bowes & Bowes). Much more than a mere retail establishment, the Macmillans' shop soon established itself as an intellectual and social center for Cambridge dons and undergraduates and for visiting literary celebrities like Tennyson and Thackeray.[26]

Hard-working, well-read and canny, the Macmillans always felt a keen sense of vocation about their trade in the printed word. While still in his twenties and employed in a Fleet Street bookshop at a salary of £80 a year, Daniel Macmillan wrote to a friend: 'We booksellers, if we are faithful to our task, are trying to destroy, and are helping to destroy, all kinds of confusion, and are aiding our great Taskmaster to reduce the world into order, and beauty, and harmony.' 'At the same time,' he added, speaking as a lay missionary who was also a Christian business-man, 'it is our duty to manage our affairs wisely, keep our minds easy, and not trade beyond our means.'[27] That strong ethic survived Daniel Macmillan and left an enduring stamp on the firm he founded with his brother.

In the 1840s, the transition from selling books to publishing them was both natural and common, and the Macmillans lost little time in making it. The first volume to bear their imprint, A.R. Craig's *The Philosophy of Training*, came out in the autumn of 1843, to be joined before the end of the year by W.H. Miller's *The Three Questions*. (The former was issued from '57, Aldersgate Street'; the latter from that address and '17, Trinity Street, Cambridge'.) There were two more books in 1844, seven in 1845, and 14, as well as the *Cambridge Mathematical Journal*, in 1846. By mid-century the business, now calling itself Macmillan and Co., was clearly off and running.

As might have been expected from its connections with Cambridge University, most of the firm's earliest books were academic, chiefly mathematical, or religious in nature. Not until 1855 did the Macmillans enter the more remunerative world of fiction publishing with Charles Kingsley's *Westward Ho!* Sutherland shows in the chapter of *Victorian Novelists and Publishers* devoted to Kingsley's book that it was this popular three-volume novel, with its powerful appeal to the patriotic sentiments aroused by the nation's involvement in the Crimean War, that placed Macmillan and Co. squarely at the center of that world.[28] The timing was perfect. One of the seven publishing houses studied by Sutherland that 'came to monopolise the best in fiction during and after the forties' (the other six were Chapman and Hall, Bradbury and Evans, Longman, Bentley, Blackwood, and Smith, Elder),[29] Macmillan and Co. had the wit and found the resources to take advantage of the precise moment in English publishing history when 'large businesses formed, then consolidated remarkably quickly becoming, as it seemed, venerable institutions almost overnight … Firms who missed the period of flux were to a large extent excluded after the period of consolidation in the 1840s and 1850s.'[30]

Already prosperous and respected, Macmillan and Co. underwent two significant changes in the late 1850s. On 27 June 1857 Daniel Macmillan died after years of struggle against a severe pulmonary ailment. Alexander Macmillan was devastated but carried on by himself, still striving as both brothers had done during Daniel's lifetime to place the firm's spiritual and intellectual calling ahead of its commercial success. The following year, acting on an idea that he and his late brother had often discussed, he opened a branch in London, at 23 Henrietta Street, Covent Garden, a step that seemed appropriate for a publishing house of the stature that Macmillan and Co. had achieved after a decade and a half of existence. Macmillan himself continued to live and work in Cambridge for the next five years but made weekly trips to London to take care of business and to preside each Thursday evening at the Henrietta Street 'tobacco parliaments', round-table gatherings of writers, scientists and artists like Alfred Tennyson, Coventry Patmore, Herbert Spencer, Thomas Henry Huxley, Thomas Hughes, David Masson, Francis Turner Palgrave, Richard Garnett, Alfred Ainger and Thomas Woolner. It was at this large table, made by craftsmen from the London Working Men's College, that the idea for *Macmillan's Magazine* took shape. However, it was not, strictly speaking, a new idea.

We have already had occasion to note that enterprising nineteenth-century publishers at a certain stage of their development considered it desirable to flesh out their lists with periodicals – not house organs in any narrow sense but certainly means whereby they reinforced their positions with the audiences they were trying to reach. John Murray's *Quarterly Review*, founded in 1809, may be regarded as the first of these periodicals;[31] other prominent early examples included *Blackwood's* (1817) and *Bentley's Miscellany* (1837). Although largely a personal vehicle for its imperious editor, Charles Dickens, the weekly *Household Words* (1850) was also a valuable asset for Bradbury and Evans; after Dickens quarrelled with them, Chapman and Hall were pleased to have him assume direction of the new *All the Year Round* (1859).[32] The proprietor of Smith, Elder, as we have seen, began laying plans for the *Cornhill* even as *Macmillan's* was being conceived; indeed, George Smith's first choice for the editorship, Thomas Hughes, who turned Smith down because Hughes 'had thrown in his lot ... with Macmillan's',[33] was a principal in those Henrietta Street deliberations. The last of Sutherland's seven dominant publishing firms to enter the magazine field was Longman, which took over *Fraser's*, established in 1830, in 1863 and continued it under its own name from 1882.

The Cambridge mathematician (and Macmillan and Co. author) Isaac Todhunter had suggested to Alexander Macmillan as early as 1855 that the time was ripe to undertake a new 'literary paper'. Also encouraged by Sir James Stephen (Regius Professor of Modern History at Cambridge, formerly a writer for the *Edinburgh Review*, whose sons James Fitzjames and Leslie Stephen were to become contributors to *Macmillan's*) Macmillan concurred. 'My idea', he wrote his brother, 'is to make a thing like the *Revue des Deux Mondes* and call it *The World of Letters*.'[34] However, Daniel Macmillan vetoed the idea: it would involve too much 'toil', he maintained; and, besides, the firm should think first about establishing itself in London.[35] In November 1856, while Hughes's *Tom Brown's School Days* was in press, John Malcolm Ludlow, a friend to both Hughes and Macmillan, urged on Macmillan a practical reason for thinking again about a magazine. Apparently assuming, correctly, that Hughes's novel was not to be the last work of fiction published by Macmillan and Co., Ludlow predicted that there would be 'some difficulty' in gaining for such a work 'all the success it deserves off hand, coming from an entirely new author', and went on to argue that

> if that same Tom Brown had been published in a magazine, for which it is admirably adapted, not only would it have increased the sale of the magazine largely as it went on, but by the time it had got to the end it would *no longer be* a book by a new hand, – it would on being republished as a whole, just step into success, instead of having to fight its way into it.[36]

Daniel Macmillan's death in 1857 and the opening of the London branch of Macmillan and Co. the following year intervened before Macmillan could act on Ludlow's advice. A letter of 27 October 1858 to Macmillan's Glasgow friend James MacLehose indicates two further reasons for hesitation: now leaning toward bringing out a quarterly, Macmillan wanted to wait and see how Bentley's forthcoming venture would fare before launching his own; and Charles Kingsley, on whom he had been counting for substantial help, 'was only half-hearted in the enterprise'.[37] As we shall see in Chapter 3, the cautious Macmillan engaged in extensive consultation with Frederick Denison Maurice and others about proceeding with the new periodical, but the Henrietta Street 'tobacco parliament' discussions, with Thomas Hughes as prime mover, revived Macmillan's flagging resolve.

Hughes knew exactly what sort of magazine he wanted – 'Everyone to sign his own name and no flippancy or abuse allowed' – and, although he turned out to be wrong in his prediction that the first number would be out before the end of 1858,[38] he kept up the pressure. 'By the spring of 1859', Hughes's biographers write, 'the original idea for a quarterly had been abandoned, and a monthly was well launched, on Hughes' suggestion.' Having lost interest in assuming the editorship, which Macmillan had offered him, Hughes joined Ludlow in persuading David Masson – a respected man of letters from Aberdeen who had been appointed Professor of English Literature at University College London a half-dozen years earlier, at the age of 31 – to fill that position.[39] It was Masson who suggested the title *Macmillan's Magazine*.[40] A great admirer of Tennyson, Macmillan had preferred an Arthurian name, possibly *King Arthur* or the *Round Table*, which would also have called to mind the venue of the Henrietta Street conversations that led to its creation,[41] but yielded to his first editor on this occasion.

The Christian Socialist element

Macmillan, Hughes, Ludlow and Masson were united by much more than their desire to found a new magazine. The four of them, and a good number of their Henrietta Street associates, had first met several years before 1859, drawn together by the need they all felt to do something to ameliorate the lot of the London working classes – exploited, subjected to appalling living conditions, and generally deprived of significant power. The Chartists' attempt to address these problems by propaganda and agitation designed to bring about political change had ended in dismal failure in 1848: on 10 April of that year, the day that 'marked the *fiasco* of Chartism',[42] their 'Great Metropolitan Demonstration' on Kennington Common fizzled out in pouring rain, and their movement turned from a perceived threat to bourgeois values into something of a laughing stock.

Certain influential and articulate members of the middle classes did take the Chartists' grievances seriously and had been doing so even before the events of 10 April 1848. One of them was the Reverend Frederick Denison Maurice, whose growing interest in social issues came to a head after his appointment as chaplain of Lincoln's Inn in 1846. Perhaps stimulated by the proximity of that venerable legal center to some of the foulest slums in London and certainly mindful of the revolutions that began erupting on the Continent early in 1848, Maurice spoke out – for example in a series of sermons on the Lord's Prayer, delivered between February and April of that year – on the urgency of dealing in some meaningful way with the misery of the unprivileged. For Maurice, despite his profound sympathy with the desperation that had led to the rise of Chartism, there could be no useful meaning in class warfare. As a Christian and a believer in Coleridge's notion of an organic rather than an atomistic state, Maurice advocated mutual understanding rather than mutual hostility, coop-eration rather than competition. Nor did Maurice share the Chartists' view that overhauling the composition of the national legislature so as to make it more democratic was the way to begin the necessary reformation of society.

The great question was what could be done beyond the preaching of sermons to put Maurice's ideas into practice. Two young admirers of his, who had started out for Kennington Common on the fateful 10th of April in hopes of reasoning the assembled demonstrators out of taking violent action but failed to reach their destination before the crowd dispersed, called on Maurice that evening to consider this ques-tion, which had become all the more pressing after the Chartists' debacle of a few hours earlier. They were the Reverend Charles Kingsley, rector of Eversley in Hampshire and not yet a well-known writer, and John Malcolm Ludlow, a largely French-educated lawyer who had been called to the bar at Lincoln's Inn in 1843.

It is generally agreed by its historians that what became known as the Christian Socialist movement grew out of this meeting at Maurice's home and that Maurice himself, although reluctant to take charge and skeptical about some of its activities, became the spiritual head of the group that soon began to form. Much was made, by critics and defend-ers alike, of the seeming oxymoron inherent in the term 'Christian Socialist', especially in the revolutionary year 1848. In fact, however, the word 'Christian' was intended to signify a comprehensive rather than an exclusive definition of the religion and the church founded by Jesus, and the word 'Socialist' was meant to apply to relatively small communities, first of producers and then of consumers, rather than to a centralized bureaucratic state in the Continental sense. In its half-dozen years as a more or (often) less coherent body, the movement accom-plished much – for instance, the formation of cooperative societies, beginning with the Working Tailors' Association (1850); the encourage-ment of legislation, such as the Industrial and Provident Societies Act (1852), to promote its goals; and the provision of adult education, culminating in the establishment of the London Working Men's College (1854) – and its influence long outlived its brief existence. Our emphasis here, however, must be placed on its faith in the word, especially the written word.

The first Christian Socialist publication was a placard addressed to the 'Workmen of England', which Kingsley sat up most of the night of 10–11 April composing and which was posted the day after the Chartists' aborted rally. Signed 'A Working Parson', it assured them of the sympathy of 'almost all men who have heads and hearts', warned them not to mistake 'licence' for 'liberty' in their justified despair and rage, and promised them that 'Almighty God, and Jesus Christ, the poor Man who died for poor men, will bring freedom for you, though all the Mammonites on earth were against you.' 'There will be no true freedom without virtue', Kingsley's text concluded, 'no true science without religion, no true industry without the fear of God and love to your fellow-citizens. Workers of England, be wise, and then you *must* be free, for you will be *fit* to be free.'[43]

Other, less ephemeral, publications soon followed. *Politics for the People*, the first Christian Socialist penny weekly, appeared between 6 May and 29 July 1848. It was edited jointly by Ludlow and Maurice, both of whom wrote extensively for it. So did Kingsley, who signed most of his contributions 'Parson Lot'. The *Christian Socialist: A Journal of Association*, whose masthead stated that it was 'Conducted by several of the promoters of the London Working Men's Associations' and which was edited by Ludlow, came along somewhat later in the history of the movement, on 2 November 1850, and lasted until 27 December of the next year. A note by Ludlow in the final number adverted to the monetary difficulties the paper had been experiencing and announced that it would henceforth be published in eight rather than 16 pages, with a more specific title and a new editor:

> my friend Mr. Hughes, – an old friend too of our readers, – who, by his position at once as a member of the Council of the Society for Promoting Working Men's Associations, and as a Trustee for the Central Co-Operative Agency, embodies most aptly the idea of the harmony which should reign between these two bodies.[44]

As the *Journal of Association: Conducted by Several of the Promoters of the London Working Men's Associations*, it struggled on for six more months, until 28 June 1852. Like the *Christian Socialist*, however, the *Journal of Association* failed to attract enough readers to enable it to make ends meet. Hughes's 'The Approaching Death of the Journal' struck an uncharacteristically peevish note: the editor seemed to be castigating the *Journal*'s intended working-class audience for not appreciating its own interests as articulated in the paper. In some sorrow, Hughes declared that the *Journal of Association* would have to close down in two weeks' time,[45] but a note on the front page of the next number indicated that Ludlow had agreed to fund it until the end of the volume;[46] he also replaced Hughes as editor for the last two months of its short and precarious life.

Such narrowly conceived periodicals could not materially advance the Christian Socialists' aims. Somewhat more successful were the 'Tracts on Christian Socialism' sponsored by Maurice, seven of which were issued in 1850 with an eighth appearing in 1851, but these too reached a restricted public. The movement had yet to find an effective voice.[47] It would be a mistake, however, to regard *Macmillan's*, which began life more than seven years after the demise of the *Journal of Association*, as merely another Christian Socialist organ. Its price of a shilling, as well as the less polemical tone conveyed by its more varied contents, significantly distanced it from *Politics for the People*, the *Christian Socialist* and the *Journal of Association*. Nevertheless, it did in its early years regularly deliver much the same message, intermingled with and embedded in the other concerns that found expression in its pages. It is not surprising that it should have been so, in view of the fact that those who made it what it was had all been connected with the Christian Socialist movement and its publications.

Maurice, Ludlow, Hughes and Kingsley all contributed frequently to the new *Magazine*. In the early 1850s, the four of them had belonged to the Council of the Society for Promoting Working Men's Associations, whose president was Maurice, along with David Masson and George Grove, subsequently the first two editors of *Macmillan's*, and Alexander Macmillan, the *Magazine*'s publisher. As we have noticed, Maurice, Ludlow and Hughes had edited the Christian Socialist weeklies between 1848 and 1852; in addition to them and Kingsley, such men as Frederick James Furnivall, Arthur Helps, E. Vansittart Neale, James Spedding and Arthur Penrhyn Stanley, who were to be associated with *Macmillan's*, all wrote for one or more of them, as did both Daniel and Alexander Macmillan. Of the eight 'Tracts on Christian Socialism' half were the work of Maurice, three of Ludlow (one in collaboration with Charles Sully), and one of Hughes.[48] Clearly, the roots of *Macmillan's Magazine* in Christian Socialism were extensive and strong.

Maurice was the 'Prophet' of the movement, Ludlow was its intellectual leader, and Kingsley and Hughes were its most popular advocates. These facts are well known. Much less appreciated, and much closer to our present purpose, are the nature and the degree of Alexander Macmillan's connections with Christian Socialism, which were to have a profound effect on the magazine that bore his name.

An Ayrshire crofter's son, Alexander Macmillan grew up in close familiarity with poverty and badly paid hard labor. His father died before Alexander was five, leaving a large family in straitened circumstances. Despite the taste for literature and the thirst for learning that the boy acquired from his mother, a university education was out of the question for him: forced to leave the Irvine Academy at the age of 15 in order to earn money, he held a succession of humble jobs for the next half-dozen years – teaching at various little schools (he served briefly as headmaster of one of them); working in shops; going on one voyage as a sailor to America, from which he returned to Glasgow 'absolutely penniless'.[49] Not until his 21st birthday, 3 October 1839, when his brother Daniel got him a position in the London bookshop where he was employed, did Alexander Macmillan enter 'on the business of his life'.[50]

'Scottish puritanism ran in the blood of him', the poet, translator and artist Sebastian Evans, who had become acquainted with Macmillan in Cambridge in the early 1850s, said about him more than a half-century later.[51] Although he joined the Church of England and held distinctly Broad Church views,[52] Macmillan never lost the Calvinist ardor that had been bred into him, and many of his letters yield eloquent testimony to the strength of his Christian faith, which remained the supreme shaper of his thoughts and guide to his actions throughout his long life. One letter he wrote to Daniel Macmillan on 6 October 1854 may be taken as typical:

> Wonderfully indeed have we been guided and blessed. When I look on your two noble boys and on my own fine fellow ... and think of the wives whom God has given us, and our position here [in Cambridge], and indeed in England, surely there is reason why we should gird up our loins to do something for God's Kingdom ... I am far from being a good man of business, brother, husband, father or citizen, and yet I feel a power of entering into the blessedness that belongs to all these that gives me hope for myself in spite of all my failings, for it makes me feel that the Spirit of God of order and love is at least strong with me, and trying to help me in spite of my worthlessness.[53]

On 17 October 1870, in a long letter to an Irvine schoolfellow, he referred again to the next generation of Macmillans (he now had two sons and two daughters): 'I pray daily that I and they may learn to be humble and helpful, and carry on the world's work as in the sight of the Lord of Man, whose very highest character was that He was humble and helpful.'[54]

Coming from such origins and holding such convictions, Macmillan was ripe for the Christian Socialist movement of 1848–54. He met Maurice, through Daniel Macmillan, several years before 1848 and quickly fell under his spell. ('I find everything he says as a new spring of life for me', he wrote to his brother on 17 October 1848.[55]) Virtually from its inception, the Macmillans' business was closely associated with

Maurice. He was a frequent caller at 1 Trinity Street, Cambridge, and that bookshop 'became a centre for Christian Socialist sympathizers'.[56] Largely through Maurice's presence and influence there, and with the active encouragement of Alexander and Daniel Macmillan, a number of gifted Cambridge undergraduates were recruited for the movement: Raven names J. Llewelyn Davies, Richard Buckley Litchfield, Vernon Lushington and John Westlake and says that there was 'many another'.[57] A book with an introduction by Maurice, William Law's *Remarks on the Fable of the Bees*, was one of the two issued by 'D.&A. Macmillan' during their firm's second year, 1844; his *The New Statute and Mr. Ward* appeared with the Macmillan imprint in 1845; and by the time the *Bibliographical Catalogue of Macmillan & Co.'s Publications from 1843 to 1889* came out no fewer than 60 of Maurice's works, in addition to several others about him, had been published by Macmillan and Co.

Besides writing for the *Christian Socialist*[58] and serving on the Council of the Society for Promoting Working Men's Associations, Alexander Macmillan was one of the founders of the Cambridge Working Men's College, modeled after the better-known London institution of the same name established by Maurice in 1854. He did some teaching there and occupied an important position on its governing board between 1855 and 1859, acting as secretary during much of that period and occasionally presiding at its meetings. In short, he was an active participant in the work of the movement.

The foregoing discussion of Alexander Macmillan's religious views and his early and close involvement with Christian Socialism would be of doubtful relevance to a study of the periodical that bore his name were it not for the fact that he was much more than its publisher: until his gradual retirement from business in the 1880s he was its guiding spirit.[59] In the next chapter, we shall examine some of the ways in which that spirit manifested itself during the first two decades or so of the *Magazine*'s existence.

Notes

1. For a heavily theoretical examination of the first number of *Macmillan's* see Parry 1993.
2. Alexander Macmillan did confess to Thomas Hughes – who, like Macmillan, had invested £250 of his own money in this new venture (Add MSS 55837, fol. 67) – that he was disappointed by the sales of the first number (Add MSS 55837, fol. 120), but as the months passed he grew increasingly sanguine about the *Magazine*'s circulation. By 25 July 1860 he wrote Daniel Wilson that

> We print 15,000 and sell at once about 13,000 and there is a
> continued & increasing demand for back numbers and for
> the volume [that is the bound Volume 1, containing the first
> six numbers, November 1859–April 1860]. We began with
> printing 10,000 and had to print of nearly all the early ones
> 16,000 and 17,000 & of none less than 15,000. So we have
> risen from an actual first sale of between 8,000 and 9,000 to
> 13,000 (Add MSS 55838, fols 208–209).

Macmillan had written to George Grove three and a half months earlier that he hoped the *Magazine* would reach a circulation of 20 000 (Add MSS 55837, fol. 369). Cf. Add MSS 55837, fols 119, 146, 252–3, 256–7 and 337. Drawing on information culled from such sources as the *Bookseller* and the *Printers' Register*, Alvar Ellegård estimated the monthly sales of *Macmillan's* during its first decade as fluctuating between 7500 and 20 000 copies, ahead of the comparable figures for such established periodicals as *Blackwood's*, the *Edinburgh Review*, *Fraser's*, the *North British Review*, the *Quarterly Review* and the *Westminster Review* ('The Readership of the Periodical Press in Mid-Victorian Britain: II. Directory', *VPN* No. 13 [1971]: 13, 18–19). Several well-known monthlies that were founded later, for example the *Cornhill*, *St Pauls* and *Temple Bar*, did enjoy higher sales. However, none of the monthlies or quarterlies reached an audience nearly so large as that of the successful penny weeklies addressed to the working class; see Appendix C of Richard D. Altick's *The English Common Reader: A Social History of the Mass Reading Public 1800–1900* (Chicago: University of Chicago Press, 1957), especially 394–5.

3. Gurr 39.
4. The most striking commemoration of the year remains *1859: Entering an Age of Crisis*, ed. Philip Appleman, William A. Madden, and Michael Wolff (Bloomington: Indiana University Press, 1959).
5. As Hertz has pointed out (1982: 1, n1), *Macmillan's* was not really the first shilling monthly.
6. See, for example, Altick, *The English Common Reader, passim*.
7. On the professionalization of periodical journalism, see John Gross, *The Rise and Fall of the Man of Letters: Aspects of English Literary Life since 1800* (London: Weidenfeld and Nicolson, 1969), especially Chapter 7 (190–210); Christopher Kent, 'Higher Journalism and the Mid-Victorian Clerisy', *VS* 13 (1969): 181–98; N.N. Feltes, *Modes of Production of Victorian Novels* (Chicago: University of Chicago Press, 1986), *passim*; and John L. Kijinski, 'Professionalism, Authority, and the Late-Victorian Man of Letters: A View from the Macmillan Archive', *Victorian Literature and Culture* 24 (1996): 229–47.
8. 'English Publishing and the Mass Audience in 1852', *SB* 6 (1954): 4.
9. Q.D. Leavis, *Fiction and the Reading Public* (London: Chatto & Windus, 1932) 37 and *passim*.
10. Leavis 185 and *passim*.
11. Patricia J. Anderson has discussed the audience for such periodicals in '"Factory Girl, Apprentice and Clerk" – The Readership of Mass-Market Magazines, 1830–6', *VPR* 25 (1992): 64–72.
12. All three of the articles cited in the following paragraph – [Margaret Oliphant,] 'The Byways of Literature. Reading for the Million',

Blackwood's Edinburgh Magazine 84 (1858): 200–16; [Wilkie Collins,] 'The Unknown Public', *Household Words* 18 (1858) 217–22; and 'Cheap Literature', *British Quarterly Review* 29 (1859): 313–45 – are mentioned by Altick in support of his point that there was 'recurrent journalistic interest in the new mass market for the printed word' during the 1850s ('English Publishing' 5).

13.   'Cheap Literature' 316.

14.   Royal A. Gettmann, *A Victorian Publisher: A Study of the Bentley Papers* (Cambridge: Cambridge University Press, 1960) 147.

15.   George Smith, 'Our Birth and Parentage', *Cornhill Magazine* ns 10 (1901): 4. Also see Spencer L. Eddy, Jr, *The Founding of* The Cornhill Magazine, Ball State Monograph 19 (Muncie, IN: Ball State University, 1970); Jenifer Glyn, *Prince of Publishers: A Biography of George Smith* (London: Alison & Busby, 1986), especially Chapters 11 and 12; and Barbara Quinn Schmidt's Introduction to a special issue of *VPR* devoted to the *Cornhill*, '*The Cornhill Magazine*: Celebrating Success', *VPR* 32 (1999) 203.

16.   Houghton 17.

17.   Altick, *The English Common Reader* 359.

18.   William Tinsley, *Random Recollections of an Old Publisher* (London: Simpkin, Marshall, 1900) 1: 323–4.

19.   Edmund Downey, *Twenty Years Ago: A Book of Anecdote Illustrating Literary Life in London* (London: Hurst and Blackett, 1905) 246–7.

20.   John Sutherland, *Victorian Novelists and Publishers* (Chicago: University of Chicago Press, 1976) 38.

21.   George Saintsbury, *A History of Nineteenth Century Literature (1780–1900)* (London: Macmillan, 1908) 166. This quotation is taken from Saintsbury's fourth chapter, 'The Development of Periodicals'; in the ninth, 'Later Journalism and Criticism in Arts and Letters', Saintsbury applies his argument to newer periodicals like *Macmillan's*, showing in some detail that 'almost all the critical work of the latter part of the century' (403) was first published in such magazines. Mark Pattison, another witness to the importance of periodicals in the nineteenth century, went further than Saintsbury: in a lecture on 'Books and Critics' delivered on 29 October 1877 and reprinted in the *Fortnightly Review* the following month, Pattison claimed that 'the monthly periodical seems destined to supersede books altogether' and held that 'the monthlies … form at this moment the most characteristic and pithy part of our literary produce' (ns 22: 663).

22.   Michael Wolff, 'Victorian Reviewers and Cultural Responsibility', *1859: Entering an Age of Crisis* 269.

23.   *The George Eliot Letters*, ed. Gordon S. Haight (New Haven: Yale University Press, 1955) 3: 214.

24.   *William Allingham: A Diary*, ed. H[elen] Allingham and D. Radford (London: Macmillan, 1907) 303.

25.   Margaret Oliphant, *The Victorian Age of Literature* (London: Perceval, 1892) 2: 301. Writing more than a century later, Mays usefully contextualizes concerns like Tennyson's and Oliphant's. Later in the chapter of *The Victorian Age of Literature* from which my quotation is taken, Oliphant voices a common estimate of *Macmillan's*, to which she was a long-time contributor: that it 'has always been remarkable for correct taste and refinement of style, though occasionally perhaps a little too academic in tone for the general reader' (2: 307).

26. See, for example, Graham Chainey, *A Literary History of Cambridge* (Ann Arbor: University of Michigan Press, 1986) 145. In his seventies, Leslie Stephen remembered visiting the Macmillans' establishment as a young man, calling it 'a literary centre'. 'In the modest shop of those days, and still more in a smoking-room at the back, I felt that I was really entering the inner shrine of a literary workshop' ('Some Early Impressions', *Atlantic Monthly* 92 [1903]: 314). For a comprehensive account of the significance of Macmillan and Co.'s presence in Cambridge see David McKitterick, *A History of Cambridge University Press* 2 (Cambridge: Cambridge University Press, 1998), *passim*, especially 386–401.
27. Thomas Hughes, *Memoir of Daniel Macmillan* (London: Macmillan, 1883) 116.
28. Sutherland 117–32. One of the 'Best-Sellers' listed by Altick in Appendix B of *The English Common Reader* (385), *Westward Ho!* went through three editions in three years (Morgan 42–3). Although these totaled only 8000 copies, a seemingly modest figure, it should be noted that Mudie's highly influential circulating library bought 350 copies of the first edition; each of them was read by numerous subscribers. Kingsley's novel enjoyed a steady sale, so that Macmillan and Co. felt justified in printing half a million copies of a sixpenny edition in 1889 (Morgan 136).
29. Sutherland 44.
30. Sutherland 52.
31. Much closer to *Macmillan's* in nature and purpose than the *Quarterly Review* was *Murray's Magazine*, which came on the scene late, in January 1887, and lasted only until 1891.
32. After the *Fortnightly Review*, which had begun publication in 1865 and which was actually a monthly from November 1866, ran into severe financial difficulties, Chapman and Hall also became its publisher in 1867.
33. Smith 5.
34. G.A. Macmillan xxvi.
35. Graves 70.
36. Graves 91–2.
37. G.A. Macmillan 4.
38. Edward C. Mack and W.H.G. Armytage, *Thomas Hughes: The Life of the Author of* Tom Brown's Schooldays (London: Benn, 1952) 107.
39. Mack and Armytage 108. Ludlow himself had been interested in serving as editor; see *John Ludlow: The Autobiography of a Christian Socialist*, ed. A.D. Murray (London: Frank Cass, 1981) 316. Parry argues persuasively that Alexander Macmillan preferred Masson over Ludlow because the latter was too radical; see Parry 1986: 149.
40. Alfred Ainger, 'Alexander Macmillan (A Personal Reminiscence)', *Macmillan's Magazine* 73 (1896): 400.
41. Add MSS 55837, fols 34–5.
42. Torben Christensen, *Origin and History of Christian Socialism 1848–54* (Aarhus: Universitetsforlaget, 1962) 69.
43. Charles E. Raven, *Christian Socialism 1848–1854* (London: Macmillan, 1920) 107.
44. 2 (1851): 406.
45. 5 April 1852: 113–14.
46. 12 April 1852: 121.

47. Ten months before the first number of *Macmillan's* appeared, Macmillan and Co. began publishing yet another periodical with strong Christian Socialist associations, the *Working Men's College Magazine*, which ran from 1 January 1859 until 1 January 1862. Primarily an in-house publication for the College rather than an outlet for Christian Socialist doctrine, it contained many contributions by Maurice, the College's principal.

48. Raven 157. Raven lists the membership of the Council of Promoters, taken from its *First Report* (26 July 1852), on 378–9. Working from marked copies, he also prints a list of contributors to *Politics for the People* on 371–5 and to the first volume of the *Christian Socialist* on 375–7. A marked copy of the single volume of the *Journal of Association* in the University of London Library gives the names of contributors and correspondents. Brenda Colloms provides much useful information about these periodicals in her *Victorian Visionaries* (London: Constable, 1982).

49. G.A. Macmillan xv.

50. Graves 19.

51. Graves 103.

52. Suspicious of such labels in general, Macmillan himself was particularly uncomfortable with the term 'Broad Church', even though it was more or less applicable to him; see his letter of 26 March 1862 to Randall Davidson (Add MSS 55841, fol. 541). In a letter he wrote to T.A. Aldis on 29 July of the following year, Macmillan explained that he was 'a Churchman by deliberate choice', disliking 'dissent because of its exclusiveness' (Add MSS 55831, fol. 348).

53. G.A. Macmillan xxiii.

54. G.A. Macmillan xiv.

55. G.A. Macmillan xx.

56. Colloms 5.

57. Raven 126.

58. Macmillan's 'The Existence of Evil and the Existence of Good' was published on 7 June 1851 (1: 250–51); a sonnet by him followed eight weeks later, on 2 August 1851 (2: 79–80). Both were signed with the pseudonym 'Amos Yates'.

59. Macmillan was excessively modest when he corrected an old friend's mistaken impression that he was '*Editor* of the magazine that bears my unworthy name. It is true I projected it: to some extent I influence his tone ... but I am only a dealer in literature as anyone might be in cheese or pork' (G.A. Macmillan xiii). He was not, of course, the only Victorian publisher who played such an active role in a magazine brought out by his firm: George Smith, to name just one other example, was similarly engaged in shaping the early *Cornhill*. As R.H. Super put it, 'the success of a periodical depended a great deal more on the publisher than the editor'; *The Chronicler of Barsetshire: A Life of Anthony Trollope* (Ann Arbor: University of Michigan Press, 1988) 273.

CHAPTER TWO

The Role of Alexander Macmillan

Throughout the editorships of David Masson (1859–1867) and George Grove (1868–1883), Alexander Macmillan did more than anyone else to shape the policies and determine the contents of *Macmillan's Magazine*. His grip loosened during John Morley's brief tenure (May 1883 to October 1885), and he finally let go altogether while Mowbray Morris was in charge from November 1885. As we shall see in Chapter 5, the fact that Macmillan was withdrawing from the direction of the *Magazine* during the dozen years before his death in 1896 helps to account for its decline under those last two editors.

While Alexander Macmillan and *Macmillan's Magazine* were in their prime, however, he energetically solicited manuscripts; he reserved, although he did not always choose to exercise, the final authority to accept or reject submitted work; and he felt free to make suggestions to would-be contributors, no matter how experienced or established they were. Generally he was far from arbitrary in his dealings with authors, nor did he deliberately ride roughshod over his editors. On the contrary, his extensive surviving correspondence with these men and women of letters evinces great patience, a wide knowledge of literature and a lofty conception of its function, and almost unfailing courtesy, kindness and good humor, shown even to those whom he could not accommodate. It is no wonder that he managed to charm a number of well-known writers into becoming *Macmillan's*, and Macmillan and Co., authors. Macmillan was also a peacemaker, imbuing a diverse group of individualists with a common purpose while giving them a great deal of freedom to write as they would, smoothing their ruffled feelings and accepting ultimate responsibility for the sometimes controversial material they produced. With his editors, as with many of his contributors, he remained on excellent personal terms, although these relationships were not always free of strains. The *Magazine* was well named after all, because, for at least its first couple of decades, it truly was Alexander Macmillan's.

Recruiting authors

Macmillan began approaching prospective contributors during the summer of 1859. On 18 July, more than three months before the first issue was published, he asked George Wilson, an old Edinburgh friend, for 'something of yours in an early number – if possible the first. You have I know that little thing, "Pens Paper, Ink", somewhere about ready for printing.' Wilson's essay did appear in the November number, under a slightly different title. A week after his letter to Wilson, Macmillan wrote to Masson informing him of what he had arranged and also praising a poem by Henry Lushington called 'A Rural Ride', which had been privately printed in a small volume of *Joint Compositions* by Lushington and George Stovin Venables. (Lushington having died in 1855, it was Venables who called it to Macmillan's attention.)

> The poem ... seemed to me so charming that I judged it worth securing if we could for the Maga, and I accordingly asked Venables for it. He has kindly consented, and if you agree with me as to its worth we will have it. I suggested that a short paragraph at the beginning had better be given to tell people a little about Cobbett & his Rural Rides, as I think a good many people have forgotten all about Cobbett but the name. This he agrees to do.[1]

'A Rural Ride' was duly published in the November *Macmillan's*, right after Wilson's 'Paper, Pen and Ink', with the 'short paragraph at the beginning' that Macmillan had 'suggested' expanded into a five-para-graph, two-page headnote. In the same letter of 25 July to Masson, Macmillan recommended the work of his young Cambridge friend Al-fred Ainger: an essay by Ainger, 'Books and Their Uses', was printed in the second number of the *Magazine*.[2]

In 1859 Macmillan's circle of literary acquaintances included writers far more famous than Wilson, Venables and Ainger. He began wooing the most eminent of them, Alfred Tennyson, as soon as plans for the *Magazine* were well under way, believing that something by the Poet Laureate in an early number would attract attention, gain readers and give the new monthly a cachet of solid respectability. Long an enthusiastic reader of Tennyson's poetry, Macmillan met him in Cambridge in the late summer of that year and lost no time in extracting from him a 'half promise' to contribute.[3] The poet and the publisher took an immediate liking to each other, initiating a personal and professional relationship that was to last for decades.[4] Before he left Cambridge, Tennyson invited Macmillan to visit him at Farringford, his Georgian house on the Isle of Wight,[5] and Macmillan accepted with alacrity, writing to Emily Tennyson on 29 September that, if it were convenient for her and her husband, he and Masson would pay them that visit the following week.[6] It was during this excursion that Macmillan induced Tennyson to turn his 'half promise' into a firm commitment: after his return from the Isle of Wight Macmillan wrote to Tennyson to express his pleasure that his 'Sea Dreams. An Idyll' would appear in the January number of the *Magazine*.[7]

One sign of Macmillan's skill in dealing with Tennyson was that he took great care to cultivate Emily Tennyson, praising her husband's work, sending her books and periodicals, and reasuring her that the publication of Tennyson's poetry in *Macmillan's* would not violate his contract with Edward Moxon, then the publisher of his books. Although 'Sea Dreams' did not have the dramatic effect on the fortunes of the *Magazine* that Macmillan had hoped for, he was correct in his prediction to Emily Tennyson that it had 'no doubt been of service to us in a permanent sense':[8] Tennyson went on contributing poetry to *Macmillan's*,[9] and from 1884 Macmillan and Co. became the publisher of his books as well. Aggressive as he was in securing writers for the *Magazine*, Macmillan also believed in taking long views, with results that almost always redounded to the prosperity of his firm.[10]

Macmillan's alertness for material that might be suitable for the *Magazine* continued, as his letters attest again and again. For instance, in June 1862 he was struck by a report on recent developments in Montenegro, then engaged in a particularly bitter phase of its perpetual struggle against domination by the neighboring Austrian and Ottoman Empires, which he had received from Georgina Muir Mackenzie, an indefatigable Balkan traveler,[11] and immediately sent her a request for an article:

> People ask where Montenegro is … Won't you write us a good clear account of how the matter stands and I will prevail on our Editor to insert it in the first possible number of our magazine after its arrival. By all means say what you think the conduct of England ought to be. We can only afford you 8 pages of the Magazine for such a subject … [12]

True to his word, Macmillan saw to it that Mackenzie's 'Montenegro, the Herzegovine, and the Slavonic Populations of Turkey' appeared in the August 1862 number: coming to eight printed pages, it began with an explanation of 'where Montenegro is' and ended with a recommendation as to 'what … the conduct of England ought to be'. ('The catastrophe of Mussulman domination is approaching; let us prepare for it by educating those Christian nationalities [like the Montenegrins] who are the lawful heirs of its inheritance.'[13])

Needless to say, Macmillan's efforts on behalf of his magazine were not always successful. For instance, although he published a number of James Russell Lowell's books in England, he could not persuade this American whom he greatly admired to write for *Macmillan's*, and his attempt, with Grove's help, to commission an article from John Bright on Gladstone's decision to retire from the leadership of the Liberal Party was equally unavailing.[14] Nevertheless, the frequency of such initiatives tells us much not only about Macmillan's enterprise as a publisher but also, and especially, about the active part he took in the affairs of the *Magazine*.

Macmillan's Magazine was of course closely linked with the principal business of Macmillan and Co., the publication of books, and Alexander Macmillan diligently fostered that connection: like Tennyson, the writers whom he recruited for the *Magazine* often turned into the authors of Macmillan and Co. books. The case of Christina Rossetti makes a good example. There is abundant, if not unfailingly clear, evidence that it was thanks to Alexander Macmillan's interest in her work, strange as it must have seemed to him, that she made her *Magazine* debut in the February 1861 number with 'Up-Hill'; the one rather diffident letter she had written David Masson the previous month[15] apparently got her nowhere, but the 79 addressed to Macmillan – 60 at the British Library and 19 in the Berg Collection – attest to an increasingly close and cordial relationship between the publisher and the poet from the early 1860s on. There were to be 22 more of Christina Rossetti's poems in *Macmillan's*,[16] and Macmillan's fascination with 'Goblin Market'[17] led to the publication of *Goblin Market and Other Poems* by Macmillan and Co. in 1862. His firm went on to bring out virtually all the rest of her books of poetry.

Relations with Masson and Grove

Although Macmillan made an elaborate show of deferring to his editors, there is much evidence that it was he who ultimately determined the magazine's contents. When R.D. Blackmore, whose first novel, *Clara Vaughan*, Macmillan and Co. had published in three volumes in 1864, sought a periodical in which to serialize his next one, *Cradock Nowell*, he submitted it not to Masson but directly to Macmillan, who accepted it for the *Magazine*, where it ran from May 1865 until August 1866. (As we shall see later in this chapter, the course of its serialization turned out to be less than smooth.) Likewise, Charles Kingsley offered *The Water-Babies* to his friend Macmillan, who told him in a letter dated 13 May 1862 that 'from your description of the Story I think it will suit us admirably, and form a new and interesting feature in our Magazine'; he asked Kingsley to send him 'any chapters you have ready … so that I may see them and consult with Masson'.[18] As a result of this overture to Macmillan, Kingsley's 'Faery Tale for a Land-Baby' began its eight-month run in *Macmillan's* in August and was published as a book the following year,[19] one of a dozen titles by that prolific clergyman issued by Macmillan and Co. in 1863 alone. Equally revealing is a letter Macmillan wrote on 4 August 1864 to a cousin, Hugh Macmillan, about his essay 'Our Garden Wall': 'Editor David', he said in part, 'has your paper. I have used all the influence I a humble publisher dare, to urge its insertion in our next number. For indeed I am proud of my clansman.'[20] Obviously Alexander Macmillan had no difficulty in persuading Masson to appreciate the virtues of his relative's piece, for it did appear in the next number of the *Magazine*.

On those rare occasions when something that offended Macmillan made its way into print during Masson's editorship, he did not hesitate to express his displeasure. Having spent two happy months in the United States and Canada in 1867, he was dismayed to find that in his absence the October *Macmillan's* had carried an article by Stephen Buckland, 'Eating and Drinking in America: A Stroll among the Saloons of New York', which Macmillan believed gave a false picture of a city where he had been cordially received and splendidly entertained. His reproachful letter of 18 November 1867 to Masson is almost unique among all his voluminous correspondence in its crossness:

> I was very sorry to see it in the Magazine, because it belongs to a class of English gossip on American subjects that gives great and, as I think, just offence to the substantial citizens of that Great Country. I have no doubt Mr Buckland describes what he saw but it is evident to me that he saw as exceptional a side of the country. I mixed with a considerable variety of people there and saw nothing like it.[21]

In the rest of a long paragraph, Macmillan went on to cite examples of the civility of New Yorkers as he had recently experienced it and pointed out that 'there are places in London' just as crude as those in New York depicted by Buckland. Apparently that unfortunate had submitted other work to Masson, and Macmillan was adamant in his instructions: 'All this means "dont take Buckland's paper." Give him any excuse you like.' Sure enough, Buckland never again made an appearance in *Macmillan's Magazine*.

Concerned about publishing anything that might exacerbate the already strained feelings between England and the United States in the wake of the American Civil War, Macmillan informed Masson about a damage-control measure that he had already taken: 'I have asked an able American to give us an article on the American Lecture System, which will be … appropriate while Dickens is there.'[22] The 'able American' was Thomas Wentworth Higginson, a highly cultivated New Englander;[23] his 'The American Lecture System' was printed in the May 1868 *Macmillan's* when Dickens was on the way home from his American reading tour of 1867–68 – itself a gesture of reconciliation.

Neither Macmillan's stern letter to Masson about the Buckland article nor his decisiveness in this and many other matters should be construed as evidence of a fundamental high-handedness. Rather, such behavior must be viewed in the light of the long and friendly association between the two men, for theirs was clearly the sort of relationship that occasional differences cannot permanently spoil. By 1867 they had known each other for nearly two decades, ever since both of them had participated in the early stages of the Christian Socialist movement. Macmillan and Co. published almost all of Masson's books, beginning with his *Essays Biographical and Critical* in 1856; Macmillan himself regarded the most ambitious of these works, the six-volume *Life of Milton: Narrated in Connection with the Political, Ecclesiastical, and Literary History of His Time* (1859–80) as 'the best history of the time, spiritual and literary, that exists'.[24] Yet theirs was a personal as well as a business connection: they frequently spent holidays together, *à deux* or with their families;[25] and after Macmillan's death, Masson, by then in his seventies, wrote that 'The memory of him will be among my possessions till I go too. He was one of the oldest of my friends, and connected with me by the most close and affectionate intimacy through many years.'[26]

Alexander Macmillan's relationship with George Grove, the second editor of *Macmillan's* and an early Christian Socialist like Macmillan and Masson, was similarly 'close and affectionate'. Speaking at a banquet celebrating the publication by Macmillan and Co. of the second volume of his *Dictionary of Music and Musicians* in 1880, Grove referred to his long 'connexion' with Macmillan, 'during which he has always shown himself a generous and sympathising friend', and expressed his gratitude for 'the liberality and generosity of my friend Mr Macmillan throughout this long and difficult undertaking'.[27] In the extensive correspondence between them preserved in the British Library's Macmillan Archive, Grove regularly addressed Macmillan more familiarly as 'Dear Mac'.

Like his predecessor, Grove was bombarded with suggestions from Alexander Macmillan regarding possible contributors and contributions, and – as he had done with Masson – Macmillan often went beyond mere advice, accepting work for the *Magazine* on the assumption that Grove would run it. Thus he sent Grove a poem by Charles Kingsley, 'The Priest's Heart', on 17 September 1873, telling his editor that he had 'promised' Kingsley that it 'shall go into the October Mag. I hope you will be delighted to have it.'[28] Whether Grove was 'delighted' or not, the poem did appear in that number. Something similar happened five years later: George Meredith gave Macmillan his poem 'Love in the Valley'; Macmillan wrote to Grove that he found it charming;[29] and it came out in the October 1878 number of *Macmillan's*.

A few of such publisher-to-editor communications concerned Alexander Macmillan's wish to publicize forthcoming Macmillan and Co. books in the *Magazine*. In early 1877, for instance, while preparing to issue a collection of Herrick's poetry edited by Francis Turner Palgrave in his firm's Golden Treasury series, Macmillan asked Grove, at Palgrave's suggestion, to print Palgrave's preface in either the March or the April issue;[30] it appeared in the latter month. In April 1879, to cite the example of a much more famous piece of prose, Macmillan took it for granted that Grove would include Matthew Arnold's essay on Wordsworth in an early number as a way of advertising the collection of *Poems by Wordsworth*, 'chosen and edited by Matthew Arnold' and containing as its introduction a slightly altered version of Arnold's *Macmillan's Magazine* text.[31] The essay appeared in the July number, the Macmillan and Co. book in September.

It would seem then that, much as he liked them personally, Alexander Macmillan was inclined to keep the first two editors of his *Magazine* on a fairly short leash. His private dealings with Masson and Grove were also not always as harmonious as their eloquent public tributes to him implied.

Thomas Hughes had objected to 'Masson's handling' of his editorial responsibilities as early as October 1860,[32] but Macmillan stood by his man for years. Things got more difficult after Masson moved from London in 1865 to take up the position of Professor of Rhetoric and English Literature at the University of Edinburgh (the Buckland episode of 1867 did not help): the arrangement whereby Masson attempted to edit *Macmillan's* from 400 miles away simply was not working. He and Grove, who was supposed to carry out some of Masson's duties in his absence, were often at 'cross-purposes',[33] and it fell to Macmillan to sort out the resulting confusion, which caused him to be 'a little over-worked – or at least over-worried – which is worse'.[34]

In a letter Macmillan wrote to Masson on 20 December 1867, he in effect dismissed him from the editorship, although in the kindest possible way. Macmillan conceded that a *modus vivendi* might be reached if he never interfered in the *Magazine*'s affairs but 'referred every body direct to you' – something that he was obviously unwilling to do. Perhaps, Macmillan mused in that letter, the *Magazine* could get along without an editor. Grove would continue to do the 'sitting and letter writing', Masson would serve as consultant at £100 a year, and (of course) Macmillan would retain the real authority. Regretting that 'we cannot go on as we did in the old pleasant days' and expressing the hope that Masson would continue to take 'a friends interest' in *Macmillan's Magazine*, Macmillan went on to propose that Masson remain nominally in charge 'till the end of the volume'[35] – that is, April 1868. That appears to have been what happened. Grove was editor in all but name from January 1868[36] and took over officially with the new volume that began in May of that year.

Like Masson, Grove had been occupying the editor's chair for several years before Macmillan put his dissatisfaction with him in writing. On the surface, at least, the trouble seemed to be mainly financial. Also like Masson, Grove was paid £25 per number, or £300 per annum, for editing *Macmillan's Magazine*. In addition, however, Grove received £600 a year for 'his assistance in managing the literary part' of Macmillan and Co. and 'a further £400 on account of half-profits on books that you were to write'. However, there had *been* no such books by December 1876, and Macmillan wrote to Grove on the 7th 'to put before you [presumably not for the first time, although no earlier letters on this delicate subject appear to have survived] how very unsatisfactory the present state of matters between us is'. (Macmillan did sign this letter 'ever affectionately yours'.) Eleven days later Macmillan informed Grove that he was willing to wait a year to make a final decision about Grove's future with the firm but added that the management would like to 'be able to count on your presence at definite times'[37] – no doubt a reference to the over-committed editor's frequent travels.

Grove's magnum opus, the *Dictionary of Music and Musicians*, did begin appearing the following year – Macmillan and Co. published the first volume in 1877, the second in 1880, the third in 1883 and the fourth in 1889 – but his role as literary adviser came to an end in 1880. 'The Editorship of the Magazine we propose shall remain in your hands', Macmillan wrote to him on 16 June, 'and after a consultation with the partners we propose to increase your salary for editing the Magazine from £300 to £500.'[38] If Grove regarded this as a blow, Macmillan had found a way to soften it, and when the time came, two and a half years later, to remove Grove from the editorship, it was Craik rather than Macmillan who administered the *coup de grâce*, as we shall see in Chapter 5.

Dealing with authors

In corresponding with contributors to his magazine, Macmillan resorted to the same tempered forthrightness that marked his correspondence with Masson and Grove. A diligent reader of their work, he never hesitated to offer suggestions or voice criticisms, assuming a tone that varied according to his perception of what he could usefully say to a particular writer.

With his old friend Margaret Oliphant, for instance, he must have thought that he could afford to indulge in banter – correctly so, for she continued to supply him copiously with fiction and nonfiction for many years. While her *A Son of the Soil* was being serialized in the *Magazine* between November 1863 and April 1865, Macmillan wrote to her more than once that, although he admired the novel, he thought it was too diffuse and too polemical. What troubled him especially were her references to the controversial religious views of Benjamin Jowett, who was mentioned by name in the February 1865 installment, in Chapter 44.[39]

> Mr Maurice was remarking on it. I said it was the wonted audacity of woman, and the wonted cowardice of man that I did not mutter a remonstrance – indeed did not even think of one. See how the coarser sex cower before you – Oh ye Tyranesses.

(Macmillan signed his letter, uncharacteristically but in keeping with the tone he had assumed in it, 'Your humble slave'.[40]) When she revised the text of her novel for the two-volume edition published by Macmillan and Co. in 1866, Oliphant obligingly changed the 'Jowett' to 'Heward' and also removed an ironic reference to Jowett as 'the great heresiarch'. As we shall notice in Chapter 4, however, Oliphant won more than her share of these epistolary exchanges with Alexander Macmillan and his associates.

Another woman who published fiction in *Macmillan's*, Caroline Norton, had to be handled with greater care, and again Alexander Macmillan took it upon himself to do the negotiating. Twenty years older and even more strong-willed than Oliphant, Norton bristled when Macmillan informed her on 24 April 1866 that he had held back a chapter called 'Royal Idols' from the May installment of her *Old Sir Douglas* because he considered it disrespectful of the Queen. Although praising her 'very beautiful novel, which is charming us all', Macmillan was quite explicit about 'Royal Idols': 'it would not do to put it in the magazine under any possible circumstances'. He went on to state his 'sincere hope that you will kindly leave it out of the novel as it appears in the Magazine' because, 'much as I feel that it would cause obloquy to us, I should regret much more what I think it would bring on you'.[41] In her reply of the same date Norton was indignant: she maintained that she had written her novel 'with a distinct purpose' and, after a long and often tumultuous career in the public eye, she had come to be indifferent to 'obloquy'; for her, she insisted, 'it is not a question of omitting a *chapter* but omitting *the book*, if one main purpose of the book is to be objected to'.[42]

Although Norton did promise to take another look at the revised proofs of the offending chapter, it began to appear that Macmillan had met his match, for the serialized version of 'the book' was actually withdrawn from *Macmillan's* for the next three months. Nothing about its absence was mentioned in the June number. In July there was a note announcing, 'with great regret, that the publication of the Hon. Mrs. NORTON'S Story of "OLD SIR DOUGLAS" is discontinued in these pages', but by August she and Macmillan must have reached some sort of agreement, for that number carried the news that 'The Editor has great pleasure in announcing that the Hon. Mrs. Norton's story, "OLD SIR DOUGLAS", will be resumed in the SEPTEMBER number.' So it was, but without 'Royal Idols'. There were to be two more interruptions in the serial run of Norton's novel: the one in January 1867 was explained as the result of 'the authoress's illness'; the other, in April of the same year, was unaccounted for, but readers were assured that the 'Story will be continued in the number for May'.[43]

Alexander Macmillan's daughter Margaret told his biographer that 'her father had a great admiration for Mrs. Norton',[44] and their differences over *Old Sir Douglas* should probably be regarded in that context. Certainly the relationship between them had begun auspiciously several years before the impasse of 1866. The granddaughter of Richard Brinsley Sheridan, Norton took grave exception to what she considered to be three scurrilous books about her famous family and wrote to Macmillan offering to supply an appropriate rejoinder for publication in the *Magazine*. As 'Books of Gossip: Sheridan and His Biographers', this appeared in *Macmillan's* in January 1861.

Macmillan agreed to accept her 'Letter to the Publisher' before he had read it, feeling strongly about the issues it addressed: 'on public, as well as on private grounds', he wrote to Norton on 19 November 1860, he would have 'the greatest pleasure in inserting your rebuke to those wretched pandarers to the depraved appetite for detraction & scandal which unfortunately generates as well as grows on what it feeds on'. A second letter from Macmillan to Norton written five days later was even more explicit in stating his view of the proper function, and the necessary limits, of literary discourse:

> I can assure you it will be a real delight to me to have this letter in our Magazine. The recklessness with which people permit themselves to speak of persons even who are alive has always stirred my anger even more than direct wilful lying would – on a mere rumour and often in mere vacant thoughtlessness reputations are gossiped away, the usefulness of many a man and woman destroyed[,] suspicion and ill blood bred to a fearful extent. I can assure you that there will be no disposition on my part – nor do I think Mr Massons – to mitigate a word of censure you have written. If you made it stronger I should not regret.[45]

By declaring his willingness to open the pages of his magazine to corrections of such illegitimate exercises of the freedom to publish, Macmillan was enlarging on Thomas Hughes's motto, 'no flippancy or abuse allowed'. On a more positive note, he always contended that *Macmillan's* should be a means of moral instruction. 'I cannot tell you how anxious I am that every thing we put into our Magazine should be manly and elevating',[46] he wrote to Franklin Lushington within a fortnight of the appearance of the first number. 'I dont in the least believe', he continued, 'that the aimless and frivolous is as interesting as that which means something'.[47] Macmillan's expression 'that which means something' must of course be understood in connection with his own beliefs and attitudes. Living in an age when received opinions and traditional ways were being subjected to unprecedented challenges was a serious business, he held, and the many fundamental problems of which thoughtful nineteenth-century men and women were all too keenly aware could not be trivialized or simply disregarded. Rather, they should be conscientiously and even reverently explored, an essential process of which responsible periodical journalism formed a vital component. Over and over again, Alexander Macmillan's correspondence articulates this credo, and its results in the contents of his *Magazine* are plain for all unbiased readers to see.

The American Civil War

While the new *Macmillan's* was establishing its position on the literary scene in the early 1860s, no question before the British public was more persistent than what the nation's stance toward the American Civil War should be. For a variety of reasons, the aristocratic, manufacturing and commercial classes, which still wielded immense power, favored the Confederacy. So did almost all the daily newspapers, most notably the *Times*, all but a few weeklies, including the influential *Saturday Review*, the *Press*, the *Guardian* and the *Examiner*, as well as *Punch* and its comic imitators and rivals, and such leading opinion-molders as *Blackwood's* and the *Quarterly Review*. Many writers and intellectuals refused to commit themselves to either side, deploring the often blatant shortcomings of North and South alike. For Alexander Macmillan, however, the complicated struggle in America tended to boil down to one simple issue: slavery. 'No one can ... feel more the iniquity of slavery than I do', he wrote to Elizabeth Gaskell.[48] Like such fellow Christian Socialists as Hughes, Ludlow and Maurice, all three of whom gave voice to their strong anti-slavery feelings in *Macmillan's*, he regarded this as so manifestly a moral and religious issue that advocacy of the Union case became imperative, despite his frequently expressed misgivings about the Northern position.

Macmillan's great fear was that political demagogs on both sides of the Atlantic and the scribblers they hired might drive a wedge, and perhaps even bring about a war, between Britain and the North; his great hope was that the right sort of articles in *Macmillan's* might lead to a better understanding between the two nations. Accordingly, he commissioned

Edward Dicey, whom Brian Jenkins has placed at 'the forefront of the pro-Union activists' in England,[49] to send back from his American travels in 1862 'a Series of articles, the great aim of which will be wisely to remove the misunderstandings between the Northern States and this country';[50] signed 'Our Special Correspondent in America', these appeared monthly in *Macmillan's* from April until September. There were many other articles like them in the *Magazine* between 1861 and 1865 – articles that plainly bore the stamp of Macmillan's own convictions.[51]

It would be misleading, however, to imply that those convictions were always clear, consistent or (from our present-day perspective) enlightened. Nor would it be accurate to say that contributors to *Macmillan's Magazine* always spoke with one voice, that of its publisher, on this or any other subject.

In some of Alexander Macmillan's letters dealing with the Civil War, his support of the North sounds less than wholehearted, at any rate not ardent enough to cause him to advocate British involvement. Well into the second year of the conflict, on 16 June 1862, he wrote to Henry Kingsley, apropos of a comment in that morning's *Times* that the American war was 'aimless':

> The aim may not be a good one, but many of less importance have served to keep blood flowing for years & years. I am thankful to see that our government is not going to attempt mediation ... Our policy is to stand by and let them fight it out. Our policy, and I suspect the just and merciful thing too in the long run. I do hope that it will drive our merchants and monied people to see what can be done in Jamaica [,] India & Australia in growing cotton for ourselves.[52]

Even about slavery Macmillan could occasionally sound ambivalent. In the August 1863 *Macmillan's* there appeared a piece that was instantly recognized as Thomas Carlyle's, so very brief that it can be given here in its entirety:

> ILIAS (AMERICANA) IN NUCE
> PETER *of the North* (*to* PAUL *of the South*). 'Paul, you unaccountable scoundrel, I find you hire your servants for life, not by the month or year as I do! You are going straight to Hell, you — !'
> PAUL. 'Good words, Peter! The risk is my own; I am willing to take the risk. Hire you your servants by the month or the day, and get straight to Heaven; leave me to my own method.'
> PETER. 'No, I won't. I will beat your brains out first!' (*And is trying dreadfully ever since, but cannot yet manage it.*)
> MAY, 1863   T.C.[53]

The publication of this outburst, quintessentially Carlylean if atypically terse,[54] aroused protests from two of Macmillan's closest Christian Socialist allies, Ludlow and Maurice. Macmillan's rather different replies to them teach us much about the man and about the view he took of his *Magazine*.

The one to Ludlow professed Macmillan's disagreement with the apparent message of 'Ilias (Americana) in Nuce' but defended Carlyle: 'He is not "a bad old man",[55] but a very noble & useful one, and even his wrong sayings have wisdom and significance in them which are wanting in the rabid vapid utterance of deepest truths.' Macmillan urged Ludlow to respond to Carlyle ('you know very well that the pages of the magazine are opener to you than to Carlyle'), which Ludlow promptly did: his 'Servitude for Life (A Brief Dialogue)' was published in *Macmillan's* the next month.[56] Throughout his answer to Ludlow, as was appropriate to the occasion, Macmillan took pains to assert his own belief in liberty, shrewdly extending the meaning of the term to apply to the point at issue between himself and Ludlow: 'Wherein does the value of a theory of human freedom consist that permits no divergence of opinion, no freedom of discussion? … I am for freedom, my most excellent & wellbeloved friend John, & mean to have it against all tyranny over others, even in thought.'[57]

Macmillan's answer to Maurice, who had taken public exception to Carlyle's American *Iliad*-in-a-nutshell in the *Spectator* of 8 August 1863, went further than his letter to Ludlow in revealing a readiness to sympathize with Carlyle's idiosyncratic argument:

> I did not agree with Carlyle as you know, and think your retort in the Spectator merited. But I did not feel that it was open to the charge of being mere folly. There is a root of wisdom in what he said. It is an element of good in slavery that the connection has a certain permanency in it. He ignores – no doubt with a humorous wilfulness the other side. But I do not think the grand old man is the fool you say. You will see a bit of John Malcolms retort in the next number.

Before turning to the 'Ilias (Americana) in Nuce', Macmillan confessed to Maurice in the same letter that he was beginning to have doubts about the North's war aims after a conversation with 'two pleasant cultivated Americans', concluding that 'Lust for empire not slavery sustains the present war' and voicing

> the feeling the sooner England recognizes the Confederacy the better for herself & humanity. God knows I hate & abominate slavery in every shape with my whole heart, but there are really worse forms of it than the planter form bad as it is. Modern Yankeedom will become old Rome without her dignity, unless in Gods providence something comes to stop her mad career.[58]

What this disturbing episode shows about Alexander Macmillan, among other things, is that he was willing to grant considerable leeway to a contributor whom he admired as much as he did Carlyle.[59] It also indicates that he refused to force the trusted men and women whom he encouraged to write for the *Magazine* into any sort of ideological straitjacket. Especially in the early volumes of *Macmillan's*, there was a perceptible tension between two potentially clashing principles: that the *Magazine* should promote what may be called the Christian Socialist agenda, and that it should permit, indeed encourage, the 'divergence of opinion', the 'freedom of discussion', to which Macmillan had alluded in replying to Ludlow's protest about 'Ilias (Americana) in Nuce'. A published comment on the second number of *Macmillan's* points to this contradiction as a flaw in an otherwise estimable periodical: although it had 'enlisted the aid of at least one set of thinking men who have not only something to say, but something of common principle to assert, and who are able to assert it with unequivocal ability and strength of conviction', that 'element of common faith which will, we trust, give a marked type to this periodical' did not 'quite sufficiently *permeate* the magazine'.[60]

Yet of course such 'divergence of opinion' or 'freedom of discussion' may also be viewed as a virtue, as Alexander Macmillan obviously did. Certainly it was a corollary of the precept Hughes had laid down while the *Magazine* was in its formative stages: 'Everyone to sign his own name'. *Macmillan's* was a pioneer among nineteenth-century periodicals not only in pricing each number at a shilling but also in identifying the great majority of its contributors, by name or by often transparent pseudonyms or initials,[61] thereby eschewing the magisterial 'we' that had been a convention of magazine and newspaper writing. The practice of attaching authors' signatures to articles, essays and reviews as well as to poetry and fiction served to demystify the *Magazine* as a corporate entity without destroying the purposes that it had been founded to serve. As Hughes remarked in *Macmillan's* just after it had entered its third year, it also tended to purify the tone of periodical journalism by counteracting both the thunderous bullying of the *Times* and the 'fine-gentlemanly airs, *insouciance*, and indifferentism' of the *Saturday Review*.[62]

Although it placed greater responsibility on contributors while giving them greater freedom, this practice did not ease the life of a publisher who conceived of his role *vis-à-vis* his firm's magazine as Alexander Macmillan did. 'Ilias (Americana) in Nuce' was by no means the first, or the only, piece in the *Magazine* that caused him discomfort.

Diversity and controversy

Beginning with its second number, which came out shortly after the publication of *The Origin of Species*, *Macmillan's* carried several articles that explained what Darwin had said and explored a wide range of implications of evolutionary theory. To someone of Alexander Macmillan's religious outlook, this must have been a deeply troubling subject, but he refused to close his mind or his magazine to it. When he wrote to Tennyson about that December 1859 issue, Macmillan went out of his way to draw the Laureate's attention to Thomas Henry Huxley's 'Time and Life':

> Darwins book which it mentions [Huxley's subtitle was 'Mr. Darwin's "Origin of Species"'] is remarkable certainly. I thought of 'Nature red in tooth & claw' as I was glancing over it. I wish someone would bring out the other side. But surely the scientific men ought on no account to be hindered from saying what they find as facts.

To be sure, 'theological asperity' was injected into the ensuing debate, as Macmillan conceded in a letter to Daniel Wilson the following July, for instance during the famous encounter between Huxley and Bishop Wilberforce at the British Association for the Advancement of Science meeting in Oxford. However, Macmillan was cheered by his belief that 'a true scientific spirit is on the whole gaining ground'. Like Huxley, he felt 'the greatest anxiety in the interests of science that all justice should be done to the theory and perfect fairplay given to its discussion untrammeled by the yelping of the curs of orthodoxy'.[63]

Like other contributors to *Macmillan's* (the *Magazine* printed eight more of his pieces), Huxley went on to publish books with Macmillan and Co. High on his list of concerns was the growing need he saw for a new kind of education in a dawning age of science and democracy, and he expounded his views on that question in such essays as 'A Liberal Education; and Where to Find It', the lead article in the March 1868 *Macmillan's*, and in such books as *Science and Culture and Other Essays* (Macmillan and Co., 1881). Through these and similar utterances, Huxley set himself in direct though invariably civilized opposition to another *Macmillan's* contributor and Macmillan and Co. author, Matthew Arnold, who took a very different view of liberal education and culture from Huxley's, and whose essays and books Alexander Macmillan was equally eager to bring out.[64] Between him and Arnold, as between him and Huxley, there existed strong ties that were personally cordial as well as mutually respectful, and Macmillan had no difficulty in acting as publisher to both men.

At least as much as Huxley, Arnold had a way of embroiling himself in controversy, often appearing to go out of his way to pick more or less good-natured quarrels with writers and other public figures whose stated opinions on a variety of subjects clashed with his. As Isobel Armstrong has pointed out, one of Arnold's crucial arguments in the Preface to his *Poems* of 1853 grew out of his disagreement with something David Masson had written in the *North British Review* about the appropriate subject matter of poetry, and Arnold was not above twisting a quotation from Masson by omitting a key qualifying phrase the better to suit his own polemical purpose.[65] This occurred half a dozen years before the birth of *Macmillan's Magazine* and nearly a decade before the first of Arnold's several appearances in it during Masson's editorship; that Arnold was willing to write for *Macmillan's* and Masson was willing to have him do so may well have been the result of Alexander Macmillan's skill in handling both men. Not unnaturally, given his genteel pugnacity, Arnold was also a favorite target for the criticism of others, and Macmillan's high regard for him did not prevent some of that from finding its way into the *Magazine*, most notably Henry Sidgwick's 'The Prophet of Culture' (August 1867), a key document in the evolution of the text that was to become Arnold's *Culture and Anarchy*.

In assessing Alexander Macmillan's influence on the *Magazine*, then, his firm belief in freedom of expression must be weighed along with, if not placed above, his deep convictions about what should be published in it. On those occasions when something in *Macmillan's* gave rise to ill feeling, directed against the publisher rather than the author or the editor, he could be counted on to come to the defense of his contributors. Three very different examples will illustrate how Macmillan was often called on to play this role.

The first of these involves, again, Matthew Arnold, whose first *Macmillan's* essay, 'The Bishop and the Philosopher' (January 1863), ridiculed the approach to biblical criticism taken by John William Colenso, Bishop of Natal, in his recent *The Pentateuch and Book of Joshua Critically Examined* by contrasting it with Spinoza's much more edifying approach in the *Tractatus Religio-Politicus*, which had just come out in a new English translation.[66] Although Macmillan was acquainted with Colenso, some of whose work he had been publishing since 1847, he agreed with Arnold that the Bishop had written a book that was foolish as well as dangerous. When Colenso complained to Macmillan about Arnold's article, Macmillan replied to the Bishop to say that, not without regret for the hurt Arnold had inflicted on 'one to whom I owe so much', he 'must accept the responsibility of the general view that Mr Arnold takes of your book', conceding – significantly – 'that you have more sympathy from Professor Masson, our editor than from either Mr. Arnold or myself. He thinks your book will do good in the long run.' On the same day, 27 December 1862, in a note enclosed with Arnold's check for the essay, Macmillan complimented Arnold on his 'admirable paper' and informed him that he was writing Colenso

> as civilly and inoffensively as I can to say that I quite accept the responsibility of your article, so far as it concerns him. It is very painful for *me* to say this, as he has always been kind & friendly to us. But he had no reason to say that he 'didn't expect it of me' for I told him here months since what I thought of the sort of thing, and in as plain terms as I could.[67]

So strongly did Macmillan feel about that 'sort of thing' that, three weeks after writing to Arnold and by then presumably taking a more relaxed view of Colenso's misguided attempt to apply statistics to his study of the Old Testament, he composed a limerick on the matter and sent it to the Cambridge mathematician Barnard Smith:

> There was a wise Bishop, Colenso,
> Who counted from one up to ten so,
>   That the writings Levitical
>   He found were uncritical
> And went out to tell the black men so.[68]

About another, much more famous, controversy involving religion into which Macmillan was drawn because of something that appeared in the *Magazine* his feelings were considerably more mixed. In his January 1864 *Macmillan's* review of Volumes 7 and 8 of James Anthony Froude's *History of England*, Charles Kingsley saw fit to include the following assertion, which was to have consequences beyond anything he could have imagined:

> Truth, for its own sake, had never been a virtue with the Roman clergy. Father Newman informs us that it need not, and on the whole ought not to be; that cunning is the weapon which Heaven has given to the saints to withstand the brute male force of the wicked world which marries and is given in marriage.[69]

Again it fell to Macmillan to deal with the objection of an aggrieved party to something published 'in a *Magazine* which bears your name' – what John Henry Newman called 'a grave and gratuitous slander, with which I feel confident you will be sorry to find associated a name so eminent as yours'.[70]

Macmillan's response, dated 6 January, to Newman's letter of a week earlier was suitably emollient: he had delayed his reply until he had had an opportunity to discuss the subject with Kingsley; he wanted 'to answer such a letter from you with peculiar care and reverence' because he treasured 'memories of more than twenty years since' when Newman's sermons 'were a delight & blessing shared, & thereby increased, with a dear brother no longer here'; he acknowledged that he could not dissociate himself 'from whatever injustice, and your letter convinces me that there was injustice, in Mr Kingsley's charge against you personally'; he admitted that, perhaps because of his limited 'intercourse with members of the Church that holds us heretics', he had shared Kingsley's view but regretted that 'I may have allowed heats of controversy to blind myself'; and affirmed his certainty 'that Mr Kingsley & Mr Masson both will do all in their power to repair any wrong & print a full retractation of what you feel unjust' and 'that both these gentlemen are incapable of wilfully slandering any man, and surely not more one whom all thoughtful Englishmen must owe so much to'.[71] However, neither Macmillan's long private letter to Newman nor Kingsley's one-paragraph Letter to the Editor in the next number of *Macmillan's*,[72] which was too brief and too grudging to qualify as 'a full retractation', satisfied Newman, who soon came to believe that the only effectual way to vindicate himself was to publish the history of his religious opinions that we know as the *Apologia pro vita sua*.[73]

As for Macmillan, there is evidence to indicate that, although he regretted the unnecessary dispute that Kingsley's rash words in the *Magazine* had provoked, he was motivated by more than a desire to make amends for what a valued contributor, who also happened to be an old friend and fellow Christian Socialist, had written to insult Newman: he believed that Kingsley did have at least a measure of justice on his side. A pair of key sentences in a letter Macmillan wrote to Froude on 23 February 1864, omitted from the version printed in *The Letters of Alexander Macmillan* as edited by his son, makes this quite clear:

> The old saying attributed to Tallyrand that the use of words is to conceal thought might be extended in certain cases to intellects which would then be described as the power of perplexing truth. In this art apparently Newman is a master, and thank God C.K. is not even a learner.[74]

A rereading of what Macmillan had told Newman in light of these later observations to Froude suggests that Macmillan himself had been forced to choose his words carefully, so as not to give away too much of what he really thought. Defending those whose work appeared in *Macmillan's Magazine* was not always easy for the man who felt obliged to discharge this responsibility.

Yet it was not always as difficult as in the cases of 'The Bishop and the Philosopher' or, especially, Kingsley's review of Froude's *History*. Macmillan had no trouble at all responding to the Oxfordshire clergyman who raised objections to the 'strong language' in two novels that were being serialized in the *Magazine* early in 1861, Hughes's *Tom Brown at Oxford* and Henry Kingsley's *Ravenshoe*. (There are some mild oaths in both, uttered by the sorts of speakers who could be expected to use such expressions; strategically placed dashes or asterisks are obviously meant to signify that they also resorted to more pungent words that are not written out.) It was important, Macmillan insisted, to keep in mind the general effect of such fiction, referring in the first of his two letters to the Reverend A.M. Morgan to the 'palpably noble tone that runs like life blood through *Tom Brown* & makes me proud to be its publisher'. Although valuing 'care and reverence in speech as well as in action' quite as much as his correspondent did, Macmillan was unsure that 'the extreme fastidiousness in reference to all such words such as you allude to ever can be carried out'. He confessed that 'personally I would prefer at any time erring on the side of art rather than on the side of taste or morals' and maintained that he had 'always urged this in the case of any writer with whom we have dealings', ending his second letter to Morgan with a promise that he was far better able to keep than the one he later made to Newman: 'I value your candid & courteous criticism, & shall certainly give it careful consideration.'[75]

The 'chaste Macmillan'?

These letters to Morgan call into question a charge that has often been made against Macmillan: that he was a prude in the way he ran his *Magazine* and his publishing house. When Swinburne referred to him as 'the chaste Macmillan',[76] he clearly did not mean to be complimentary. Nor was he disinterested, for he and Macmillan differed sharply about the nature and function of poetry. Macmillan turned aside Dante Gabriel Rossetti's persistent advocacy of Swinburne's work, which, he wrote to Rossetti, he regarded as showing 'genius' but also as 'very *queer* – very'. Rossetti failed to make the case for Swinburne, and nothing by him ever appeared in the *Magazine* or on Macmillan and Co.'s list of books.[77] Our best clue to what lay behind Macmillan's unwillingness to publish Swinburne may be another sentence in his letter to Rossetti: 'Whether the public could be expected to like [Swinburne's poetry] was doubtful.'[78] Reason or pretext, the concern of Macmillan the businessman for what 'the public could be expected to like' was genuine. It had to be. A year and a half later, the same concern led him to abandon his idea of issuing a selection of classic English novels. 'The difficulty is the selection', he wrote to James MacLehose on 24 February 1866. 'You begin with Richardson, Fielding, Smollett, Sterne. But what are you to do with their dirt? Modern taste won't stand it. I don't particularly think they *ought* to stand it.' However, he added, 'Still less would they stand castration.'[79]

A comment by a woman who contributed to *Macmillan's Magazine* in the 1860s, Anne Gilchrist, was closer to the mark than Swinburne's flippant characterization of Alexander Macmillan's outlook. Left with the task of completing her late husband's substantial *Life of William Blake* (Macmillan and Co., 1863) after Alexander Gilchrist's death in 1861, she complained to William Michael Rossetti about the difficulty of getting past Macmillan 'that most vigorous and admirable little bit apropos of "The Daughters of Albion"'. Macmillan was vigilant: he 'reads all the proofs' and 'would take it out again'. Gilchrist's perception of him was just: 'Mr. Macmillan is far more inexorable against any shade of heterodoxy in morals than in religion.'[80]

No attempt to assay how much of Macmillan's caution about what he published was attributable to his prudishness and how much to his prudence can have any verifiable outcome. What is indisputable, however, is that he brought to bear on submissions to the *Magazine* a much broader set of concerns than the moral rigor to which Gilchrist alluded. He knew and loved literature, and he drew on his extensive reading and his discriminating taste in arriving at his judgments of what would work in literature and what would not.

An avid bookman throughout his life, Macmillan was conversant with much English poetry and drama. When he was barely into his twenties, he edited a volume of selections from Shelley, which was published anonymously in 1840.[81] Among contemporary poets, Tennyson was his favorite: one of Macmillan's few contributions to the *Magazine*, in December 1859, was an incisive defense of *The Princess* and, especially, of *Maud* against the strictures of a recent *Quarterly* reviewer.[82] His acquaintance with English fiction was somewhat more selective – he once confessed that he could not remember having read anything by Jane Austen[83] – but he kept abreast of current literature of all kinds and often set down his reactions to it in his letters. He also had some familiarity with foreign literature. Macmillan knew German well enough to translate Heine's version of 'Die Lorelei' (this translation was published in the *Magazine* in May 1872) and to hold some strong opinions about what should be included in an anthology of *Deutsche Lyrik* brought out by his firm in 1875. Even though its editor, Karl Adolf Buchheim, was Professor of German Literature at King's College London, Macmillan disagreed vehemently with him about Heine's merits as a lyric poet. Macmillan's letter of 3 November 1874 to Buchheim is worth quoting here at some length for several reasons, quite apart from the unmistakable irritation with the professor that it betrays:

> On my return to business yesterday Mr Craik put your letter into my hands in which you seek to re-open a question which we discussed & settled some two or three years since, and I certainly

thought with your concurrence. It is with no depreciation of Goethe, even as a Song Writer that Heine was preferred, but that Goethe was so much *besides*, and your parallel between Shakespeare & Sheridan is not in the least to the point. Shakespeare was far more conspicuous by his dramas than by his poetry. He was *the* dramatist of England. Sheridan wrote plays, but he was even more eminent as a political speaker. Besides which surely Heine is far nearer Goethe in genius, I do not say he was his equal, than Sheridan was to Shakespeare. The real parallel would be that in a selection of British Songs, we would rather choose Burns than Shakespeare, because though Shakespeare has written exquisite songs, that is not the specific quality which marks him. So with Heine. He wrote no dramas like Faust, or Romances like Meister. When one thinks of Heine it is preeminently as a Singer.[84]

Although Macmillan would sometimes cite the exigencies of business – his need 'to calculate what will commercially pay' – when he tried to let down disappointed contributors as gently as possible, he normally invoked literary criteria in justifying his decisions. About English prosody, for instance, he held firm views, referring on one occasion, in 1860, to 'an old quarrel of mine with young authors – that about rhythm':

I dont think that it is a mere love of smoothness that induces me to cry out against imperfect rhythm. I can get at and even intensely admire Tennysons queerest metres, because after due pains taken I can get them to go and can gallop on or canter or trot along them without breaking my poor nags knees. The reading of imperfect rhythm puts my teeth on edge like saw sharpening. Our greatest poets *never could help* writing sweetly and not the less sweetly when most mighty. I remember long (twenty years) ago a young poet – who hasn't come to much in that line – prophecying to me about the grandeur of the rugged verse, and my challenging him to find an example in Milton, Shakespeare ... or any really great poet – and he couldn't.[85]

Macmillan's role in the so-called bowdlerization of two works that appeared in the *Magazine*, the serial version of R.D. Blackmore's *Cradock Nowell* and Tennyson's 'Lucretius', has been the subject of much valuable scholarship,[86] but, if viewed in the light of the argument I have been developing, the available data suggest a somewhat different conclusion from the one usually reached: it seems clear that Macmillan's interventions in the textual histories of these works were not grounded primarily in his squeamishness. Moreover, they did not bring about any serious breach in his friendly relations with Blackmore and Tennyson.

Even a brief sketch of Macmillan's dealings with the author of *Cradock Nowell* should begin with the publishing history of *Clara Vaughan*, brought out in three volumes by Macmillan and Co. in 1864, because going back to Blackmore's first novel provides a revealing context in which to judge the fortunes of *Cradock Nowell*, his second. Although apparently there had been no question of running *Clara Vaughan* as a serial in *Macmillan's*, Alexander Macmillan did recommend it to John Willis Clark, editor of *Cassell's Illustrated Family Paper*, and handled the often delicate negotiations that ensued, at one point offering Blackmore £100 when the payment proposed by Clark fell short of what he required. The grateful Blackmore called Macmillan's intercession 'wonderfully kind'; it was also successful, for the novel did duly appear in *Cassell's*, between 12 March and 8 August 1864. Macmillan had won Blackmore's confidence to such an extent that it was to him that Blackmore complained about the way *Cassell's* had tampered with his text, making '72 alterations (every one of them for the worse)' in the first number alone, thereby 'converting Clara's hot strong English into diluted & stale pig's wash'.[87] Blackmore was not much happier about his experience with the three-volume *Clara Vaughan*, but most of his displeasure was aroused by the errors committed by Macmillan's printer rather than by anything that could be construed as stylistic meddling or censorship perpetrated by Macmillan himself.

Despite such problems with *Clara Vaughan*, Blackmore did send *Cradock Nowell*, his next novel, to Alexander Macmillan, who after some delay accepted it for the *Magazine*, offering £250 for the serial version.[88] Even before the first installment appeared in May 1865, however, Blackmore began objecting to Macmillan's and Masson's attempts to smooth down the rougher features of his language, and these protests continued throughout the novel's 16–month run. On 2 August 1865, for instance, Blackmore expressed puzzlement about the changes that had been made to two sentences in the latest number, professing his failure to understand how they could have been 'objectionable to the very mildest society'. 'I must entreat you', his letter continued,

> to let me have the last supervision of what is inserted. All my sentences are so cast & turned in the brain-lathe afterwards, that they cannot be meddled with by any but the author without destroying the balance. ... You will think all this great prudery, just as I do your social exigencies; but by this time we can, I think, allow for one another.[89]

The conciliatory note Blackmore struck in that sentence continued to be heard, along with his protests, through the rest of his correspondence with Macmillan about *Cradock Nowell*; after the final installment was published in the *Magazine* a year later he wrote to thank Macmillan for his friendship and understanding even though 'we differ about little questions of art'. 'A book "without a d—n in it" seems to suit people best', Blackmore conceded; 'perhaps you are right in your knowledge of their taste'.[90] Although Blackmore clearly did not like having the text of *Cradock Nowell* interfered with, he was much more disturbed by

Macmillan's wish that he abridge the novel so as to make room in the *Magazine* for Henry Kingsley's *Silcote of Silcotes*,[91] but again he complied, reluctantly.

Whatever Blackmore's feelings about his treatment over *Cradock Nowell* may have been, however, he did try Macmillan with his third novel. That he failed – 'I came to offer you "Lorna Doone" for the Magazine; but you could not see me', he wrote on 26 April 1871[92] – was more Macmillan's misfortune than Blackmore's, for *Lorna Doone* turned out to be a great success. Not even this contretemps put Blackmore permanently off *Macmillan's*: his *Perlycross* was first published in the *Magazine*, although much later, from June 1893 until July 1894.

As to 'Lucretius', what students of Tennyson may remember about the *Macmillan's* text, published in May 1868, is that the poet had consented to remove some erotic language from his description of a nymph whom Lucretius sees in a vision induced by a love potion administered by his 'wrathful, petulant' wife: gone are the Oread's 'slippery sides', her 'rosy knees', her 'supple roundedness' and her 'budded bosom-peaks', so that the *Magazine* reader's impression, instead of being rendered vivid by the diction of the several luscious lines that Tennyson had originally devoted to her, was reduced to a mere glimpse: 'And here an Oread, and this way she runs/Before the rest'.[93]

Edgar Shannon's detailed reconstruction of the complicated textual history of 'Lucretius' indicates that more was involved in this curtailment than mere prudery, for example Macmillan's acceptance of Tennyson's request that the poem be set up in larger-than-usual type, a change that appeared to Macmillan to call for some condensation. He wrote to Tennyson on 27 February 1868 that 'Grove seemed to prefer the shorter description of the Oread', adding that '[o]n the whole the balance of taste seems in favour of it'.[94] Tennyson yielded to Macmillan's wish, telling Grove on 3 March: 'With respect to the Oread please yourself but send the full passage to America. They are not so squeamish as we are.'[95] (Macmillan had arranged with James T. Fields for the publication of 'Lucretius' in the *Atlantic Monthly* simultaneously with its appearance in *Macmillan's*; because it was received in Boston too late for inclusion in the May number, the poem was printed instead in *Every Saturday* on 2 May, with the Oread's charms intact.)

There is, of course, much more to this story than can be repeated here, but one additional point does need to be made. Early in his correspondence with Alexander Macmillan about 'Lucretius', on 8 January 1868, Tennyson had given Macmillan an opening 'to reject Lucretius after you have seen it if you don't like it.' The explanation of this remark given by the editors of Tennyson's *Letters* seems inadequate: 'Macmillan was a prude, and Tennyson knew it'.[96] Macmillan did 'like' the poem, as did Grove,[97] and even the text printed in the *Magazine* with his approval is drenched in frustrated sexual passion expressed in insistently explicit language, for instance in its depiction of Helen of Troy as seen by the drugged Lucretius:

> Then, then, from utter gloom stood out the breasts,
> The breasts of Helen, and hoveringly a sword
> Now over, now under, now direct,
> Pointed itself to pierce, but sank down shamed
> At all that beauty; and as I stared, a fire,
> The fire that left a roofless Ilion,
> Shot out of them, and scorch'd me that I woke.[98]

It will not do, then, to dismiss Macmillan as a spokesman for Mrs Grundy; on the contrary, he deplored Grundyism as a serious obstacle to the appreciation of Tennyson's poetry.[99]

Thomas Hardy

Later in 1868, Macmillan began a correspondence with a much younger author, Thomas Hardy, which also reveals a great deal about the bases on which he formed his literary judgments and which resulted in the same outcome as his long and patient dealings with Tennyson: like Tennyson, Hardy ultimately decided to make Macmillan and Co. the publisher of his books. Not even the treatment Hardy would endure at the hands of Mowbray Morris, who edited *Macmillan's Magazine* during the serialization of Hardy's *The Woodlanders* between May 1886 and April 1887, could erode the foundation of a warm relationship with Hardy that Macmillan had started to lay two decades earlier.

On the recommendation of his friend Horace Moule,[100] Hardy submitted the manuscript of his first novel, *The Poor Man and the Lady*, to Alexander Macmillan on 25 July 1868. On 10 August, along with John Morley's reader's report, Macmillan sent Hardy a four-page critique of his own, one that was 'so long and detailed that it represents the clearest surviving indication of what the novel was like'.[101] If there was potentially offensive sexual matter in that lost manuscript, neither Macmillan nor Morley alluded to it; what Macmillan concentrated on in his assessment of *The Poor Man and the Lady* were questions of characterization, verisimilitude and tone, and he found much to praise in Hardy's text.[102]

Encouraged by the care that Macmillan had lavished on this first attempt at long fiction, even though he had not accepted it for publication, Hardy subsequently turned to him with the manuscripts of his second and third novels, *Desperate Remedies* and *Under the Green-*

wood Tree. Again Macmillan, Morley and (in the case of *Under the Greenwood Tree*) Macmillan's son Malcolm did not find the novels suitable, but again their rejections contained much constructive advice. John Sutherland sums up their responses to Hardy's early work by saying that 'they perceived in the young writer an outstanding talent – even if they were unprepared to put their money behind it' and continues: 'Hardy derived from his experiences with *Macmillan's* what amounted to an education in writing fiction', acquiring 'a practical acquaintance with the mores, fashions and taboos which regulated the selection of novels for publication, for purchase by the circulating libraries and reading by the general public.'[103] No wonder that Hardy felt a great sense of indebtedness to Macmillan and his firm.

As was the case with such other writers as Tennyson, Alexander Macmillan went far beyond the call of professional duty in his connection with Hardy, extending to him the hand of friendship long before he became a Macmillan and Co. author. Soon after the Hardys moved to South London in 1878, they began visiting the Macmillans at Knapdale, their nearby house in Upper Tooting, where they encountered such men as Huxley, Morley and Hardy's American publisher Henry Holt; a thunderstorm that doused a Knapdale garden party in July 1879 gave Hardy the idea for a similar occurrence used to telling effect at the end of the first book of his *A Laodicean*.[104] In October of the next year, when Hardy became alarmingly ill, 'Mrs Hardy, in her distress, called on their neighbours the Macmillans, to ask their opinion, and they immediately sent their own doctor.'[105] While Hardy was convalescing, the Macmillans' daughter Margaret looked in on him, and the novelist recalled how she and his wife took tea at his bedside: 'She and Em worked, watching the sun set gorgeously. That I should also be able to see it Miss Macmillan conceived the kind idea of reflecting the sun into my face by a looking-glass.'[106] Again Hardy was to make use in his fiction of an incident in his social intercourse with the Macmillan family: he had Sue resort to the same device in order to enable the ailing Phillotson to see 'such a beautiful sunset' in Chapter 6 of Part Fourth of *Jude the Obscure*. Only a wrong-headed cynic would suggest that Macmillan deliberately fostered such close relations with Hardy so that he might eventually secure his work for the *Magazine* and his publishing house; however, although there were clearly other motives involved, his long association with Hardy did bring about that result.

We have seen how Alexander Macmillan was able to put his personal stamp on the *Magazine* and to use it both as a vehicle to express his most cherished ideas and as a device to attract and retain authors. The case of Thomas Hardy, with which this chapter has ended, helps us to understand how closely the *Magazine* was bound up with Macmillan's principal business, the publication of books, for it is impossible to disentangle his transactions with writers for the former from those with writers of the latter, who were often the same people. Certainly Macmillan was always the same man, displaying the same qualities, throughout these relationships. Yet that man was not free of contradictions, as shown for example by his hesitations and ambivalences about issues raised by the American Civil War. Internally divided as he himself could be, Alexander Macmillan would not – perhaps could not – impose conformity on those who contributed to his *Magazine*. The resulting freedom of writers to express their own views within rather loose ground rules was on the whole a source of strength in the early *Macmillan's*, as long as he kept his hand in. After Macmillan began withdrawing from its affairs, however, the *Magazine*'s hospitality to diverse positions became less an expression of its founder's principles than of an apparent purposelessness that strayed from the moral earnestness of its founders.

Notes

1. Add MSS 55836, fols 359 and 372.
2. That turned out to be Ainger's only contribution during Masson's editorship, but he later wrote for *Macmillan's* while Grove, Morley and Morris held that position. One of the Cambridge undergraduates whom the Macmillan brothers took under their wing at 1 Trinity Street in the 1850s, Ainger had been an admirer of Maurice before that time. His last contribution to *Macmillan's* was the obituary 'Reminiscence' of Alexander Macmillan cited in Chapter 1, n. 40.
3. G.A. Macmillan 21.
4. For a full account of this relationship, see June Steffensen Hagen, *Tennyson and His Publishers* (London: Macmillan, 1979), especially her sixth chapter, 'Final Choice: Alexander Macmillan (1884–92)', 158–85. Hallam Tennyson was one of those who considered it quite special: *Alfred Lord Tennyson: A Memoir by His Son* (London: Macmillan, 1911) 2: 383.
5. Charles Tennyson, *Alfred Tennyson* (New York: Macmillan, 1949) 320.
6. Hagen 164–6.
7. Add MSS 55837, fol. 81.
8. Add MSS 55837, fol. 253.
9. Tennyson's later *Macmillan's* poems were 'Wages' (February 1868), 'Lucretius' (May 1868), 'The Charge of the Heavy Brigade at Balaclava. October 25th, 1854' (March 1882), 'Freedom' (December 1884), 'Vastness' (November 1885), and – probably the one that attracted the most attention – 'Carmen Secularae. An Ode in Honour of the Jubilee of Queen Victoria' (April 1887).

10. Although Alexander Macmillan courted George Eliot (and her partner, George Henry Lewes) as diligently as he did the Tennysons, and in most of the same ways, his success with her was less striking. She did contribute three poems – 'The Legend of Jubal' (May 1870), 'Armgart' (July 1871), and 'A College Breakfast-Party' (July 1878) – to the *Magazine*, but none of her books was published by Macmillan and Co. Macmillan wanted Eliot to write the Shakespeare volume in the English Men of Letters series but failed to persuade her to do so (*The George Eliot Letters*, ed. Gordon S. Haight [New Haven: Yale University Press, 1955] 6: 416–17). Their letters attest to their mutual esteem. Macmillan regarded her as the foremost living novelist (Add MSS 55380, fol. 295), and Eliot was an attentive and generally approving reader of the reviews of her books in *Macmillan's*. She was so pleased by 'George Eliot's Novels' (August 1866), which John Morley had written at Macmillan's suggestion, 'that she had GHL[ewes] call upon Macmillan to thank him for it, and an introduction to GE followed' (*The George Eliot Letters* 4: 309n).

11. Earlier in 1862, Macmillan and Co. had published Mackenzie's *Across the Carpathians*, written in collaboration with Adelina Irby, her companion on these journeys. A more famous woman traveler, Lucy (or Lucie) Duff Gordon, also contributed to *Macmillan's* during the 1860s; seven of her pieces about Egypt appeared in the *Magazine* between January 1865 and June 1868. Like Mackenzie, she had started out as a Macmillan and Co. author: her 'Letters from the Cape' were first published in *Vacation Tourists and Notes of Travel in 1862–63*, ed. Francis Galton (1864), and her *Letters from Egypt: 1863–65* (1865) went through three printings in seven months. Some of her *Magazine* work was included in *Last Letters from Egypt: To Which are Added Letters from the Cape*, also brought out by Macmillan and Co., in 1875. Duff Gordon was the subject of a *Macmillan's* obituary tribute, Caroline Norton's 'Lady Duff-Gordon and Her Works' (September 1869), a month and a half after her death in Cairo.

12. Add MSS 55380, fols 149–50.

13. 6 (1862): 345, 352.

14. Add MSS 55387, fols 852–3; Add MSS 55396, fol. 812.

15. Add MSS 54975, fols 1–2.

16. 'A Birthday' (April 1861), 'An Apple-Gathering' (August 1861), 'Light Love' (February 1863), 'The Bourne' (March 1863), 'The Fairy Prince Who Arrived Too Late' (May 1863), 'A Bird's-Eye View' (July 1863), 'The Queen of Hearts' (October 1863), 'One Day' (December 1863), 'Sit Down in the Lowest Room' (March 1864), 'My Friend' (December 1864), 'Spring Fancies' (April 1865), 'Last Night' (May 1865), 'Consider' (January 1866), 'Helen Grey' (March 1866), 'By the Waters of Babylon. B.C. 570' (October 1866), 'Seasons' (December 1866), 'Mother Country' (March 1868), 'A Smile and a Sigh' (May 1868), 'Dead Hope' (May 1868), 'Autumn Violets' (November 1868), 'They Desire a Better Country' (March 1869), and 'A Wintry Sonnet' (April 1883).

17. Macmillan wrote to Dante Gabriel Rossetti on 28 October 1861 describing what must have been one of the oddest public occasions in the history of the Cambridge Working Men's College: he told Rossetti that he had read 'Goblin Market' to a gathering there, and those in attend-

ance 'seemed at first to wonder whether I was making fun of them; By degrees they got as still as death, and when I finished there was a tremendous burst of applause. I wish Miss Rossetti could have heard it' (Add MSS 55841, fol. 4).

18. Add MSS 54965, fols 30–31, 39–40 and *passim*; Add MSS 55380, fol. 107.

19. See Larry Uffelman and Patrick Scott, 'Kingsley's Serial Novels, II: *The Water-Babies*', *VPR* 19 (1986): 122–31. Although they concentrate on Kingsley's revisions of the serial text for book publication, they also stress Alexander Macmillan's role in the acceptance of the novel for *Macmillan's Magazine*.

20. Add MSS 55383, fol. 253.

21. Add MSS 55387, fol. 687.

22. Add MSS 55387, fol. 688.

23. Macmillan and Co. published one of Higginson's books, *Malbone*, in England the following year.

24. G.A. Macmillan 6.

25. Graves 180, 256; Add MSS 55841, fol. 253; Add MSS 55390, fol. 793.

26. G.A. Macmillan lviii.

27. Charles L. Graves, *The Life & Letters of Sir George Grove, C.B.* (London: Macmillan, 1903) 254.

28. Add MSS 55394, fol. 371. There is more about this in a letter Macmillan wrote to Grove the following day (fol. 374).

29. Add MSS 55406, fol. 805.

30. Add MSS 55401, fol. 93.

31. Add MSS 54793, fol. 129. For a discussion of the genesis and nature of Arnold's essay, see Vol. 9 of *The Complete Prose Works of Matthew Arnold*, ed. R.H. Super: *English Literature and Irish Politics* (Ann Arbor: University of Michigan Press, 1973) 336–40.

32. Add MSS 54918, fol. 99. Hughes apparently felt that the *Magazine* under Masson was turning out to be insufficiently Christian Socialist: he found it 'intensely disgusting that Ruskin should have come out in the Cornhill [rather than in *Macmillan's*] with a profession of Christian Socialism' (*Unto This Last* was published in the *Cornhill* from August until November 1860), and he reported to Macmillan that the ardently Christian Socialist J.M. Ludlow believed that he was being muzzled, 'not allowed to write on the subjects he cares about' in the *Magazine*. For whatever unknown reason, the more even-tempered Hughes sold his share of the *Magazine* back to Alexander Macmillan, but not until 14 June 1865 (Add MSS 54917, fol. 38).

33. Add MSS 55387, fol. 597. At least some of the fault was apparently Grove's: a letter from Masson to Craik dated 4 October 1867 is full of complaints about his deputy (Add MSS 54792, fols 83–4).

34. Add MSS 55387, fol. 778.

35. Add MSS 55842, fol. 91.

36. Hertz 1981: 120.

37. Add MSS 54793, fol. 77; Add MSS 55842, fols 485 and 487.

38. Add MSS 55843, fol. 16.

39. This was actually Chapter 45. In the June 1864 *Macmillan's*, Chapter 20 had been printed as Chapter 19, and this error threw off by one the chapter numbering of the rest of the serial version of *A Son of the Soil*.

40. Add MSS 55384, fol. 135.
41. Add MSS 55842, fol. 41. Masson, who had moved to Edinburgh by this
     time, did not enter the fray until 10 days later; the five-page letter he
     wrote to Norton on 4 May was deferential to the point of fulsomeness,
     but he nevertheless expressed complete agreement with what Macmillan
     had done. Although Masson implied that it was he who had suppressed
     the chapter – 'when I did read that last chapter, I telegraphed to stop it
     until we could refer it to you' (Add MSS 54964, fol. 14) – the fact that
     Macmillan had been the first to write to Norton assumes considerable
     significance in the light of the argument I have been developing.
42. Add MSS 54964, fols 7 and 9.
43. 14 (1866): 240, 320; 15 (1867): 256, 536. Although *Old Sir Douglas*
     finally completed its run in the *Magazine* in October 1867, that was not
     the end of Alexander Macmillan's trouble over that novel. Macmillan
     and Co. had bought 'the right to print Old Sir Douglas, in their maga-
     zine'; Hurst and Blackett was to bring out a three-volume edition, after
     which the copyright was to be 'the exclusive property of Macmillan &
     Co.' (Add MSS 54964, fol. 21). The same agreement stated that 'Messrs
     Hurst & Blackett and Macmillan & Co. jointly granted Baron Tauchnitz
     permission to print Old Sir Douglas in his series.' Norton was dismayed
     about all the errors she found in Macmillan and Co.'s 1868 one-volume
     edition of *Old Sir Douglas* and complained vigorously (Add MSS 54964,
     fol. 23); she was even more upset about the way the publication of her
     novel in Tauchnitz's Collection of British Authors (vols 922 and 923;
     Leipzig, 1867) had been handled and threatened to take legal action
     (Add MSS 54964, fols 25–40). Alexander Macmillan's replies to her
     angry letters were scrupulously courteous and forbearing (Add MSS
     55391, fols 741, 755 and 881).
44. Graves 164.
45. Add MSS 55839, fols 9 and 25–6.
46. The words 'manly' and 'manliness' were given a much broader and less
     gender-specific meaning by mid-Victorian writers than contemporary
     readers may suppose. See my 'Of Muscles and Manliness: Some Reflec-
     tions on Thomas Hughes' in *Victorian Literature and Society*, ed. James
     R. Kincaid and Albert J. Kuhn (Columbus: Ohio State University Press,
     1983) 308–11.
47. Add MSS 55837, fol. 133.
48. Add MSS 55841, fol. 318. Gaskell's sole contribution to the *Magazine*
     was a tribute to Colonel Robert Gould Shaw of the 54th Massachusetts
     regiment, who had been killed while leading his African-American troops
     in an assault on Fort Wagner, South Carolina, on 18 July 1863. Her
     article appeared in the December 1863 number.
49. Brian Jenkins, *Britain and the War for the Union* (Montreal: McGill-
     Queen's University Press, 1974) 2: 34.
50. Add MSS 55841, fol. 319.
51. For more on this subject, see my article '*Macmillan's Magazine* and the
     American Civil War: A Reconsideration', *VPR* 26 (1993): 193–8; and
     my Letter to the Editor of the same journal, 27 (1994): 282.
52. Add MSS 55380, fol. 164.
53. 8 (1863): 301.
54. Carlyle's best-known statement on the subject is his 'Occasional Dis-

course on the Negro Question', *Fraser's Magazine* 40 (1849): 670–79. This was later expanded and published separately under the more inflammatory title *Occasional Discourse on the Nigger Question* (London: Bosworth, 1853).

55. Ludlow had called Carlyle that in an intemperate letter of 29 July 1863 to Alexander Macmillan (Add MSS 55253, fol. 43): 'I did not think your magazine would ever fall so low as to insert that thing signed T.C. in the new no. ... It is a *lie*, & the bad old man who wrote it knows it to be such, as well as you or I.'

56. Ludlow's piece was enclosed with a letter to Macmillan dated 1 August 1863 (Add MSS 55253, fol. 44), which was as angry as his original complaint of three days earlier had been. Ludlow repeated his charge that Carlyle was dishonest, grumbled about the way his own recent contributions to *Macmillan's* had been treated, and demanded that 'Servitude for Life' be printed in the next number (which it was). He had not calmed down four weeks later: on 28 August he expressed displeasure to Macmillan about the shape in which the proofs of the article had reached him (Add MSS 55253, fols 56–7). Ludlow was a hard man to please: after his 'Mr. Tennyson's "Northern Farmer"' had come out in the October 1864 number, he challenged Macmillan's statement that he was glad to see his work in the *Magazine* again, pointing out that 'out of the 5 papers last offered by me, 3 were refused (one of the accepted moreover going in by you)' (Add MSS 55253, fol. 101). Ludlow made two more appearances in *Macmillan's* in 1865, and then vanished from its pages for nearly 20 years.

57. Add MSS 55381, fol. 347.

58. Add MSS 55381, fols 399–400.

59. Another, even stronger, indication of Macmillan's feelings about Carlyle may be found in a letter he wrote on 2 July 1860 to William Stigant:

> I probably do not hold an opinion in common with him on some of the most vital points. The opinions concerning Christianity which appear to be his I certainly dont hold ... But, look here, there is to my mind ... a deep and kind and wise truth which only genius of the very highest order, and moral natures of the highest and purest order can give or can reach to. Thomas Carlyle belongs to the Immortals as indubitably as Dante – who said a good many somewhat brutal things, which your small Leigh Hunts of after ages can discover to their huge delight – or John Milton who was not always wise ... I daresay he has be[en] the occasion of as large an amount of unwisdom as most odd humorous men of genius must be among those who go to them for opinions. (Add MSS 55838, fol. 151.)

Four years after the publication of 'Ilias (Americana) in Nuce', Carlyle's 'Shooting Niagara: And After?', an attack on the Second Reform Bill and what lay behind it, appeared in the August 1867 *Macmillan's*. His only other contribution to the *Magazine*, this equally notorious piece was also out of line with the opinions that then characterized most of the contributions to *Macmillan's*, which were strongly pro-Reform and pro-democracy.

60. *Economist* 17 (1859): 1377.
61. Of the prose writings from *Macmillan's* cited in *Wellesley* 1, approximately 78% were signed, 'though not infrequently with a single initial or a title' (556). If one includes initials, titles and pseudonyms, the figure for poetry, which is not included in *Wellesley*, is comparable: about 82%; see my 'Poetry in *Macmillan's Magazine*', *VPR* 23 (1990): 56.
62. 'Anonymous Journalism', 5 (1861): 165–6.
63. Add MSS 55837, fol. 156; Add MSS 55838, fols 207–208.
64. One way Macmillan went about wooing Arnold was to pay him handsomely for his contributions to the *Magazine*. Arnold's first poem in *Macmillan's*, 'Thyrsis' (April 1866), brought him £25, which, in a letter to Macmillan of 30 March 1866, he called 'a splendid, extraordinary payment'. Writing to his mother the next day, Arnold told her that 'this is the best pay I have yet had' (*The Letters of Matthew Arnold* 3, ed. Cecil Y. Lang [Charlottesville: University Press of Virginia, 1998] 25, 26). A dozen of Arnold's books were published by Macmillan and Co.; he also edited and wrote the introductions to a number of others. For a helpful account of the Macmillan–Arnold relationship, see William E. Buckler's *Matthew Arnold's Books: Toward a Publishing History* (Geneva: Droz, 1958), which also treats Arnold's dealings with George Smith of the *Cornhill* and the firm of Smith, Elder. A number of interesting contrasts emerge: Buckler argues that Arnold's relations with Macmillan were less 'distinctly personal' than those between Arnold and Smith, 'but there was always a fine respect and friendliness between them; and the intellectual rapport between Arnold and Macmillan seems to have been a great deal more vital than that between Arnold and Smith' (15). Arnold felt free to approach Macmillan for cash advances, for instance when his life insurance premium fell due (*passim*, especially 169).
65. Isobel Armstrong, *Victorian Scrutinies: Reviews of Poetry 1830–1870* (London: Athlone Press, 1972) 32. Also see Michael W. Adams, 'David Masson's Theory of Imagination and Matthew Arnold's 1853 *Preface*', *Studies in Scottish Literature* 11 (1974): 141–55.
66. A later *Macmillan's* article by Arnold, 'A Word More about Spinoza' (December 1863), was included, under the title 'Spinoza', in Arnold's *Essays in Criticism* (Macmillan and Co., 1865). For the second edition of *Essays in Criticism* (Macmillan and Co., 1869), Arnold expanded 'Spinoza' by incorporating in it material from 'The Bishop and the Philosopher'; now called 'Spinoza and the Bible', this version omitted the unflattering references to Colenso contained in the January 1863 piece. Arnold could not leave the poor Bishop alone: he also poked fun at him in the first essay in the volume, 'The Function of Criticism at the Present Time', but abridged and thereby toned down his comments for the second edition. Much has been written about the complicated textual history of the *Essays in Criticism*. In addition to Buckler, cited in n. 64 above, see E.K. Brown, *Studies in the Text of Matthew Arnold's Prose Works* (1935; reprinted, New York: Russell & Russell, 1969); Matthew Arnold, *Lectures and Essays in Criticism*, ed. R.H. Super with Sister Thomas Marion Hoctor (Ann Arbor: University of Michigan Press, 1962); and *Matthew Arnold's Essays in Criticism: First Series*, ed. Sister Thomas Marion Hoctor (University of Chicago Press, 1968).

67. Add MSS 55380, fols 591–2, 588.
68. Add MSS 55830, fol. 653.
69. 9 (1864): 217.
70. Nowell-Smith 46–7.
71. Add MSS 55382, fols 18–19.
72. 9 (1864): 368.
73. The steps by which Kingsley's outburst led to the writing of the *Apologia* are traced by Martin J. Svaglic in the 'Editor's Introduction' to the Oxford English Texts edition of that work (Oxford: Clarendon, 1967): vii–lx; and, more briefly, in 'Why Newman Wrote the *Apologia*', in *Newman's* Apologia: *A Classic Reconsidered*, ed. Vincent F. Blehl and Francis X. Connolly (New York: Harcourt, 1964): 1–25. Along with some documents relating to the Kingsley–Newman controversy, the latter is reprinted in the Norton Critical Edition of the *Apologia* (New York: Norton, 1968): 373–88. Neither Svaglic nor the Norton text, however, mentions Macmillan's letter of 6 January 1864 to Newman; in the correspondence between himself and Kingsley that Newman published the following month as *Mr. Kingsley and Dr. Newman*, the earliest letter from Kingsley, obviously written after Macmillan had shown him Newman's protest, bears the same date. In March Macmillan and Co. put out a further contribution by Kingsley to the escalating debate, *What, Then, Does Dr. Newman Mean?*. See Hertz 1986 for further evidence of the extent of Macmillan's involvement in the Kingsley–Newman controversy; a passage inadvertently omitted from Hertz's article is printed in *VPR* 20 (1987): 79.
74. Add MSS 55382, fol. 209.
75. Add MSS 55839, fols 428 and 451.
76. *The Swinburne Letters* 1, ed. Cecil Y. Lang (New Haven: Yale University Press, 1959) 60.
77. Swinburne did contribute an essay on William Collins to the third volume of *The English Poets*, ed. Thomas Humphry Ward, published by Macmillan and Co. in 1880. Whatever his reservations about Alexander Macmillan may have been, he was a faithful reader of *Macmillan's Magazine*, as his letters frequently testify. He drew largely on T. Wemyss Reid's three-part 'Charlotte Brontë: A Monograph', which appeared in the *Magazine* from September until November 1876, in writing his *A Note on Charlotte Brontë* (1877); see *The Swinburne Letters* 3 (1960): 220, 260.
78. Add MSS 55383, fol. 64.
79. G.A. Macmillan 203. Six years earlier, Macmillan had expressed his distaste for Sterne in a letter to Charles Allston Collins but did not interfere when Masson decided to run a sketch by Collins describing a visit to Sterne's supposed grave in the churchyard of St George's, Hanover Square (Add MSS 55837, fol. 360). Collins's piece, 'Poet's Corner; or, An English Writer's Tomb', appeared in the June 1860 number.
80. Herbert Harlakenden Gilchrist, *Anne Gilchrist: Her Life and Writings* (London: Fisher Unwin, 1887) 128.
81. Graves 22.
82. Although Macmillan probably did not know it at the time, that reviewer was William Ewart Gladstone. His essay in the October 1859 *Quarterly* treated the 1842 two-volume edition of Tennyson's *Poems*, *The Prin-*

cess, *In Memoriam*, *Maud and Other Poems*, and the first four *Idylls of the King*.

83. Add MSS 55380, fol. 295.
84. Add MSS 55396, fol. 394.
85. Add MSS 55380, fol. 361; Add MSS 55839, fol. 63.
86. The best sources are William E. Buckler, 'Blackmore's Novels before "Lorna Doone"', *NCF* 10 (1955): 169–87; and Edgar F. Shannon, Jr, 'The Publication of Tennyson's "Lucretius"', *SB* 34 (1981): 146–86.
87. Add MSS 54965, fols 12 and 23.
88. Add MSS 55383, fol. 107. The book version was published by Chapman and Hall in 1866.
89. Add MSS 54965, fol. 66.
90. Add MSS 54965, fol. 82.
91. Buckler attributes Macmillan's request to his 'high regard for Kingsley ... coupled with the facts that Kingsley's *Ravenshoe* had had a marked success in the magazine and *Cradock Nowell* was attracting little popular attention' ('Blackmore's Novels' 183–4). There is some irony here: Blackmore had been much impressed by *Ravenshoe*, which had run in *Macmillan's* between January 1861 and July 1862, and apparently borrowed from it in writing his *Clara Vaughan*; see Max Keith Sutton, *R.D. Blackmore* (Boston: Twayne, 1979) 42–3.
92. Add MSS 54965, fol. 83.
93. 18 (1868): 6.
94. Add MSS 55388, fol. 66. Still nominally the editor of the *Magazine*, Masson wrote to Macmillan from Edinburgh a month later to offer a different opinion: he believed that 'some flash of the figure of the running Oread, more than is given in the abbreviated form of the passage, is necessary for the full effect of what is to follow', recommending that the 'slippery sides' and the 'rosy knees' be left in but that the 'budded bosom-peaks' and the 'supple roundedness' be removed – not so much because of the 'chance of a row ... with Mrs Grundy' as because the former struck him as 'too hackneyed and too physically-harsh an indelicacy' and the latter seemed, 'though innocent enough, not new enough, & rather insipid' (Add MSS 54792, fol. 95). Masson was, however, overruled. Malcolm Macmillan might have been referring to the passage depicting the Oread in a story he told about Tennyson's reading of 'Lucretius' after one of his parents' dinner parties 'early in 1868': 'Kingsley [certainly no prude] remonstrated with him about some descriptive lines being too warm, and tending to revive the fashion of the lesser Elizabethan dramatists. These lines were, in fact, excised till the poem appeared with others in a collected form' (*Selected Letters of Malcolm Kingsley Macmillan* [London: privately printed, 1893]: 291).
95. *The Letters of Alfred Lord Tennyson* 2, ed. Cecil Y. Lang and Edgar F. Shannon, Jr (Cambridge, MA: Harvard University Press, 1987): 483.
96. 2: 476.
97. Shannon 'The Publication' 168, 164.
98. 18 (1868): 3.
99. Graves 86.
100. Moule had met the Macmillan brothers when he was a Cambridge undergraduate; see Michael Millgate, *Thomas Hardy: A Biography* (Ox-

ford: Oxford University Press, 1985) 109. He contributed one article to *Macmillan's*: 'Achilles and Lancelot' (September 1871).

101. Millgate 110.
102. Add MSS 55388, fols 646–8.
103. *Victorian Novelists and Publishers* (Chicago: University of Chicago Press, 1976) 212–13.
104. Michael Millgate, ed., *The Life and Work of Thomas Hardy* (Athens: University of Georgia Press, 1985) 131.
105. Millgate, *Life and Work* 149.
106. Millgate, *Life and Work* 152.

CHAPTER THREE

The Role of
Frederick Denison Maurice

As we have seen, *Macmillan's Magazine* was not a Christian Socialist organ. Nevertheless, Frederick Denison Maurice, regarded by others if not by himself as the founder and leader of the Christian Socialist movement, was a central figure in the early history of that periodical, perhaps second in importance only to Alexander Macmillan himself. Maurice was prominent among those whom the founders of the *Magazine* consulted as it was taking shape during the late 1850s; he contributed to it frequently during the first decade of its existence; and, most significantly, his articles, reviews and long Letters to the Editor expressed concerns that were also addressed by other contributors and defined what may be called the position of the early *Macmillan's* on some of the most pressing issues of the day.

During the spring and summer of 1858, when Alexander Macmillan and Thomas Hughes were still thinking of their projected periodical as a quarterly rather than a monthly, Maurice's name kept appearing in their correspondence about this new venture. On 13 April, Hughes, who was then expecting to serve as editor, wrote to Macmillan that Llewelyn Davies would speak to 'the Prophet' (that is, Maurice) about 'this regenerating journal, review, magazine, or whatever it is to be' and invited Macmillan to join in the discussion. In a letter of 7 May to Austen Henry Layard in which he solicited 'an article on India' at 'the best quarterly pay, a guinea a page', the ever-sanguine Hughes mentioned Maurice, along with Charles Kingsley and W.E. Forster, as one of the 'good men' who 'are going to start a quarterly in which the contributors are to sign their names', whose 'first number' he then assumed would 'come out towards the end of the year'. Two weeks later, in a letter to Alexander Macmillan, Hughes listed a review of Froude's *History of England* by Maurice among the planned contents of that initial number.[1] (By the time he wrote that letter, Hughes was thinking of John Malcolm Ludlow, rather than Layard, as the author of the 'article on India', adding that 'Maurice is ... strongly for the idea'.)

More cautiously, Macmillan himself assured Maurice on 22 July that he and Hughes were in agreement that Maurice would be consulted before they decided finally whether or not to go ahead with 'our Review Scheme'. Apparently Maurice advised against proceeding in 1858, and that, Macmillan wrote to Maurice on 27 July, 'of course decides the matter for the present'; Macmillan would defer the project for a year. On the next day, Macmillan went into further detail to Charles Kingsley, whose lukewarm attitude toward the idea of starting a new periodical served as another deterrent:

> I had a good deal of discussion with Hughes when I was in town last week and the result was that we agreed to put the whole of our difficulties before Mr Maurice and abide by his decision. He has written very emphatically saying that under the circumstances we must give it up. I have no doubt that your dislike of the scheme has weighed with us all considerably & it seemed a growing feeling with some of us that you were right. I had taken a small London house which I should perhaps not have taken for a year or two, but for the Review. As it is however no harm is done, for we must have had it before long ... [2]

Maurice's own Life and Letters, edited by his son, contains little explicit information about his involvement with *Macmillan's Magazine* but does suggest his strong interest in 1858 in 'a scheme for a magazine with Mr. Hughes as editor, in which the articles should all be signed',[3] and two letters from Maurice printed there, the first written on 27 May to Charles Kingsley and the second written on 23 August to R.H. Hutton, do indicate Maurice's strong support both of Hughes as a potential editor and also of Hughes's notion of a periodical in which each contributor was 'to sign his own name'.

That Hughes was 'not a professional literary man' was no disqualification in Maurice's view. 'I say boldly', he wrote to Kingsley, 'we must have done with professional *littérateurs* if we are to have any honest, manly literature.' Maurice regarded the *Edinburgh Review* as 'the most successful periodical of the nineteenth century; the one which gave the new tone to periodical literature', and 'it was begun by a set of young men, chiefly barristers [like Hughes], who looked upon literature as subordinate to life and action'; it went into decline, according to Maurice, when 'it fell so much into the hands of literary hacks'.[4]

In that letter to Kingsley, Maurice also expressed himself forcefully on what he regarded as the evil of 'the "We" spirit' of mid-century periodical literature as manifested, for instance, in the recently founded *Saturday Review*:[5]

> It seems to me that if the time is come, as you tell us it is, in which nuisances that pollute the air are to be abated – if, as you say, every one is guilty of a sin who is not labouring that cesspools should be drained, and disinfecting fluids of all kinds be sought for – the time is come when those whose circumstances or whose ignorance disqualify them for those higher tasks, but who feel that there is a foul stench sent forth by our anonymous periodical literature and that

they in times past if not now have contributed, as I have, to the increase of it, may think that they are bound before they die to do something, be it ever so little, for the purpose of purifying the moral atmosphere of the vanity, cruelty, falsehood with which it is impregnated.[6]

To Hutton, who had apparently perceived a contradiction between Maurice's notion that all humans are 'members of a body', presided over by God and dedicated to carrying out God's will, and his 'eagerness that in their writings they should throw off the symbol of a corporation and each present himself as an *I*', Maurice maintained that it was the 'symbol We' of periodical journalism that encouraged the sectarianism Maurice abhorred: individuals writing as individuals were in a much better position 'to bear witness against the sectarian spirit'. 'I think we have most of corporate sensibility when we most take all the burden of our position as actual men.'[7]

Although Maurice was often at odds with all the leading schools of the mid-century Church of England, his importance in the history of that institution can hardly be overestimated.[8] In the *Macmillan's* obituary of Maurice, Charles Kingsley paid eloquent tribute to his unceasing efforts in behalf of the English Church and the nation it served:

> he had done more than any man of that generation to defend the Church's doctrines; to recommend her to highly cultivated men and women; to bring within her pale those who had been born outside it, or had wandered from it; to reconcile the revolutionary party among the workmen of the great cities with Christianity, order, law; to make all ranks understand that if Christianity meant anything, it meant that a man should not merely strive to save his own soul after death, but that he should live here the life of a true citizen, virtuous, earnest, helpful to his human brethren.

Kingsley rightly stressed Maurice's aversion to sects and schools, his unshakable faith in the Kingdom of God – God who 'was His own system' – and his conviction that our task on earth was, 'instead of building systems of our own, to find out His eternal laws for men, for nations, for churches; for only in obedience to them is Life'.[9]

Maurice's widespread influence made itself felt in a variety of ways: through his many books, chiefly perhaps *The Kingdom of Christ* (1837) and the *Theological Essays* (Macmillan and Co., 1853); through his preaching, his teaching and his lecturing, in London, Cambridge, and elsewhere; and not least through a personal magnetism that exerted a strong pull on many younger men despite his humility and his great reluctance to think of himself, or to be thought of by others, as the head of a school. When he wrote for *Macmillan's*, Maurice was generally responding to specific events that seemed to him to demand that he speak out for the edification of an audience of like-minded men and women.

It would be going too far to claim that Maurice's 18 contributions to *Macmillan's* between 1859 and 1869 touched on every one of the issues that were extensively dealt with in the *Magazine* during that decade. That would, clearly, have been impossible. Maurice took no part, for example, in the outpouring of articles describing and commenting on recent scientific developments: not only the work of Darwin and others on evolutionary theory but also that done in such fields as chemistry, physics, astronomy, mineralogy, botany, mathematics, psychology, philology, historiography, archaeology, anthropology, meteorology and genetics and their practical applications, as well as the history and philosophy of science and scientific education. Nor, with a few significant exceptions to be noted below, did Maurice express himself, as a large number of writers for the *Magazine* were doing, about events that were occurring in Europe or overseas and their implications for the British national interest. Nevertheless, on those occasions when Maurice did venture beyond his compelling concern with religious questions he struck keynotes that resonated throughout the pages of *Macmillan's*. Moreover, although the continuing agenda of what had been the Christian Socialist movement, particularly as it endured in the cooperative societies it had fostered, was articulated by others (chiefly Hughes, Ludlow and Henry Fawcett)[10] rather than by 'the Prophet' himself in the *Magazine*, Maurice's spirit permeated much of the writing on such issues published in *Macmillan's* during his lifetime, whether or not his name appeared in those articles.

No public question was of greater importance to Maurice than the position of the established Church. Maurice believed that it could retain its spiritual health and play a significant role in the life of the nation only if it regarded itself as the embodiment of God's will, expressed primarily in the Bible but also in the *Book of Common Prayer* and the 39 Articles, and that it could not accomplish its mission if it allowed itself to get embroiled in sectarian controversies or to be trapped into taking narrowly dogmatic stands that were bound to alienate large numbers of believers. Maurice had ample opportunity to express these convictions in the pages of the *Magazine*.

In those of his contributions to *Macmillan's Magazine* that were not explicitly based on his deep concern over the future of the Church of England, Maurice took the lead in outlining positions that were subsequently developed by other contributors. During the 1860s, a decade marked by a rapidly growing awareness that many inequities and abuses in the British electoral system had survived the implementation of the 1832 Reform Act, Maurice was the first to advocate further corrections. Of the many *Macmillan's* articles arguing that women should play a more active role in British society, one by Maurice came earliest, and, even before the outbreak of the American Civil War, Maurice stated the moral and religious case against slavery and for its abolition – a case that was to be asserted repeatedly in the *Magazine* by his colleagues and admirers.

Church reform

Although Maurice held that the Church of England should be a truly national institution, he could not align himself with those who argued that one way to realize this desirable objective would be to make it more attractive to Protestant Dissenters by recasting the *Book of Common Prayer*, which had governed Anglican worship since the Reformation, so as to remove some of its more controversial features.[11] When he wrote his 'On the Revision of the Prayer-Book and the Act of Uniformity', which appeared in *Macmillan's* in April 1860, Maurice had in mind two particular exponents of this superficially attractive but in his view very dangerous idea: Lord Robert Grosvenor, first Baron Ebury, who had founded an organization called the Association for Promoting a Revision of the Book of Common Prayer the previous year; and Isaac Taylor, who had recently published *The Liturgy and the Dissenters*, a pamphlet that was attracting considerable notice.

Any reform in the Prayer Book, Maurice insisted, must conform to what he regarded as the principles of a national Church, closely related to the state but neither subservient to it nor in control of it – a connection between Church and state that 'stands upon no decrees or acts of parliament, but exists in the laws of society, in the nature of things'. Taylor's proposal that Dissenters could be drawn to the Church by sacrificing 'a few words in our Baptismal Service, in our Catechism, in our Burial Service' would not only fail to achieve this commendable goal but would also mean surrendering 'something that has been connected with our spiritual interests for the sake of defending our material interests', a compromise that Maurice rejected. He opposed any measure that would challenge the premises on which he believed the *Book of Common Prayer* to be based: that the people of the nation 'are members of Christ, children of God, inheritors of the Kingdom of Heaven' – premises that had deepened in Christians inside and outside the Church of England 'the feeling that there must be a fellowship which is not a sectarian one, and which cannot be created by an amalgamation of sects'.

That the *Book of Common Prayer* was open to a variety of interpretations Maurice regarded as a virtue rather than a defect, and he was uneasy about the growing practice of subjecting to the discipline of

Church courts clergymen whose interpretations clashed with those of their congregations or of the Anglican hierarchy. Maurice's preferred solution to the potential conflict between an individual's freedom of conscience and prevailing doctrine was to repeal the 1662 Act of Uniformity, which required clergymen to assent to the *Book of Common Prayer*, rather than to undertake the impossible task of revising the Prayer Book so as to make it more generally acceptable.

> If we take this course, those Clergy who have difficulties about the use of one or another part of the Liturgy will not be forced to smother those difficulties, to affect a belief which they have not, and so to injure the effect of all their ministrations.[12]

Allowing diversity within unity in this manner would, in Maurice's judgment, serve the end of confirming and strengthening the national character of the English Church better than airing doctrinal quarrels in ecclesiastical courts under the gaze of the entire nation.

The following year, Maurice again had occasion to state his views concerning this sort of conflict within the Church in *Macmillan's Magazine*. The Bishop of Winchester, Charles Richard Sumner, had brought suit against the Reverend Dunbar Isidore Heath, Vicar of Brading on the Isle of Wight, for having published a book of sermons (*Sermons on Important Subjects* [1860]) that allegedly challenged portions of the *Book of Common Prayer* and the 39 Articles, the 1571 statement that attempted to define the Church of England's dogmatic position regarding a number of theological controversies of the Reformation era. The case was heard before Stephen Lushington, Dean of the Court of Arches, the consistory court of the Province of Canterbury. Lushington pronounced Heath guilty on 2 November 1861. The *Spectator* carried an editorial about the case a week later, and this prompted Maurice to respond in a long Letter to the Editor of *Macmillan's* (December 1861) entitled 'Dr. Lushington, Mr. Heath, and the Thirty-Nine Articles'.

What particularly concerned Maurice about the *Spectator*'s comment was the assertion 'that clergymen of this day who subscribe to a document which was compiled in the sixteenth century, involve themselves in an ignominious slavery, and in probable, almost certain, falsehood'. If this was true, it was an unfortunate consequence of 'the construction which nineteenth century wisdom puts upon the Articles, exceedingly hard and narrow'. Such a reading seemed to Maurice grossly at variance 'with the Theology of the Fathers or of the Reformation, of the Creeds and of our Prayers' – and deeply inimical, he might have added, to his cherished ideal of the Church of England as a comprehensive body that had embraced a broad range of beliefs since its founding. Nineteenth-century interpretations of Church doctrines, Maurice insisted, must preserve a sense of history and tradition, appealing 'to the past against the present' rather than exalting the present over the past.

Maurice believed that Lushington's verdict, which deprived Heath of his living, was regrettable, for both of the principals in the case and, especially, for the Church as a whole. Heath was clearly a man of good will, no more eccentric than a number of his fellow clergymen who were not required to answer for their unorthodox opinions before the Court of Arches; and Lushington, despite his excellent intentions, found himself articulating an excessively strict interpretation of the Articles, especially 11 and 12. Maurice hoped – and he thought that Lushington did too – that an appeal by Heath to the judicial committee of the Privy Council, which included lay as well as clerical members, would result in a reversal of his conviction.[13] Believing, like Lushington, in the importance of 'maintaining the credit of the Articles', Maurice felt that such an outcome would do more to strengthen the Church than would a denial of Heath's appeal. 'Should it be found necessary for their [the Articles'] credit, for the interests of Theology, for the peace of the Church, to deal more gently with the defendant – a few bitter divines may be angry, a benevolent layman will certainly rejoice.'[14]

A much more eminent churchman and scholar than Heath whom Maurice also defended in *Macmillan's*, on principle rather than because he agreed with him, was Benjamin Jowett, Regius Professor of Greek at Oxford University. Jowett had made important enemies by virtue of his liberal theological views, expressed for instance in his *The Epistles of St. Paul to the Thessalonians, Galatians, and Romans* (1855) and his contribution, 'On the Interpretation of Scripture', to the notorious *Essays and Reviews* (1860), and Jowett's alleged heterodoxy was used as a pretext by university authorities to freeze his stipend at a derisory £40 per annum. Although he 'burnt with indignation'[15] at such treatment of a man whose competence as a professor of Greek was questioned by no one, Maurice apparently did not speak out in public until the Anglican weekly *Guardian* printed a letter from C.A. Heurtly, Lady Margaret Professor of Divinity at Oxford, protesting a £2000 subscription that had been raised by friends and admirers of Jowett to augment his salary. Heurtly's letter appeared on 19 February 1862; Maurice's rejoinder – also in the form of a Letter to the Editor, under the heading 'The New Morality: Worship of Majorities' – was published in the April 1862 *Macmillan's*.

In his letter to the *Guardian*, which Maurice reproduced in full, Heurtly had complained that the donors of the £2000, whom he branded as 'restless spirits', were flying in the face of a 'course deliberately determined upon, after a free and full discussion, by that body whose decision is definitive in such matters' and that their refusal to acquiesce 'in the sentence of authority, unless perchance that sentence happens to be in their own favour' would perpetuate institutional 'strifes'. Although the corporate institution whose governance was at issue in this dispute was a university and not the Church of England, that distinction was still quite blurred in the 1860s, and it seemed to Maurice that the conduct of the University Senate in attempting to penalize an advocate of unpalatable views bore a disquieting resemblance to the behavior of the Church under similar circumstances. Quite apart from the injustice of denying 'the maxim that a labourer is worthy of his hire',[16] the university's position as defended by Heurtly would justify the condemnation of all those, including Christ and his Apostles, who dared to differ with duly constituted authority. Maurice was deeply suspicious of hegemonic hierarchies, whether academic or ecclesiastical, that placed their own authority above what he regarded as the will of God. What that will was could not, in the nature of the case, be a matter on which all conscientious and learned persons would agree in every detail, and to attempt to legislate such agreement was a vain and harmful undertaking.

Maurice saw the danger of conflict between his notion of 'the Kingdom of Heaven' and the pronouncements of church hierarchies in the colonies and abroad as well as at home, and he tried to demonstrate the applicability to English conditions of such foreign developments in two *Macmillan's* essays late in 1864 and early in 1865.

In 'A Letter to a Colonial Clergyman on Some Recent Ecclesiastical Movements in the Diocese of Capetown and in England', Maurice drew a parallel between the misfortunes of John William Colenso, Bishop of Natal in South Africa, and Henry Bristow Wilson, Vicar of Great Staughton, Huntingdonshire, in England. Both the bishop and the vicar had run afoul of their superiors in the Church because they had published theological views that were at variance with accepted Church doctrine, Colenso in *The Pentateuch and Book of Joshua Critically Examined* and Wilson in 'Séances Historiques de Genève: The National Church', one of the seven *Essays and Reviews*. Both had been disciplined by the Church: Bishop Robert Gray of Capetown deposed Colenso from his bishopric on 16 December 1863 and excommunicated him when Colenso disregarded that sentence; Stephen Lushington, who had heard Wilson's case in the Court of Arches on 25 June 1862, found him guilty of three charges of heresy and suspended him from his living for a year. Both Colenso and Wilson appealed to the judicial committee of the Privy Council, and both were exonerated by that body.[17]

For Maurice, the central issue in these two cases had nothing to do with the substance of Colenso's or Wilson's unorthodoxy, which he found as troubling as Jowett's; in fact, he had severed an old friendship with Colenso over *The Pentateuch and Book of Joshua* and urged him to resign his bishopric.[18] The real question as Maurice saw it was whether or not a 'mixed' court of appeal like the judicial committee of the Privy Council, rather than some sort of Church tribunal, should have the last word in disputes like those in which Colenso and Wilson had been caught up, and his answer was an unequivocal 'yes'.

Maurice's study of Church history had persuaded him that there had been a continuing battle 'of those who believed in a righteous Ruler of the earth – in an actual kingdom of God – against the ecclesiastical rulers and ecclesiastical tribunals that were exalting their own authority and calling that the divine authority'. The judicial committee of the Privy Council, speaking as it did for 'our people generally' and for those 'theologians and ministers of the Gospel' who 'derive their idea of theology and of the Gospel from the Bible and the Catholic creeds', had been playing a constructive role and one that was in accord with long tradition in overruling the misconceived verdicts of Bishop Gray and Dr Lushington. It had upheld religious freedom and fostered a broadly based Church of England, and Maurice applauded it for the spirit of its judgments in vindication of Colenso and Wilson.

To replace the judicial committee of the Privy Council with a totally ecclesiastical court of appeal – as had recently been urged by Edward Bouverie Pusey, Regius Professor of Hebrew at Oxford – would, in Maurice's view, be a tragic mistake. Such a body would inevitably do 'exactly the reverse of that which the mixed Court of Appeal already existing has done': it would 'decree exactly where [the present court] has refused to decree' and 'condemn those whom it has refused to condemn'. An ecclesiastical court of appeal, Maurice feared, would enforce the kind of theological rigor whose absence hitherto had made the Church of England a comprehensive body rather than a sect and whose presence in the governance of the Roman Catholic Church had had lamentable results.[19]

As if to confirm Maurice's worst fears about the pernicious example the Roman Catholic Church might set for Anglicans, Pope Pius IX's encyclical *Quanta cura* along with other writings was published as *Syllabus complectens praecipuos nostrae aetatis errores* ('list of the principal errors of our times') on 8 December 1864, within a few days after the appearance of Maurice's 'Letter to a Colonial Clergyman' in the December 1864 *Macmillan's*. The Pope's attack on liberalism and freedom of conscience, with its insistence that the Church be independent of state control and make itself responsible for all education, science and culture, prompted Maurice's next contribution to *Macmillan's*, 'A Few Words on the Pope's Encyclical Letter', in the February 1865 number.

Maurice could understand the force of the Pope's appeal to the great unsatisfied yearning of nineteenth-century Christians for fellowship in an all-embracing Church, but he totally rejected the authoritarian path to that goal laid out by the Pontiff. His encyclical clearly confirmed to Maurice 'that the Pope is not the Uniter of Christendom – that he is emphatically its DIVIDER'; by asserting his role as 'the dogmatist of the Christian Church', Pius had destroyed his credentials as 'the head and centre of its fellowship', and his encyclical was in fact a fierce 'attack upon the faith and unity of Christendom'.

However, Maurice was less interested in *Quanta cura* and its accompanying documents as a demonstration of the reactionary nature of the Roman Catholic Church under Pius IX than as a warning of the great danger then facing the Church of England as it attempted to deal with disturbing manifestations of theological liberalism and freedom of conscience in his own country. He took it for granted that the 'creeds' of Christianity 'set forth Him who is, and was, and is to come', and it followed that 'any attempt to put decrees and dogmas for truth must be a subversion of them'.

> If the Sacraments of the Church assert the unity of man in a living and immortal Head, they must be the great antagonists of him who wishes to cut men off for not accepting his opinions. But that assertion is two-edged. It strikes as sharply against all Protestant, all English dogmatism, as against all Romish. The Pope's Encyclical Letter should be framed and glazed, and hung up in the house of every English clergyman [as a somber warning], that he may understand what *he* is aiming at.[20]

Closer to home than the Pope and fundamentally at odds with him and his Church, another foreigner had published a book outlining an approach to Christianity, and particularly to its founder, that was causing Maurice profound concern at about this time: Ernest Renan's demythologizing *Vie de Jésus* (1863). As Maurice read Renan, his Jesus denied the fatherhood of God in the traditional Christian sense, not only with regard to his own filial relationship to God but also with regard to God's paternal relationship to humankind in general, although in most of his preaching he claimed and caused others to believe the contrary; Jesus was, therefore, a fraud, and so Renan's book constituted yet another challenge to faith of the kind Victorian believers had been confronting for at least the past two decades. A bestseller in France from its publication in June 1863, the *Vie de Jésus* appeared in an authorized English translation before the end of the year, and this occasioned Maurice's 'Christmas Thoughts on Renan's Vie de Jésus' in the January 1864 *Macmillan's*.

Maurice's great fear was that English Christians trying to define a viable Jesus during this troubled period had been insufficiently strengthened to resist such a depiction as Renan's by a Church that lacked a clear and coherent notion of the Kingdom of God. They were only too ready to be seduced by a plausible thinker who asserted that it was 'the most wonderful step in human progress' to believe that Jesus was born and died like other men, 'that He had no life before, or has had since'. In making this claim, Renan had fallen into the error of denying 'a common humanity' – an error that stems from 'the disposition to glorify the past, or the present, or the future, at the expense of the other; to deny the Eternal in which they meet'. Yet, as would be the case 13 months later with Pius IX's encyclical, Maurice saw in the *Vie de Jésus* an opportunity as well as a warning: the inadequacies of Renan's reductive portrayal of Christ, confused and inconsistent as they were, might actually serve to show forth more clearly the true 'Living Christ', as he is and not as he has been appropriated and distorted by biblical critics (like Renan) and by narrow-minded divines (like some in positions of authority in the Church of England):

> Every great reformation, every assertion of the true glory of our race, every overthrow of imposture and fraud, has had its root in the conviction that there is a direct relation between the God of Heaven and His creatures on earth. If we would cast down the thrones of the oppressor, civil or spiritual – if we would really believe the progress of our species – being content to part entirely with the fame and honour of believing it; if we would be in the true sense humanists, being willing to be denounced as bigots by those who usurp the title, we shall speak of a Living Christ – of One who is, and was, and is to come; we should declare that from the highest throne of all, whether it sound from any altar on earth or not, a voice is saying, 'Children, you have a Father. I am the way to Him.'[21]

Long before the appearance of Renan's unsettling book, Maurice had looked abroad to the ideas of another writer that might yield useful lessons for Anglican believers. This was Christian Carl Josias von Bunsen, who had served as Prussian ambassador to London from 1841 to 1854 and whom Maurice had admired even before his arrival in England.[22] Bunsen's death on 28 November 1860 had inspired an obituary notice by Edmond de Pressensé in the *Revue chrétienne* that was translated in the *Times* of 9 January 1861; this in turn prompted Maurice's 'Baron Bunsen', which was printed in the March 1861 *Macmillan's*.[23] In this article and in a later one, also called 'Baron Bunsen' (a review of two new books about him in the June 1868 number), Maurice paid tribute to Bunsen as a man who had tried to reintroduce his countrymen and countrywomen to the Bible as 'treat[ing] history as the revelation of the purposes of God, as exhibiting the order of His government' so that it might play for them the same central role it had played in

England and Scotland; 'chiefly he desired to bring his own people, learned and unlearned, to receive the Bible in what he took to be its simple sense'[24] – not the debased sense of Renan.

Maurice had reservations about Bunsen's efforts to accommodate the Bible to present-day Germany, for its message is universal and not time-bound: 'a message to those wants which are *not* satisfied by, nor expressed in, the peculiar tendencies and conceptions of any age or place, rather which are crying to be emancipated from those tendencies and conceptions'. However, Maurice did applaud Bunsen's 'belief of a special vocation for his people' and his conviction that domestic 'evils' can only be extirpated by 'native methods', both of which he regarded as salutary examples for the English to emulate.[25] Bunsen's writings about the importance of *Gemeinde*, or community, in religion especially appealed to Maurice, for they pointed out both the dangers and the opportunities facing a national body such as Maurice wanted the Church of England to be: it should not degenerate into a branch of civil government but – ever mindful of its divine origins – must conform to the national character and national traditions.

Maurice's contributions to *Macmillan's* during its first decade or so were hardly unique – either in their advocacy of a truly national Church embracing a variety of theological opinion and of an ultimate unity of Christians of all persuasions based on liberty of conscience, or in their opposition to ecclesiastical dogmatism, sectarianism and authoritarianism. Indeed, the great majority of the dozens of articles on religious questions in the *Magazine* from its founding in November 1859 until his death on 1 April 1872 took positions in striking agreement with Maurice's views.

Perhaps the title of the lead article in the March 1870 number by Sir John Duke Coleridge, the solicitor-general, said it all: 'The Freedom of Opinion Necessary in an Established Church in a Free Country'. Originally delivered before a clerical audience at Sion College, London, on 20 January 1870, Coleridge's paper made it clear that he was speaking as a layman deeply concerned about the preservation of 'a very wide latitude of opinion' in the national church. Coleridge praised what he took to be the 'moderate and comprehensive views' embodied in the 39 Articles and the *Book of Common Prayer* and claimed to see no danger in the continuing existence within the Church of England of 'the Catholic or High Church school' alongside 'the Protestant or Low Church school'; indeed, he said, he was persuaded that both were 'essential to the maintenance of the historical character of the Church of England'. Like Maurice and a number of other writers whose work appeared in *Macmillan's* during these years, Coleridge approved of the judicial committee of the Privy Council as 'a lay tribunal, speaking for and in the name of the Queen', and so carrying out a mission that was entirely appropriate in view of the Church of England's character as 'a national institution like the Houses of Lords and Commons, the Universities, the courts of law, the army and navy, the municipal corporations'.[26]

Coleridge's point was particularly timely, for the judicial committee was much in the news late in 1869 and early in 1870. The cases of two controversial clergymen – the ritualist Reverend W.J.E. Bennett, Vicar of Frome Selwood, Somerset, and the Reverend Charles Voysey, Vicar of Healough, Yorkshire, who had questioned the strict truthfulness of the Bible's statements about God – were about to be heard by that body, and readers of the *Magazine* were duly exposed to a good deal of factual information and commentary about its workings. Francis W. Rowsell's 'Ecclesiastical Courts' (November 1869) was a historical account of how the Privy Council had come to be involved in such Church disputes and took no stand, but an article by a distinguished churchman whose name will recur in this chapter, Arthur Penrhyn Stanley, Dean of Westminster ('Consultative Committees in Matters Ecclesiastical', April 1870), was emphatic in insisting on the indispensability of the judicial committee of the Privy Council 'to the security of freedom and independence in the Church'.[27] Earlier, James Fitzjames Stephen, writing in *Macmillan's* as 'A Lay Churchman', had applauded its refusal to take action against two clerics, Henry Bristow Wilson (whom Maurice had defended in his 'Letter to a Colonial Clergyman') and Rowland Williams (Vicar of Broad Chalk, Wiltshire), for their contributions to *Essays and Reviews*; the judicial committee of the Privy Council, Stephen wrote in 'The Law and the Church' (March 1864), was the only appropriate tribunal to rule on what the 39 Articles actually mean, and in the cases of Wilson and Williams it had reaffirmed the traditional Anglican tolerance of 'great differences of opinion' within a Church whose doctrines are 'wide enough to cover fundamental human differences'.[28]

In 'The Freedom of Opinion Necessary in an Established Church in a Free Country', Coleridge also maintained that a national Church 'must widen its limits and abolish its tests if, as they exist, they exclude large and increasing portions of that national religion',[29] continuing a line of argument against religious tests taken by two earlier contributors to *Macmillan's*: Henry Fawcett in 'On the Exclusion of Those Who Are Not Members of the Established Church from Fellowships and Other Privileges of English Universities' (March 1861) and Henry G. Liddell, Dean of Christ Church, Oxford, in 'Subscription No Security' (April 1864). By the time Coleridge's paper appeared in the *Magazine* in March 1870, one battle in this ongoing struggle for religious liberty had already been won: from 1865, clergymen were no longer required to subscribe to the 39 Articles but rather 'only to affirm that the doctrine of the C of E as set forth in the BCP and the Articles is agreeable to the Word of God',[30] the kind of 'simple and general form of Declaration' advocated by Liddell in 'Subscription No Security'.[31] Religious tests at Oxford and Cambridge were virtually done away with in the University Tests Act of 1871, the year following the publication of Coleridge's lecture in *Macmillan's*.

One source of divisiveness within the Church of England was the Athanasian Creed, printed in the *Book of Common Prayer* immediately before the Litany, especially its so-called damnatory clauses, which denied everlasting salvation to those who did not 'keep whole and undefiled' 'the Catholick Faith'. Beginning with the first Lambeth Conference of 1867, presided over by Charles Thomas Longley, Archbishop of Canterbury, efforts were made to remove this creed from the Anglican service – efforts with which Maurice found himself in sympathy.[32] In *Macmillan's Magazine*, a pair of articles by Thomas Fowler – then Fellow of Lincoln College, Oxford, and later President of Corpus Christi College and Vice Chancellor of the university – argued for its elimination: 'The Athanasian Creed' (November 1867) and 'A Few More Words on the Athanasian Creed' (November 1869). Signing himself 'Presbyter Academicus', Fowler adverted to the mounting uncertainty regarding the date, authorship, authenticity, authority and precise meaning of the creed and its disruptive effect in a Church trying to come to terms with inescapable nineteenth-century realities. He appealed to 'our ecclesiastical rulers' to 'attempt to provide in the Church of England a religion which, while it satisfies the deepest cravings of the spiritual nature, shall not be inconsistent with the most profound knowledge of the age' rather than to repudiate 'all the discoveries of history, criticism, and science' by declaring 'themselves at open war with intellect and learning'.[33]

Fowler's argument was continued and extended in a series of three *Macmillan's* articles (November 1869 to January 1870), each called 'Lambeth and the Archbishops', by an author identified in the *Magazine* as the 'Lambeth Librarian' – John Richard Green, who subsequently became famous as a historian.[34] Taking as his focus Lambeth Palace, the London residence of the archbishops of Canterbury and site of the 1867 Lambeth Conference, which had tried to bring about greater harmony within the Anglican communion, Green stressed the all-encompassing nature of the modern Church of England and the vital lesson to be derived from 'the whole political history' of the physical structure on the Thames so long associated with that spiritual entity: Lambeth Palace had been and remained a 'voice' calling on the Church of England to 'break with the dead traditions of the past, and fling herself boldly on the living sympathies of a free people'. Green had nothing but praise for that Church 'as it stands to-day', 'the quiet illogical compromise of past and present', which 'has found room for almost every shade of religious opinion', and for the outcome of the recent Lambeth Conference: the 76 Anglican bishops from all over the world who attended

> were sent home again, without one doctrinal decision, without a single new dogma, without the addition of one iota to Creed or Articles, with the formal condemnation of not a single heretic, but simply with an increase of charity, and a widening of spiritual communion: this is the proof of the quiet power that Lambeth still possesses.[35]

Another contributor to *Macmillan's*, Goldwin Smith, followed Maurice in drawing an unfavorable contrast between the rigidity of the Roman Catholic Church and the tolerance of the Church of England and in contending that, in its present Ultramontism – characterized by its promulgation of such dogmas as the immaculate conception of the Virgin Mary and papal infallibility – the Roman Church might conceivably swallow up the Anglican but not reach an accommodation with it that would be acceptable to the vast majority of English believers. Smith was moved to make this point by the publication of two pieces of religious polemic: Pusey's *The Church of England a Portion of Christ's One Holy Catholic Church, and a Means of Restoring Visible Unity: An Eirenicon* (1865) and John Henry Newman's reply, *A Letter to the Rev. E.B. Pusey, D.D., on his recent 'Eirenicon'* (1866). The first of Smith's *Macmillan's* articles, 'Dr. Pusey's Eirenicon' (February 1866), argued that, in view of the Roman Catholic Church's intransigence on fundamental doctrinal issues, Pusey's appeal for the removal of barriers to reunion was useless; the second, 'Dr. Newman's Reply to Dr. Pusey's Eirenicon' (March 1866), cited Newman's unyielding *Letter* as a confirmation of the position Smith had taken in the *Magazine* the month before.

However, readers of *Macmillan's Magazine* were told, the historic character of the Church of England as a comprehensive institution was threatened by internal as much as by external forces, for instance by its powerful Evangelical contingent. In 'The English Evangelical Clergy' (December 1860), C.S.C. Bowen, although commending the good work that Evangelicalism was doing in the parishes, presented it as a great threat to the well-being of the Anglican Church as a whole in its intolerance and its 'direct antagonism to intellectual progress and research'. If ever the national Church is 'to lead a grand attack on vice, and folly, and worldliness', Bowen wrote, 'it cannot be by the continuance among this large portion of her clergy of the spirit which seems to animate their collective action'.[36]

An example of the kind of 'intellectual progress and research' Bowen must have had in mind was the biblical criticism of Joseph Barber Lightfoot, Hulsean Professor of Divinity and Fellow of Trinity College, Cambridge, whose *St. Paul's Epistle to the Galatians: A Revised Text with Introduction, Notes, and Dissertations* was published by Macmillan and Co. in 1865. In a pair of articles in the *Magazine* on 'Modern Commentaries on the Bible' (December 1865 and July 1866), Reginald Stuart Poole praised Lightfoot's work as confirming the divine nature of Jesus and the essentials of a Christian faith that rose above sectarian dogma.

A much more popular book than Lightfoot's *St. Paul's Epistle to the Galatians*, also brought out by Macmillan and Co. in 1865, was *Ecce Homo: A Survey of the Life and Work of Jesus Christ*.[37] Published anonymously, it was written by John Robert Seeley, then Professor of Latin at University College London and later Charles Kingsley's successor as Professor of Modern History at Cambridge. Maurice was one of those who regarded *Ecce Homo* as a corrective to the *Vie de Jésus*, succeeding where Renan had failed in attributing 'entire veracity' to Christ.[38] Reviewing it in the June 1866 *Macmillan's Magazine*, A.P. Stanley took Seeley's work as a significant contribution to a healthy sense of unity among all Christians. Better than 'a hundred artificial "Eirenicons"', Stanley held, *Ecce Homo* spoke to 'a wide-spread conviction that the essence of Christianity must be found in the doctrines which those persons have in common, not in the doctrines which divide them asunder', and it refuted the position of those narrow-minded people 'who place the salvation of the world in precise forms of dogmatic statement', valuing 'what they think orthodoxy as the first of virtues, and what they know to be truth and charity as the second and third virtues'.[39]

Stanley's comments in *Macmillan's* on another new book, Sir John Taylor Coleridge's *A Memoir of the Rev. John Keble* (1869), nearly three years later (March 1869) similarly emphasized the necessity of religious tolerance. A leader of the Tractarian movement who maintained a firm High Church stance, Keble, who had died in 1866, personified to the Broad Church Dean of Westminster what was best in nineteenth-century Anglicanism. Keble 'never took active steps in the persecutions and personal attacks by which the High Church school has distinguished itself in later years', Stanley pointed out, nor had Keble himself been subjected to the sort of 'legal persecutions and judgments of late set on foot and threatened by one ecclesiastical party against the other'. In Stanley's view, such willingness to countenance internal disagreement unquestionably redounded to the benefit of the national church.

If a judgment had been pronounced in his lifetime which had rendered it penal for an English clergyman to profess his belief in the Real Presence in the Eucharist, and in the lawfulness and duty of adoring that Real Presence, John Keble, if any man, would have been struck at, and excluded from the pale of the Church of England. We ask, without fear of contradiction, Is there any English Churchman – nay, we might almost say, is there any English Nonconformist – who would not have regretted such a consummation?[40]

Like notices of new books, obituaries of eminent churchmen were used by contributors to *Macmillan's* to articulate their convictions about what the Church of England had been and should continue to be. In 'The Late Bishop of Calcutta' (December 1866), for instance, George Edward Lynch Cotton was commended for having stood in a 'loving relation ... to all sections of the Church', a latitudinarian position he had jeopardized only once, in 1862, when he allowed Presbyterian soldiers to attend worship services in Anglican chapels on government posts in India, to the dismay of 'a small fraction of the Church, or rather of the clergy, at home'.[41] The author of this tribute to Bishop Cotton was George Granville Bradley, who had succeeded Cotton as headmaster of Marlborough; the man whom Bradley was to follow in 1881 as Dean of Westminster, A.P. Stanley, bestowed similar posthumous praise on Henry Hart Milman in 'The Late Dean of St. Paul's' (January 1869). Milman had died on 24 September 1868, and Stanley's article in the *Magazine* was partly an appreciation of Milman's life and partly a review of his *Annals of S. Paul's Cathedral* (1868). In characterizing Milman's work, Stanley singled out his contributions to maintaining 'the freedom, the generosity, and the justice of the English Church' as a national institution, and his profound understanding of 'that subtle framework of social and religious life which has hitherto afforded scope for the gradual and free development of all the diverse elements of the English Church and nation'.[42]

In the view of Maurice and a number of his fellow contributors to *Macmillan's*, it was entirely proper that the Church of England, embodying the national religion as it did, be established by law in a uniquely intimate connection with the state.[43] In the contentious atmosphere of the mid-nineteenth century, however, this view was challenged by a growing number of persons inside and outside the Anglican Church. The debate about the implications and the likely consequences of disestablishment was placed in a new framework by the introduction and enactment in 1869 of the Irish Church Bill, which dissolved the union between the episcopal churches of Ireland and England and cut the ties of the Church of Ireland to the government. Was this a body-blow to the principle of a national Church so long urged by Maurice

and others, or was it rather an act of simple justice to the overwhelm-
ingly Roman Catholic population of Ireland?

Maurice himself inclined to the latter position,[44] but two contributors
to *Macmillan's* voiced troubled doubts. In his October 1868 'A Free
Anglican Church', Edwin Hatch, Vice Principal of St Mary Hall, Oxford, who had recently held academic posts in Toronto and Quebec,
argued that the disestablishment of the Anglican church in Canada had
led to an unfortunate fragmentation that might well be replicated in
Ireland; two months later, in 'Luther on Church and State, with Some
Considerations on the Irish Church', Henry Wace, a curate at St James's,
Piccadilly, expressed the fear that similar disestablishment in Ireland,
much nearer home, would sever the existing near-identity between 'the
interests of the Church' and 'the interests of the nation' and threaten the
present 'close connexion between religion and national feeling'.[45] Wace,
of course, was taking an unexceptionably Mauricean position concerning Church–state relations, but was begging the question of what 'the
nation' really was in his application of that position to the particular
case at hand. As Maurice recognized, the 'connexion between religion
and national feeling' across the Irish Sea was not what it was in England by virtue of the fact that the Church there was not an expression of
Irish religious feeling but had been imposed on the indigenous inhabit-
ants by their English conquerors.[46]

There is probably some significance in the appearance of a footnoted
editorial disclaimer – rare, although not unique, in *Macmillan's* – on the
first page of Wace's article:

> We willingly give insertion to the above able argument against the
> disestablishment of the Irish Church, though without pledging the
> Magazine to that view. It is one of the advantages of signed arti-
> cles, that, the writers being responsible for the opinions they express,
> scope is given for a less rigid treatment of a question than where
> the articles are anonymous.[47]

Whatever lay behind the insertion of that note, the treatment of the
Irish Church Bill in *Macmillan's* serves as another useful reminder that
the *Magazine* did not impose a monolithic uniformity on its contributors. In fact, yet another article on this subject, published two months
after Wace's, 'Disestablishment and Disendowment', by a resident of
Belfast, W.D. Henderson, took a much more benign view of what was
about to happen in Ireland than either Hatch's or Wace's did. It seems
clear that Alexander Macmillan and David Masson were able to rec-
oncile their profound respect for Maurice and his vision of a national
Church with the principle on which *Macmillan's Magazine* had been
founded: that it should be open to opinions that strayed from what
some might consider its editorial policy – a principle that, after all, did

not differ substantially from Maurice's own belief in freedom of thought.

Political reform

On 1 March 1860, Lord John Russell, who had been active in the cause of Parliamentary reform for three decades, introduced into the House of Commons a measure that would have lowered the property qualifications for the franchise and brought about a redistribution of seats. The bill died in consequence of legislative maneuvering and popular indifference, and the status quo remained inert until later in the decade. No authority on political infighting, Maurice did ask himself why the working classes had not bestirred themselves more vigorously on behalf of Russell's bill, which would have significantly advanced their interests, and he answered his own question in the lead article of the June 1860 *Macmillan's*: 'The Suffrage, Considered in Reference to the Working Class, and to the Professional Class'.

The problem as Maurice saw it was that, unlike those who had worked successfully for the passage of the 1832 Reform Bill, '[t]he popular agitator' of 1860 addressed 'himself directly to the material interest' of the working classes, but such appeals, however plausibly and ably delivered, could not and did not achieve their intended effect. A different, loftier kind of argument was needed, he believed, to 'move the hearts of men more than these'. 'Working men ... demand that you should do homage to something in them which is not material, which is not selfish.' As their predecessors had done 30 years earlier, according to Maurice, proponents of extending the franchise should instead evoke the 'high, national, divine interests' that were alive, at least in latent form, in all English people, including workers. For, Maurice insisted, they too 'wish to be recognised as members of the nation, not to stand aloof from it; to have a common interest with other classes, not an interest which is opposed to theirs or destructive of theirs'. Maurice concluded by urging those whom he regarded as the opinion-molders of his day, 'the professional men and literary men', to base their pro-reform rhetoric on this premise and to agree on 'the ground of manhood' rather than 'the ground of possession' as the appropriate qualification for the right to vote, because 'our common object' must be 'to get all the manhood we can into our constituencies, and into our representatives'.[48]

Of course Maurice's reference to 'high, national, divine interests' shared by all Englishmen and Englishwomen regardless of class is reminiscent of his writings, in *Macmillan's* and elsewhere, about the Church of England as an embodiment of these same exalted feelings latent in all the people of the nation.[49] However, a further element in this June 1860 essay on 'The Suffrage' links the article with other, more secular work in the *Magazine*. As one way 'to get all the manhood we can into our constituencies, and into our representatives', Maurice recommended the plan for proportional representation of 'Minorities' set forth by Thomas Hare in his *A Treatise on the Election of Representatives, Parliamentary and Municipal* (1859) and given wider currency by John Stuart Mill in a supplement to the recently published second edition of his *Thoughts on Parliamentary Reform* (1859).[50]

In the years that followed the publication of Maurice's 'The Suffrage', other writers in *Macmillan's* also advocated the Hare plan as an essential ingredient in any further Parliamentary reform: Henry Fawcett (June 1861),[51] Thomas Hare himself (February 1862), Vere Henry Hobart (January 1866 and November 1866), and Millicent Garrett Fawcett (September 1870 and April 1871). Not surprisingly, however, in view of the *Magazine's* openness to conflicting opinions, contrary views regarding the Hare plan also appeared in its pages on two occasions during the decade. G.O. Trevelyan's 'A Few Remarks on Mr. Hare's Scheme of Representation' (April 1862) called it unnecessary, because the established mode of representation worked well enough; unrealistic, because there existed no great popular demand for it; and vulnerable to abuse, because in Trevelyan's judgment the two major political parties would soon learn to bend it to their advantage in the unlikely event it were adopted. An essay purporting to review a collection of 12 *Essays on Reform* (April 1867), far from 'puffing' that new Macmillan and Co. book, also took issue with the arguments of several of the contributors, especially Bernard Cracroft, and ended by denouncing the Hare plan as undesirable and impractical.[52]

That these two pieces may be considered dissenting opinions in the *Magazine* is clear from the fact that – like Henry Wace's 'Luther on Church and State' but unlike any other *Macmillan's* article treating the subject of Parliamentary reform – both were printed with editorial footnotes expressing Masson's, and probably Alexander Macmillan's, reservations about what they were saying.[53] No such editorial demurral accompanied the most famous article on the Parliamentary reform question in *Macmillan's*: Thomas Carlyle's strident response to the 1867 Reform Act, 'Shooting Niagara: And After?' (August 1867). Although other writers in the *Magazine* expressed various shades of apprehension about the emergence of 'democracy', none was anything like as shrill as Carlyle in his dire predictions of the consequences that would follow the resort to 'new supplies of blockheadism, gullibility, bribeability, amenability to beer and balderdash, by way of amending the woes we have had from our previous supplies of that bad article'.[54] One such writer in particular, J.R. Seeley (the author of *Ecce Homo*), in a series of three articles on 'The English Revolution of the Nineteenth Century' (August to October 1870), offered a much more cogent analysis than Carlyle's of the causes underlying the ascendancy of public opinion and the reasons behind its successes as well as its failures. The already-mentioned contributions by Maurice himself, the Fawcetts, Hare and Hobart, as well as Goldwin Smith's 'The Philosophy of the Cave' (June 1866) and the April 1867 review, possibly by Leslie Stephen, of *Essays on Reform*, were all favorable to the idea of extending the franchise.[55]

Another long-standing abuse in the British political system that cried out for correction as insistently as the still-restricted franchise and the inadequate, or non-existent, representation of minorities was the widespread practice of bribery at elections – personally experienced by Anthony Trollope in 1868 as a candidate for election to the House of Commons from the Yorkshire borough of Beverley and vividly described by him in his novel *Ralph the Heir* (1870–71) and later in his *Autobiography* (1883). Again it was Maurice who gave the lead to other *Macmillan's* contributors in voicing his dismay at this grave moral and social malady. His 'Corruption at Elections' (July 1864) praised a paper by William Dougal Christie called 'Suggestions for an Organization for Restraint of Corruption at Elections' that had been delivered before the National Association for the Promotion of Social Science in February and was subsequently published by the Association. Christie's proposals for the suppression of bribery were especially timely, Maurice held, because there was once again much talk of electoral reform and, if that reform were to be meaningful, it would have to be responsive to national indignation at such malfeasance:

> there must be a cry raised which shall not be against particular offenders, but against the offence – not against some flagrant exhibitions of it, but against the principle from which it has issued – not against those who take [bribes], but against those who give.[56]

Maurice's *Macmillan's* article was reprinted by the Social Science Association, and that pamphlet – and, more generally, the efforts of Maurice, Christie, John Stuart Mill, Edwin Chadwick and others to confront the question of electoral bribery – drew the cynical scorn of the *Saturday Review*, which maintained that this kind of corruption appealed to something base inherent in the nature of voters and so could not be expunged.[57] Christie immediately struck back in *Macmillan's* with his 'Corruption at Elections and the "Saturday Review"' (October 1864), complaining about the 'ridicule and unfair treatment' to which Maurice and he had been subjected by the *Saturday Review*, challenging the 'ribaldry' and 'nonsense' in that weekly's approach to a serious question of 'political morals and philosophy' and deploring the 'peculiar taste' that had led it to include among its targets

> Miss Emily Faithfull, who is the printer and publisher for the National Association for the Promotion of Social Science, as she is also 'printer and publisher in ordinary to Her Majesty,' and who has no more to do with the proceedings of the Association than the printer of the *Saturday Review* with the authorship of its articles. But the Saturday Reviewer thinks it becoming to try to turn ridicule on this movement by sneers at the lady printer.[58]

Having effectively silenced the *Saturday Review*, Christie returned to the subject of bribery in British politics seven months later. His 'Mr. John Stuart Mill for Westminster', which appeared in *Macmillan's* in May 1865, argued that the Parliamentary candidacy of this intellectual giant – 'one of the kings of thought' – served as proof that an incorruptible man of stature who refused to canvass, to make promise-filled speeches or to spend his own money could successfully defy the debased standards to which his less-principled contemporaries clung. 'The electors of Westminster who have brought forward Mr. Mill have set the nation a fine example.'[59] Vere Henry Hobart, in 'Bribery at Elections' (November 1866), also linked that evil to the need for Parliamentary reform and for proportional representation, a subject that Maurice had broached in *Macmillan's* some six and a half years before. Most of the remedies for electoral corruption that had been prescribed, Hobart held, would address symptoms rather than causes, the same point Maurice had made in 'Corruption at Elections'. What was wanted, according to Hobart, was equalization in the size of constituencies, which would diminish the susceptibility of electors in small districts whose votes loomed disproportionately large, and adoption of the Hare plan, which would give voters a much larger stake in government owing to their ability to vote for candidates with whom they felt some affinity rather than candidates who had been imposed on them by powerful and partisan political officials. Hobart's article demonstrated yet again how ideas first expressed in the *Magazine* by Maurice had a way of turning up in new combinations.

Women's issues

Unlike John Stuart Mill, who tried in vain during his sole term as a Member of Parliament to amend the 1867 Reform Bill to provide for women's suffrage, the great majority of those contributors to *Macmillan's* who concerned themselves with political questions in the 1860s did not explicitly advocate the removal of the barriers that confined the franchise to men. Yet women's issues did loom large in the pages of the *Magazine* during those years, and once again it was Maurice who – inadvertently, to be sure – set the agenda.[60]

Recent feminist scholars and critics have had their doubts about Maurice's credentials as an advocate for women. June Purvis, for example, argues that his 'ideas about women can be interpreted as part of a broader world view upholding not only the supposed "natural" hierarchy between the sexes but also the established hierarchy between social classes'.[61] Janet Horowitz Murray also quotes Maurice at considerable length to the effect that women should be educated for work as teachers and nurses rather than 'for the kinds of tasks which belong to our professions'.[62] Frank McClain, on the other hand, claims that Maurice was remarkably respectful of the intellectual as well as the spiritual endowments of women and attributes to him a 'deep concern for the feminine cause', which he goes on to document. Like Purvis, McClain connects that concern with 'a broader world view' but points out that to speak of separate spheres for men and women is not to place one sex hierarchically above the other:

> As a theologian and as an author, Maurice brought a new vision to what it means to be a woman. Members of the one family of God, women share equal rights with all other children of the same parent. In the creation story of Genesis God had said, 'Let us make man in our image, after our likenesss ... So God created man in his own image, in the image of God created he him; male and female created he them.' Women, though different from men, are yet integral and complementary parts of a whole. Along with the male, the female stands conjointly in the position of man-as-Image of God.[63]

Despite such disagreements among late-twentieth-century writers on Maurice, it is indisputable and probably more significant that many Victorian champions of women's rights regarded him as an inspiration and an ally. Even a short list of those who acknowledged his influence, profited from his help and claimed his friendship reads like a Who's Who of mid- and late-nineteenth century feminism. None of these women was more eloquent about her indebtedness to Maurice than Millicent Garrett Fawcett, the early campaigner for women's suffrage, who regarded herself as 'fortunate to have heard Maurice repeatedly at a time when my own mind was in process of formation'; he seemed to her 'a modern Isaiah who awakened in me new thoughts and ... new reverences'.

Yet Fawcett was not the only female activist who looked up to Maurice as a mentor and supporter. Her sister, Elizabeth Garrett Anderson, the pioneering English woman physician, gained Maurice's help in the course of her unsuccessful struggle to matriculate at London

University. Like Fawcett, the social reformer Octavia Hill was deeply impressed by Maurice's sermons when she was a young woman and regarded herself as one of Maurice's disciples. Emily Davies, the founder of Girton College, Cambridge, was the sister of Maurice's fellow-Christian Socialist J. Llewelyn Davies, who introduced her to Maurice and his circle, where she was cordially received. Two other women who blazed new trails in education – Dorothea Beale, the long-time principal of Cheltenham Ladies' College, and Frances Mary Buss, founder and first headmistress of North London Collegiate School for Girls – had been among Maurice's first pupils at Queen's College (of which more below). Such prominent Victorian feminists as Barbara Leigh Smith Bodichon and Josephine Grey Butler were also on excellent terms with Maurice.[64]

It is also of interest here that four of these women – Hill, Fawcett, Anderson and Bodichon – were among the dozens of female contributors to *Macmillan's* during the 1860s:[65] two of Fawcett's essays, on the Hare plan, have already been mentioned; a third will be treated shortly; and brief discussions of pieces by Anderson and Bodichon are yet to come. Another remarkable woman whom we encountered earlier in this chapter, the printer and publisher Emily Faithfull, was frequently associated with Maurice; the long and eloquent obituary of Maurice that she wrote for her *Victoria Magazine* makes a persuasive case for him as one who 'was always ready to forward the true interests of women'.[66]

Although Maurice's utterances about women's issues could be as cryptic as his pronouncements about theological and political questions, to which of course they were closely related, there can be no doubt about his lifelong keen interest in the education of women – an interest that was recognized for decades after his death; the article on 'Women' in the 11th edition of the *Encyclopaedia Britannica* (1911) refers to him approvingly as the 'pioneer' of the movement to 'put [women's] education on a sounder basis in the nineteenth century'.[67]

One of Maurice's earliest publications – in the *Metropolitan Quarterly Magazine*, which he co-edited as a 20-year-old Cambridge undergraduate – was an article on 'Female Education' in which he vigorously attacked the 'industrious malice and wilful perverseness' of the existing pedagogical system administered at 'those awful prison-houses called establishments, or at home under the vigilant eye of an enlightened French or English governess',[68] based as it was on stifling the mind and the imagination of girls and young women and fostering instead the memory and meaningless mechanical skills. That was in 1826; 17 years later, he helped to found the Governesses' Benevolent Institution, and this venture in turn led to the creation in 1848 of Queen's College, London, in which Maurice also played a leading role.[69]

In January 1855, within weeks of the opening of the London Working Men's College, of which Maurice served as first principal, it began offering classes for women; Maurice recruited the 17-year-old Octavia Hill as a teacher of arithmetic and administrative secretary for those classes.[70]

Four months later, on 21 May, Maurice delivered a lecture at the Working Men's College on a 'Plan for a Female College for the Help of the Rich and the Poor', in which he expressed the misgivings about women entering professions like medicine or law quoted by Murray and contended that women are divinely endowed with the capacity to be nurses and teachers and to minister to the poor as social workers, and that these innate nurturing attributes should be cultivated in a female college.[71] Throughout this lecture, Maurice respectfully cited the ideas of Anna Brownell Murphy Jameson, whose *Sisters of Charity, Catholic and Protestant, Abroad and at Home*, which took a very similar view of women's capacities, had just been published. Three and a half months after Jameson died on 17 March 1860, the July *Macmillan's* printed Maurice's 'Female School of Art: Mrs. Jameson', which not only paid generous posthumous tribute to her as an art educator and art critic and pointed to the enduring social significance of her life's work, but also indicated a softening of the position Maurice had taken five years earlier.

Perhaps Jameson's most important contribution, Maurice believed, was her successful attempt 'to counteract ... the male vulgarity which, under pretence of teaching women to keep their right place, deprives them of any place but that of their servants or playthings'. Nearly half of Maurice's article was given over to four lengthy quotations from Jameson's prefatory letter to Lord John Russell that took up the first 34 pages of a new 1859 edition of her *Sisters of Charity and the Commun-ion of Labour*, along with Maurice's admiring comments about them. The first two extracts plead for the collaboration of both sexes in working toward desirable social ends. The third pours scorn on the misogynistic diatribes of some men. The last advocates an extension of the kind of education available at Jameson's Female School of Art and Design so as to open up wider professional opportunities for women; Jameson said, in part:

> We wish to have some higher kinds of industrial, and professional, and artistic training more freely accessible to women. We wish to have some share, however small, in the advantages which most of our large well-endowed public institutions extend to men only ... [A]s I am sure men have no reason to fear women as their rivals, so I hope women will, in all noble studies, be allowed henceforth to be their associates and companions.[72]

Maurice's inclusion of this passage may be taken as a retraction of one of the arguments he had advanced in his 'Plan for a Female College'. Implicitly if not explicitly, he now seemed to be endorsing the notion of equal professional opportunities for women.

Later in the 1860s, other writers in *Macmillan's* echoed, and went beyond, the position taken by Jameson and endorsed by Maurice. Anne Jemima Clough – who was to become the first principal of Newnham College, the next college for women founded at Cambridge after Girton – proposed in her 'Hints on the Organization of Girls' Schools' (October 1866) that greater emphasis be given to academic subjects in female education; one result of such curricular reform, Clough predicted, was that 'many new paths of useful occupation may be opened to women'.[73] Millicent Garrett Fawcett went further in 'The Education of Women of the Middle and Upper Classes' (April 1868). The superficial and insufficiently demanding education of girls between 12 and 17, she maintained, was based on the assumption that the female mind is inherently inferior to the male – an assumption that current educational practice made it impossible either to prove or refute. 'Let all, both men and women, have equal chances of maturing such intellect as God has given them.' Moreover, Fawcett declared her desire 'to open all the professions to women; and, if they prove worthy of them, to share with men all those distinctions, intellectual, literary, and political, which are such valuable incentives to mental and moral progress'. Fawcett presented her vision as something much more comprehensive than the aspiration of one woman or even a group of like-minded women, for, she predicted, such 'increased diffusion of sound mental training … would add as much as any other proposed reform to the general happiness and welfare of mankind'. Clearly, however, it would make women happier, better and more productive, and it would bring about 'the extension to women of those legal, social, and political rights, the withholding of which is felt, by a daily increasing number of men and women, to be unworthy of the civilization of the nineteenth century'.[74] Fawcett's linking of sounder education with 'political rights' for women was subtle (the fraught phrase 'women's suffrage' is not to be found in this article) but nonetheless real.

The twin questions 'What are women capable of?' and 'How can they be enabled to reach their potential?' were repeatedly addressed by other post-Mauricean contributors to *Macmillan's* during the 1860s. As was to be expected given the *Magazine's* openness to diverse views, these questions were phrased and answered in varying ways, but certain common themes did emerge. Not only did these writers agree with Maurice, Clough and Fawcett in calling for a reform of women's education, but like them they also proposed specific remedies by which that might be accomplished.

In her *Macmillan's* article on 'The Education of Women of the Middle and Upper Classes', Millicent Garrett Fawcett had suggested how women, who could not then belong to any of the Cambridge colleges, might nevertheless qualify for degrees from that university. As an alternative, J. Llewelyn Davies in 'A New College for Women' (June 1868) drew his readers' attention to the imminent establishment of a new independent college for women, located between Cambridge and London and 'easily accessible to both', which would be organized very much like an Oxford or Cambridge college and offer its members the intellectual and social advantages that had long been available to male students at the two old residential universities. Davies conceded that there were objections not so much to this scheme in particular as to the idea of higher education for women in general, but persuasively refuted each of them in turn and ended his article with an appeal for sympathy and financial help for 'this enterprise which will be unique not only in England but in Europe'.[75] Conceivably family interest as well as high-mindedness lay behind Davies's argument, for the unnamed 'enterprise' he had in mind was the College for Women at Hitchin in Hertfordshire, established by his sister that very summer; in October 1873 it moved to Cambridge and became Girton College, with Emily Davies as head.[76]

Frederic W.H. Myers's proposal for strengthening the education of women, 'Local Lectures for Women', which appeared in *Macmillan's* six months later, sounded more modest than Davies's but, even more obviously than his, was also based on a venture recently launched by a group of resourceful women: the North of England Council for Promoting the Higher Education of Women, with Josephine Butler as president and Anne Jemima Clough as secretary. The idea behind this organization was

> that girls' schools, by co-operation, might secure first-rate teachers [often, as it turned out, *university* teachers], who should give lectures of a strictly educational character, to be accompanied by reading at home and supplemented by examinations or subsidiary classes, where the pupils might be questioned and their knowledge tested.

The North of England Council began its life in 1867; by the end of 1869 its success was such that counterparts had sprung up all over the British Isles, including one in Edinburgh, where David Masson – by then a professor at the university there – was one of the lecturers. Although Myers's concern in this article was with what we would call continuing or further, rather than higher, education, he based his case on the same premises as Maurice, Clough, Fawcett and Davies: that, as Myers put it, God has given women 'an intelligence which it is their duty to cultivate, and energies which it is their duty to employ' and that women are just as much in need as men of 'liberal education', 'which is intended to fit its recipients for *all* duties and for *any* position'.[77]

Another view shared by these writers was to find its most famous expression at the end of the decade in John Stuart Mill's *The Subjection of Women* (1869): that it is foolish to speak of the 'natural' abilities or disabilities of women in the absence of any opportunity to test them – in higher education or the professions, for instance. An earlier exposition of that view appeared in a *Macmillan's* article, 'Women and Criticism' (September 1866), by Mill's stepdaughter, Helen Taylor.[78] Just as people who had been blinded by received ideas about economics had resisted free trade, she argued, so people with traditional notions about what women could do were resisting the idea of letting them try anything else. Taylor used this analogy to urge the removal of those restrictions in law and custom that had been used to keep women down. The success of free trade, she wrote,

> remains an example of how human energy can find the best and easiest examples for itself when relieved of all restrictive legislation; an example likely in time to modify old opinions on many topics, and perhaps on none more than on the freedom that can safely be allowed to women.[79]

The Subjection of Women itself was reviewed, in glowingly favorable terms, by Charles Kingsley in the October 1869 *Macmillan's*; his 'Women and Politics' also dealt with a collection of essays called *Woman's Work and Woman's Culture* (edited by Josephine Butler and published by Macmillan and Co.), W.B. Hodgson's *Education of Girls and Employment of Women*, and Lydia Ernestine Becker's *Contemporary Review* article 'On the Study of Science by Women'.

More openly than any of the *Macmillan's* writers discussed so far, Kingsley emphasized the case for women's suffrage – partly in the name of 'fair play', because women were entitled to 'a share in making those laws and those social regulations which have, while made exclusively by men, resulted in leaving women at a disadvantage at every turn', and partly in the name of accepting new realities, because women's role in the work force was demonstrably growing and because women's education was rapidly improving. How, Kingsley asked, could people go on pretending that women have nothing to do with the world outside the home when the 1861 census showed that 3.5 million women (2.5 million of them unmarried) were then working for a living in England?[80] Why should many ill-educated men now be allowed to exercise the franchise as a result of the 1867 Reform Act when that right was denied to all women, however well educated they might be? Even in the areas of employment and education a great deal remained to be done,

Kingsley conceded, but that did not mean that women should not be granted the vote.

> Though the demands of women just now are generally urged in the order of – first, employment, then education, and lastly the franchise, I have dealt principally with the latter because I sincerely believe that it, and it only, will lead to their obtaining a just measure of the two former.[81]

No woman at mid-century faced greater educational or occupational obstacles than Elizabeth Garrett, later Elizabeth Garrett Anderson, in her attempts to become a physician. Because of her gender, she was not allowed to enroll in an English medical school but was given special permission by Apothecaries' Hall to attend lectures 'privately', passed its examinations and became a licentiate of the Society of Apothecaries in 1865. Garrett started practicing the next year, was placed on the medical register in 1869, and received her MD in 1870 – not from a British university, where women were still not allowed to take medical degrees, but from the Sorbonne.

Garrett told her story, or as much of it as had by then occurred, in the September 1868 *Magazine* – not as an appeal to readers' pity but as a plea that others be spared what she had been put through. Stated simply, it was the thesis of Garrett's 'Women Physicians' that no Englishwoman bent on becoming a physician should be denied the opportunity to receive normal medical training and qualify for a medical degree in her own country. Well aware 'that both the professional and the non-professional public have to be converted to the *idea* of women-physicians',[82] she tried to show how shallow were the objections of those who held that women were inherently unfit – intellectually, physiologically, emotionally and morally – to become doctors, very much as J. Llewelyn Davies had done in 'A New College for Women' when he laid bare the weakness of the conventional arguments against higher education for women. The core of Garrett's case, however, was the familiar Helen Taylor–Millicent Garrett Fawcett–John Stuart Mill position that, although there was plenty of evidence in the actual accomplishments of actual women to indicate that such theoretical arguments were at best highly questionable, they could be proved or disproved only on the basis of additional experience: there was no way to be sure how well female physicians would function, as doctors or as women, until society could base such a judgment on the performance of a sufficiently large number of them.

That same position was taken by other *Magazine* contributors. In a pair of articles about 'Women in the Fine Arts' (June and July 1865), for instance, Francis Turner Palgrave argued that, although it was undeniable that women's achievements in 'Poetry, Painting, Sculpture, and

Music' had been quantitatively fewer than and qualitatively inferior to those of men, 'It is altogether premature to decide whether women are not intended for such successes by natural organization until they have, for a sufficient period, received intellectual advantages equal to those achieved by men.' Writing from a male perspective, Palgrave was harder on his fellow men than most of the female writers in *Macmillan's* who addressed women's issues: in concluding his presentation in the second of these essays, Palgrave went beyond the speculative posture he had assumed in the first and questioned whether the 'limited and imperfect' success of women 'in the Fine Arts' might not be 'a law of man – man emphatically' rather than 'a law of Nature', pointing out not only that women had 'been hitherto debarred' from the 'prerequisites and circumstances of success' as a consequence of their 'deficient education', but also that 'the contemptuous treatment in regard to these matters which they receive at the hands of men' must bear at least a portion of the blame for the slightness of their success.[83]

As if to strengthen the case of those contributors to *Macmillan's* who upheld the intellectual capabilities of women, Leonard Benton Seeley devoted a May 1866 article, 'The Education of Englishwomen in the Sixteenth Century', to demonstrating how classical and modern learning had flourished among middle- and upper-class women under the last Tudor monarchs: Mary Tudor, Lady Jane Grey and Elizabeth I, he held, were the most prominent examples of such female erudition rather than exceptional cases. One prodigious near-contemporary of theirs not mentioned by Seeley was Elizabeth Joan Weston (1582–1612), an English poet of great learning who wrote in Latin and spent most of her life in exile in Bohemia, where her Roman Catholic family had taken refuge after her father aroused Queen Elizabeth's enmity. However, Mary Brotherton made Weston the subject of a whole *Magazine* essay, 'A Forgotten English Poetess', four years later, in the June 1870 number. It was not Brotherton's purpose to revise the male-dominated canon of what was already being called Renaissance poetry, nor did she believe herself qualified to engage in high-powered literary criticism of Weston's verses, which she characterized and from which she quoted; rather, she was attracted to the human interest of Weston's story:

> I cannot but think that many of us would gladly breathe the sweet savour of this long-dead violet; that many of us would gladly hear how it bloomed so brave and lovely amidst the wintry bleakness of adverse circumstance, and, when the brief sunshine found it, among the majestic growths of German literature.[84]

Other *Macmillan's* writers saw fit for purposes of their own to draw their readers' attention to obscure or oppressed women in countries outside Britain. One was Barbara Bodichon, recalling in 'A Dull Life'

(May 1867) an encounter she had had nine years earlier during a visit to Louisiana with 'a pale uninteresting young lady' identified only as 'Cecilia'. She was stirred out of her torpor by Bodichon's sketching and told her her dreary story: orphaned at five, she lived quietly with her grandmother and could look back to only one memorable interruption of her monotonous existence, a spell of nursing during an outbreak of yellow fever. Had 'Cecilia' been English, Bodichon observed, her life would have been considerably more interesting. Writing as a humanitarian rather than as a feminist (which she assuredly was), Bodichon concluded as follows:

> The life of this poor young lady was the dullest life I ever knew – dull, because her domestic life happened to be sad, lonely; dull, because she was poor; dull, because she was in a slave state; dull, because the country was dull and dreary; dull, because she was a young lady with nothing to do and very little education. Happily, such a dull life is not possible in many countries, and was rare no doubt in the country where I came across it.[85]

The subtext of an earlier *Macmillan's* article, by Frances Power Cobbe, was more telling. Drawing a depressing picture of the bleak, idle and intellectually impoverished existences of 'Women in Italy in 1862' (September 1862), Cobbe conceded that the lives of their English counterparts were more satisfactory but issued a baleful warning in her opening sentence: 'It has become almost a truism to observe that the progress of a nation in civilization must, in a considerable measure, depend on the condition of its women.'[86] Especially coming from such a well-known feminist, that thesis statement was clearly meant to apply at home as well as abroad.

Similar statements showed up elsewhere, sometimes in unexpected places, in the *Magazine* of the 1860s. For instance, in a review of a book of verses published by Macmillan and Co. in 1864, Lucy Fletcher's *Thoughts from a Girl's Life*, Dinah Mulock maintained that 'on the women of a nation does its virtue, strength, nobility, and even its vitality, rest'. The context here was, however, quite different from Cobbe's, for Mulock's view of what the role of women should be was considerably more moderate. She had begun the quoted sentence by exclaiming, 'From a gynocracy, or even a self-existent, self-protecting, and self-dependent rule, heaven save us, and all other Christian communities!' Although herself a prolific author, Mulock – who became Dinah Mulock Craik on marrying Alexander Macmillan's partner, George Lillie Craik, in 1865 – was even reluctant to have Englishwomen become professional writers, deploring 'that *cacoethes scribendi*, that frantic craving for literary reputation, which lures a girl from her natural duties, her safe shut-up home life', and expressing the hope that Lucy

Fletcher, whose poems she was reviewing, would not 'join the band of writing women – of which the very highest, noblest, and most successful feel, that to them, as women, what has been gained is at best a poor equivalent for what has been lost'.[87]

As this example will suggest, there was no *Macmillan's* 'party line' on women's issues, any more than there was on theological and political issues, during the 1860s, even though in each of these three areas a kind of Mauricean consensus did emerge. Another female contributor who took a more traditional stand than the others whom we have encountered so far was Anne Gilchrist, whose 'A Neglected Art' (October 1865) took it for granted that the sphere of the British middle-class matron was, and would continue to be, the home and urged her to take a more active role in household management so as to save money that would otherwise be wasted by the profligacy of cooks and other servants. Gilchrist did distinguish such a modern woman from her own grandmother, who had lived in a simpler age and was content to spend her 'whole time and thoughts in domestic affairs', but this was too restrictive; basing her argument on 'twelve years' experience', Gilchrist believed that the wife who expected to be her husband's friend and partner should do her share in managing the family's finances.[88]

At the end of the decade, *Macmillan's* played its part in a controversy regarding the position of women that dwarfed in liveliness anything it published about educational, professional or political reforms that might benefit, or harm, them. It all began with the appearance in another periodical, the *Saturday Review* of 14 March 1868, of an essay called 'The Girl of the Period' – unsigned but immediately known to be the work of Eliza Lynn Linton, a prolific novelist and journalist who was vehemently opposed to women's rights. Lamenting the disappearance of a bygone 'ideal of womanhood', 'when English girls were content to be what God and nature had made them', Linton pulled out all the stops in her demolition of this nineteenth-century forerunner of what a hundred years later would come to be called the liberated woman, labeling 'the girl of the period', among her other failings, as vain, unmanageable, rude, mercenary, immoral, thrill-seeking, grotesquely turned out, loose tongued, foul mouthed and unfit to be a wife and mother. Seeing no immediate cure for this pandemic social affliction, Linton counseled her readers 'to wait patiently until the national madness has passed, and our women have come back again to the old English ideal, once the most beautiful, the most modest, the most essentially womanly in the world'.[89]

Merle Bevington, the historian of the early *Saturday Review*, called Linton's diatribe the culmination of 'an attack on the modern girl of the sixties' that had been launched by others in the same weekly earlier in the decade. He referred to 'The Girl of the Period' itself as 'perhaps the most sensational middle article that the *Saturday Review* ever published', and described the 'extraordinary' 'furore aroused by this article'.[90] Nearly a year passed before *Macmillan's* took part in the commotion, and the *Magazine*'s response to Linton, when it finally came, was extended, complex and at times oblique.

A kind of keynote was struck in the editorial note preceding a pair of articles in the February 1869 number headed, as if to go one better than Linton, 'Two Girls of the Period':[91]

> The two following papers have come into the hands of the Editor of *Macmillan's Magazine* at the same time. He has reason to know that both are genuine; and as they are written with reality and earnestness, and describe with apparent fidelity the wants and complaints of persons at opposite ends of the social scale, he has ventured to print them together, in the hope that they may prove not uninteresting or uninstructive illustrations of one of the great social problems of our day.[92]

Neither of these articles directly attacked Linton's; rather each used 'The Girl of the Period' as a point of departure to make its own case; and together – although there is no reason to doubt that they were written and submitted independently of each other – they constituted an eloquent statement concerning the position of women in the England of the late 1860s.

The first, 'The Upper Side: Our Offence, Our Defence, and Our Petition', written by Penelope Holland, was signed 'A Girl of the Period' at the end – the only place in either article where Linton's by then notorious phrase appeared. Yes, Holland conceded, affluent young women did indeed devote too much of their time to 'frivolities' and 'vices', for a very simple reason: 'Up to this time the only employment in which a girl is not hindered is the pursuit of pleasure. We now ask for more liberty of choice.' Such freedom, she affirmed, was increasingly becoming available to middle-class women; why not to upper-class women as well? What was needed more urgently than anything else, according to Holland, was an extension of appropriate educational opportunities for such women so that they might qualify themselves to spend

> a portion of their young lives in the service of their God and of their fellow-creatures. We implore for them a release from their present bondage of idle selfishness, and the means not only of cultivating their talents, but of exercising them in the cause of good and not of evil.[93]

The companion piece to Holland's essay, 'The Under Side' by Agnes T. Harrison, is totally different in genre and effect. In a 'sketch' that

Harrison claims 'is literally true, an uncoloured picture of life', she describes her encounter with one Sarah Kidd, a poor girl who has suffered great hardship while walking from Ipswich to London in futile search of her brother and sister and of work, and who is first taken to a shelter for the homeless run by a Sister Priscilla and then placed 'in an Industrial Home for female servants'.[94] In the course of Harrison's narrative, she also describes a number of other destitute, hopeless people, both male and female. What does 'The Under Side' have to do with 'The Girl of the Period' or Holland's article? Explicitly, nothing, but by itself and especially in juxtaposition to 'The Upper Side' this sketch conveys the unmistakable suggestion – smacking, one might say in this chapter centered on the Mauricean element in the *Macmillan's Magazine* of the 1860s, of Christian Socialist doctrine – that English society must confront other, more pressing, concerns than the plight of idle rich girls and that it must not overlook the lower orders in its efforts to improve the lot of women.

Penelope Holland's February 1869 essay called forth a response the following month, Daniel Fearon's 'The Ladies Cry, Nothing to Do!' Discounting Holland's *'nom de plume* as a description of what she is', Fearon wrote that '[s]he may be a girl *in* the period, but she is no more *of* it than Miss Cobbe, Miss Clough, Miss Jex Blake [Sophia Jex-Blake, who was then attempting to earn a medical degree at the University of Edinburgh], Miss Davies, or any other earnest English gentlewoman'. Fearon's rather muddled argument was that there was already plenty of work, some of it admittedly quite humble, for women like Holland to do and that 'the would-be reformers of women', following Emily Davies rather than the suffragist Lydia Becker, should work for improved education rather than greater access to professional and public life.[95]

However, Holland was quite capable of speaking for herself and did so in another *Macmillan's* article, published the month after Fearon's, 'A Few More Words on Convents and English Girls'.[96] This was not so much Holland's reply to Fearon as it was her reaction to a court case that had recently been attracting considerable attention, an action brought by one Susanna Mary Saurin against the superioress of a convent in Hull, charging her and another member of the order with conspiracy and a number of related offenses.[97] For Holland, the chief question raised by the three weeks of testimony before the Lord Chief Justice in the Court of Queen's Bench, and the ensuing comments in the press and elsewhere, was exactly the same as the one that lay behind the whole 'Girl of the Period' debate: what was the appropriate role of women in Victorian England?

The trouble with convents, in Holland's view, was not that they subjected their inmates to great hardships: presumably those nuns had known what they were doing when they entered and what they might expect once they had subjected themselves to conventual discipline. For Holland it was a more serious problem that in their excessive concern with human souls such establishments stunted and punished human minds and human bodies that God had also created, cultivating 'Christian humility' and 'Christian obedience' to the detriment of 'Christian pride' and 'Christian independence'. Yet 'the worst part of the convent system', Holland contended, was 'that it sifts society, and leaves only the frivolous in the world', depriving the nation of the talents and energies of women who could make important contributions to its betterment if granted the opportunity to do so. Her reflections on *Saurin v. Star* in the April 1869 *Macmillan's* led her to a conclusion very similar to the one she had reached in her meditation on 'The Girl of the Period' two months earlier: give women the opportunity to do something worthwhile, and they will seize it, to their great benefit and society's.

> Let us take advantage of the spirit which is now abroad – a spirit of keen religious feeling and consciousness of responsibility; and by guiding it, and permitting it to perform God's work in the world, prevent it from taking refuge in the moral suicide of monastic institutions.[98]

There is a certain fitness and even symmetry in the fact that Eliza Lynn Linton herself had the last word in the debate that 'The Girl of the Period' had stirred up in *Macmillan's*: 'The Modern Revolt', her only contribution to the *Magazine*,[99] appeared in the December 1870 number. In this essay, Linton took a position that could be construed as much friendlier to the feminist cause than her diatribe against restless and irresponsible women in the *Saturday Review* had been nearly three years earlier, but it was also less coherent than 'The Girl of the Period' and therefore less effective as a piece of rhetoric.[100]

Linton began by distinguishing between two forms of 'The Modern Revolt' by women: 'the one, a noble protest against the frivolity and idleness into which they have suffered themselves to sink; the other, a mad rebellion against the natural duties of their sex, and those characteristics known in the mass as womanliness'. Although she declared herself in favor of the former and in opposition to the latter, Linton's very opening served to muddy the polemical waters, for even her first category of 'protest' implied that women were responsible for their present condition ('into which they have suffered themselves to sink'). Covertly or, more often, overtly, this strategy of blaming the victim persisted almost all the way through Linton's discussion of employment for women, which took up most of her essay. Echoing Fearon, she contended that there was already a great deal of work for them to do if they will do it: work waiting for them, and sadly needing their doing. But this is not the work they want to do. What they want is a share in that which men have appropriated, and which is undeniably better fitted for men than for women.

How, other than on the basis of custom, one might determine what work was 'better fitted' for which sex Linton did not bother to explain. Many careers, she insisted, were already open to women but she immediately had to qualify, fatally, her own assertion: 'To be sure the law and the church, the army, navy, and Parliament, are crypts into which they may not penetrate … ' What dissatisfied women really wanted, Linton seemed to have decided, was not work but 'public applause, an audience, excitement, notoriety', to gratify their 'personal ambition' rather than to satisfy some exalted sense of public service. However then, having made, not very adeptly, a case for keeping women in their traditional sphere, Linton inexplicably turned right around and conceded that they ought after all to have the opportunity to work in whatever field they liked: 'the best thing that could be done for women would be to open all careers to them with men, and to let them try their strength on a fair field, and no favour'. What more could a Millicent Garrett Fawcett or an Elizabeth Garrett Anderson or a Helen Taylor – or, for that matter, a Frederick Denison Maurice – have asked for?

Having got all that out of her system, Linton went on, with relative brevity, to voice her support of two other causes advocated by 1860s reformers, women's suffrage and 'the right of married women to their own property', but without the ambivalent fervor that she had devoted to the subject of employment for women: both objectives would in time be fully achieved, Linton complacently believed, as the second had already begun to be through the Married Women's Property Act of 1870. Nevertheless, she did not forbear to end her article, or further to confound her readers, with the declaration of her hope and trust that 'the main body of Modern Revolters' would want to retain their essential womanly qualities while gaining their rights.[101]

More than anyone else, then, F.D. Maurice defined an agenda, set a tone and established a context for much of the writing on controversial issues that appeared in *Macmillan's* during the 1860s, as we have seen in this chapter with regard to the reforms he advocated in the Church of England, in the political system and in the position of women. This seems clear despite the obvious fact that not all those who dealt with such subjects after him accepted his premises (the example of Eliza Lynn Linton comes immediately to mind) or arrived at his conclusions. Maurice also played a similar role with regard to the *Magazine*'s stance on the internecine struggle in the United States, which was treated in Chapter 2.

Five months before the outbreak of the Civil War, in November 1860, Maurice was among the first to express himself on American affairs in *Macmillan's*, arguing that the abolitionist cause was rooted in the 'reverence for the law and a Divine lawgiver' that was a prominent part of the heritage shared by 'Old England' and 'New England'.[102] Unlike Alexander Macmillan, Maurice did not waver in his opposition to slavery or in his conviction that it was the overriding issue in the War between the States – a moral and religious issue of profound significance rather than a spurious *casus belli*. He made that point, with uncharacteristic sarcasm, in his answer to the 'Ilias (Americana) in Nuce' when he had his Southern spokesman say, turning Carlyle's own ideas against him:

> A scoundrel of the old country scattered books up and down the States against Gigmanity [Carlyle's derisive term for smug respectability]. He preached the doctrine of the old Scotch ploughman, 'A man's a man for a' that.' He canted about a judgment of God which came upon the French nobles of the last century for denying that doctrine. Certain fools at the North fancied he was in earnest. They believed what he told them, and said that they should act upon it. Idiot parsons went so far as to say that the words we use on Sunday about a Person who was put to death as a slave being the corner-stone of the universe were true. What could we do? It was a matter of life and death. We raised the shout for Gigmanity. We affirmed that slavery itself, not the Person who suffered the death of the slave, was the corner-stone of the universe.

Perhaps significantly, Maurice's response was published in the *Spectator*,[103] rather than in *Macmillan's Magazine*, where Carlyle's offending, and offensive, piece had appeared. Thus, enormous as Maurice's role in the early *Macmillan's* clearly was, there were also limits to his influence on its publisher and on its contents before the end of the 1860s and his death on 1 April 1872.

Notes

1. Add MSS 54918, fol. 67; Add MSS 38986, fols 94–5; Add MSS 54918, fols 70–71. There may well have been some communication between Hughes and Maurice about Maurice's undertaking such a review. In a letter of 27 May 1858 to Charles Kingsley, Maurice mentioned 'a review of Froude's History' as something he might 'do' for 'some journal which shall discard anonymous writing' (Frederick Maurice, *The Life of Frederick Denison Maurice Chiefly Told in His Own Letters* [New York: Scribner, 1884] 2: 321–2); under the circumstances, this seems

like more than a hypothetical example, especially in view of the fact that Maurice did ultimately review Volumes 6 and 7 of Froude for *Macmillan's*: 2 (1860): 276–84; also see Maurice's 'History and Casuistry', 2 (1860): 505–12.

2. Add MSS 55836, fols 9–10, 11–12 and 14. Several other letters from Alexander Macmillan to various correspondents in Add MSS 55836 mention the delay in the appearance of the *Magazine*: to F.J.A. Hort, 27 July 1858 (fols 12–13); to F.J. Furnivall, 17 August 1858 (fol. 24); to J. W. Blakesley, 17 August 1858 (fol. 25); to J.W. Blakesley again, 23 August 1858 (fol. 39); and to T.H. Huxley, 26 August 1858 (fols 43–4).

3. Frederick Maurice 2: 321.

4. Frederick Maurice 2: 323.

5. Maurice's first contribution to *Macmillan's*, a Letter to the Editor that appeared in the second number, challenged the assumption of the anonymous reviewer of Kingsley's *Miscellanies* in the *Saturday Review* of 12 November 1859 that Kingsley had borrowed some of his ideas from Maurice: 'Mr. Kingsley and the "Saturday Review"', 1 (1859): 116–19.

6. Frederick Maurice 2: 322.

7. Frederick Maurice 2: 326.

8. See, for example, Desmond Bowen, *The Idea of the Victorian Church: A Study of the Church of England 1833–1889* (Montreal: McGill University Press, 1968) 311–38 and *passim*; Owen Chadwick, *The Victorian Church*, Part I (New York: Oxford University Press, 1966) 346–63 and *passim*; Bernard M.G. Reardon, *From Coleridge to Gore: A Century of Religious Thought in Britain* (London: Longman, 1971) 158–215 and *passim*; and Alec R. Vidler, *The Church in an Age of Revolution: 1789 to the Present Day* (Grand Rapids: Eerdmans, 1962) 83–9, 95–9, and *passim*. More recently, Frank M. Turner has called Maurice 'the most important liberal Anglican theologian of the mid-century' (*Contesting Cultural Authority: Essays in Victorian Intellectual Life* [Cambridge: Cambridge University Press, 1993] 344).

9. 26 (1872): 84, 87–8.

10. Examples include Hughes's 'More about Masters and Workmen' (October 1861) and 'Trades' Unions, Strikes, and Co-operation' (November 1865), Ludlow's two-part 'Trade Societies and the Social Science Association' (February and March 1861) and Fawcett's 'Co-operative Societies: Their Social and Economical Aspects' (October 1860), 'On the Present Prospect of Co-operative Societies' (February 1862) and 'Inaugural Lecture on Political Economy' (April 1864). For more on Fawcett, see n. 51 below.

11. See R.C.D. Jasper, 'The Prayer Book in the Victorian Era', *The Victorian Crisis of Faith*, ed. Anthony Symondson (London: SPCK, 1970) 107–21.

12. 1 (1860): 424, 419, 420, 422, 428.

13. In fact the Privy Council upheld Lushington's verdict, on 6 June 1862.

14. 5 (1861): 153, 156.

15. Frederick Maurice 2: 400.

16. 5 (1862): 504, 505.

17. Each of them retained his post until his death, Colenso's occurring in 1883 and Wilson's in 1888; but for each man life became considerably more difficult as a result of the ordeal through which he had passed.

18. Frederick Maurice 2: 421–35 and 485–7.

19. 11 (1864): 99–100, 105, 107.

20. 11 (1865): 277–8, 278.
21. 9 (1864): 197.
22. Frederick Maurice 1: 167–8, 286, 287, 291.
23. For an account of a much less benign English reaction to the Baron's passing, in the Evangelical *Record*, see Josef L. Altholz, 'Bunsen's Death: Or, How to Make a Controversy', *VPR* 30 (1997): 189–200.
24. 18 (1868): 149–50.
25. 3 (1861): 380, 375.
26. 21 (1870): 370, 371, 373–4.
27. 21 (1870); 500.
28. 9 (1864): 442–3. Writing to the editor of *Macmillan's*, Harvey Goodwin, Dean of Ely, had supported the right of the seven authors of *Essays and Reviews* to speak out as they did: 'A Letter on "Essays and Reviews"' (May 1861). Joseph L. Altholz has shown that those Anglicans who publicly denounced *Essays and Reviews* were more numerous and more typical than those, like Goodwin, who came to its defense: 'The Mind of Victorian Orthodoxy: Anglican Responses to "Essays and Reviews", 1860–64', *Church History* 51 (1982): 186–97.
29. 21 (1870): 372.
30. My telegraphic wording is taken from *The Oxford Dictionary of the Christian Church*, ed. F.L. Cross (London: Oxford University Press, 1958) 1349.
31. 9 (1864): 471.
32. See Maurice's 'A Few More Words on the Athanasian Creed', *Contemporary Review* 15 (1870): 479–94; and Frederick Maurice 2: 618–19.
33. 21 (1869): 42.
34. Encouraged by his friend Alexander Macmillan, Green was working on his *A Short History of the English People* while writing these and other articles for the *Magazine* between 1869 and 1871. The *Short History* became a bestseller on its publication by Macmillan and Co. in 1874, and Green remained a Macmillan and Co. author until his death in 1883, also editing some popular historical and literary 'primers' by other hands for that firm.
35. 21 (1869–70): 7, 99, 208, 104.
36. 3 (1860): 120, 119.
37. See Owen Chadwick, *The Victorian Church*, II, 2nd edn (London: Black, 1972) 64–6 for a brief account of *Ecce Homo* and the contemporaneous reactions to it, including Stanley's in *Macmillan's*.
38. Frederick Maurice 2: 466n, 511–12.
39. 14 (1866): 140, 141.
40. 19 (1861): 461, 463, 464.
41. 15 (1866): 109.
42. 19 (1869): 182.
43. See, for instance, Thomas Hughes's *The Old Church: What Shall We Do with It?* (London: Macmillan, 1878).
44. See his 'The Irish Church Establishment', *Contemporary Review* 7 (1868): 54–65. William Connor Magee, Dean of Cork, answered Maurice in 'The Irish Church Establishment: A Reply to Professor Maurice', *Contemporary Review* 7 (1868): 429–44; and Maurice answered Magee in a Letter to the Editor of the *Contemporary*: 'The Dean of Cork and the Irish Establishment', 7 (1868): 586–90.

45. 19 (1868): 172.
46. Frederick Maurice 2: 586.
47. 19 (1868): 170n.
48. 2 (1860): 89, 90, 93, 94, 95.
49. This feature of Maurice's article on 'The Suffrage' calls into question a point made by Ann Parry in her discussion of his role in shaping the early *Macmillan's*: that in Maurice's writing for the *Magazine* 'the innovative, disaffected tendencies of his theology did not receive direct political application'. See Parry 1988: 25.
50. Maurice subsequently made this case more fully in his *The Workman and the Franchise: Chapters from English History on the Representation and Education of the People* (London: Strahan, 1866), where he praised 'the skilful and laborious contrivance of Mr. Hare, for giving every person in the country an opportunity of expressing a judgment, if he has one, in favour of some candidate' and predicted that it would be found 'easy and simple in its operation' (230–31). For a more recent treatment of this subject see Jenifer Hart's *Proportional Representation: Critics of the British Electoral System 1820–1945* (Oxford: Clarendon Press, 1992); she devotes her second chapter (24–55) to Hare and Mill and mentions the sympathetic attention given to the Hare plan in *Macmillan's* by Maurice and others (67–8).
51. Fawcett was one of the young university men whom Macmillan befriended while his business was still based in Cambridge. It was Macmillan who suggested that Fawcett write his influential *Manual of Political Economy*, published by Macmillan and Co. in 1863; early in the same year Macmillan persuaded Fawcett to become a candidate for the vacant Cambridge seat in the House of Commons, taking the chair at Fawcett's public meetings. See Leslie Stephen, *Life of Henry Fawcett*, 3rd edn (London: Smith, Elder, 1886) 116–17, 203–204. Knowing what we know about Alexander Macmillan and his early *Magazine*, it is not surprising that another of Fawcett's biographers, Winifred Holt, states that it was also he who recruited Fawcett as a contributor; see *A Beacon for the Blind Being a Life of Henry Fawcett* (London: Constable, 1915) 104.
52. Having identified this anonymous review as the work of Leslie Stephen, one of the contributors to *Essays on Reform*, Alan Hertz calls it an example of 'puffery', not only in that it was a Macmillan and Co. book that was being prominently noticed in *Macmillan's Magazine* but also in that here was 'an author surreptitiously recommending his own work' (Hertz 1981: 119). However, as we have seen, the review was hardly a recommendation; moreover, it did not mention Stephen's 'own work' in the collection, his essay 'On the Choice of Representatives by Popular Constituencies'. The enduring significance of *Essays on Reform* was attested to by the publication in 1967 of two volumes commemorating its hundredth anniversary: W.L. Guttsman, ed., *A Plea for Reform* (London: Macgibbon & Kee); and Bernard Crick, ed., *Essays on Reform, 1867* (London: Oxford University Press).
53. 5 (1862): 480n; and 15 (1867): 536n.
54. 16 (1867): 323.
55. D.J. Trela has speculated that the appearance of such an anomalous article as 'Shooting Niagara' in *Macmillan's* 'may well have had its

origin in Carlyle's friendship with David Masson, which dated to 1844' ('Carlyle's *Shooting Niagara*: The Writing and Revising of an Article and Pamphlet', *VPR* 25 [1992]: 30).

56. 10 (1864): 194.

57. 18 (3 September 1864): 292–3. The following week, in 'Representation of Minorities' (18 [10 September 1864]: 322–3), the *Saturday Review* also attacked the Hare plan, pointing to the disastrous results of the adoption of a similar scheme in Denmark.

58. 10 (1864): 518, 519, 520.

59. 12 (1865): 94, 96.

60. Andrea Broomfield has counted 'over 25 articles in *Macmillan's* between 1859 and 1883' that 'advocated women's rights' ('Towards a More Tolerant Society: *Macmillan's Magazine* and the Women's Suffrage Question', *VPR* 23 [1990]: 121). Broomfield's own article discusses two from the 1860s, Helen Taylor's 'Women and Criticism' and Charles Kingsley's 'Women and Politics', which I shall treat later in this chapter. Maurice himself was won over to the cause of women's suffrage by 1870, when he wrote an eloquent letter on 'Female Suffrage' to the *Spectator* (43 [5 March 1870]: 298).

61. June Purvis, *Hard Lessons: The Lives and Education of Working-class Women in Nineteenth-Century England* (Minneapolis: University of Minnesota Press, 1989) 165.

62. Janet Horowitz Murray, *Strong-Minded Women and Other Lost Voices from Nineteenth-Century England* (New York: Pantheon, 1982) 313.

63. Frank McClain, 'Maurice on Women', *F.D. Maurice: A Study*, ed. Cynthia Logan (Cambridge, MA: Cowley, 1982) 29–30, 30.

64. The quotations from Millicent Garrett Fawcett are taken from her *What I Remember* (London: Unwin, 1924) 44 and 45. On the attitudes toward Maurice of the other women mentioned in the last two paragraphs, see Nancy Boyd, *Three Victorian Women Who Changed Their World: Josephine Butler, Octavia Hill, Florence Nightingale* (New York: Oxford University Press, 1982); Barbara Caine, *Victorian Feminists* (Oxford: Oxford University Press, 1992); Brian Harrison, *Prudent Revolutionaries: Portraits of British Feminists between the Wars* (Oxford: Clarendon, 1987); Josephine Kamm, *Hope Deferred: Girls' Education in English History* (London: Methuen, 1965); and McClain.

65. Rosemary T. VanArsdel has counted 63 of them during the period 1859–74 and points out that women writers were far more of a presence in *Macmillan's* during those 15 years than in its contemporaneous shilling magazines *Blackwood's* and the *Cornhill*. See her two-part '*Macmillan's Magazine* and the Fair Sex: 1859–1874', *VPR* 33 (2000): 274–96 and 34 (2001): 2–15.

66. *Victoria Magazine* 19 (1872): 51. I am grateful to Maria Frawley for supplying me with a copy of this article. On Emily Faithfull, the Victoria Press and *Victoria Magazine*, see William E. Fredeman, 'Emily Faithfull and the Victoria Press: An Experiment in Sociological Bibliography', *Library* 5th series 29 (1974): 139–64; and Sheila Herstein, 'The Langham Place Circle and Feminist Periodicals of the 1860s', *VPR* 26 (1993): 24–7. For a book-length study of Faithfull's life and work, see James S. Stone, *Emily Faithfull: Victorian Champion of Women's Rights* (Toronto: Meany, 1994).

67. *Encyclopaedia Britannica* 28: 785. For a discussion of the mystery surrounding the authorship of this seven-page *Britannica* entry, the only one in the 11th edition signed with the initial *X*, see Gillian Thomas, *A Position to Command Respect: Women and the Eleventh* Britannica (Metuchen, NJ: Scarecrow, 1992): 37–9.

68. *Metropolitan Quarterly Magazine* 2 (1826): 268.

69. See Elaine Kaye, *A History of Queen's College, London: 1848–1972* (London: Chatto & Windus, 1972) 20–9 and *passim*. Kaye calls Maurice's 'the greatest intellect and the greatest character connected with Queen's' (104). Maurice's inaugural lecture, 'Queen's College, London: Its Objects and Methods', which he gave in the Hanover Square Rooms on 29 March 1848, was published as the first piece in *Introductory Lectures, Delivered at Queen's College, London* (London: Parker, 1849) 1–27.

70. There was considerable controversy about the place of women in what was explicitly a college for men. See J.F.C. Harrison, *A History of the Working Men's College: 1848–1954* (London: Routledge, 1954) 106–10; and Purvis 161–92. As Purvis observes, both Elizabeth Malleson, the honorary secretary of the London Working Women's College, established in 1864, which evolved into a College for Men and Women, and Frances Martin, who founded the London College for Working Women 10 years later, believed themselves and their rival institutions to be operating under Maurice's aegis even though the two women held opposing views about the connection between gender and education: 'just as Elizabeth Malleson had asserted that the inspirational force for mixed education was to be found in Maurice's educational thinking, so Frances Martin claimed that Maurice had supported single-sex education!' (174) – a good example of how Maurice's words could lend themselves to contradictory interpretations.

71. This lecture was published by Macmillan and Co. in 1855 in two forms: first as a free-standing 24-page pamphlet and then as the 'Introductory Lecture' (1–25) in *Lectures to Ladies on Practical Subjects*.

72. 2 (1860): 229, 235.

73. 5 (1866): 439. In a later *Macmillan's* article, 'Suggestions on Primary Education, and a Short Notice of the Method of Teaching Reading and Writing in Germany' (August 1868), Clough cited the successful German experience in beginning such rigorous education with young pupils. Clough was one of those early *Macmillan's* contributors who submitted work to the publisher rather than the editor of the *Magazine*. On 10 August 1866, Alexander Macmillan wrote to Masson: 'Miss Clough, a sister of Arthur's, sends us a paper on female Education, which seems to me good and important. I have had it set up and you will have a proof in a day or two' (Add MSS 55386, fol. 328). Macmillan went on to tell Masson that he 'should like to see it in this number' (that is September 1866), but in the event it did not appear until the next month.

74. 17 (1868): 513, 514, 515, 517.

75. 18 (1868): 169, 175.

76. In 1869 Macmillan and Co. published a 30-page pamphlet called *College for Women, Hitchin: Examination Papers for the Examination Held in July, 1869, to Which Are Added, Lists of Committees, the Prospectus for the College, the Regulations for the Entrance Examination, &c, &c.*

77. 19 (1868): 160, 169.
78. Unlike Andrea Broomfield (see n. 60 to this chapter), I am unable to find
     in Taylor's essay an explicit argument for women's suffrage. Apparently,
     though, it was welcomed and used by suffragists in the late 1860s as
     part of a carefully orchestrated campaign to gain favorable attention to
     their cause in the periodical press. See Theodora Bostick's 'The Press and
     the Launching of the Women's Suffrage Movement, 1866–67', *VPR* 13
     (1980): 125–31.
79. 14 (1866): 340.
80. Frances Power Cobbe had made a similar point in *Macmillan's* in the
     year of that census; see her 'Social Science Congresses, and Women's
     Part in Them' (December 1861).
81. 20 (1869): 555, 559.
82. 18 (1868): 374.
83. 12 (1865): 119, 218. In his *Macmillan's Magazine* review of *In the Fir
     Wood*, a children's book written and illustrated by Eleanor V. Boyle and
     published by Macmillan and Co. in 1866 ('A Few Words on "E.V.B."
     and Female Artists', 15 [1867]), Palgrave claimed that the creations of
     'our female artists, whether they work with the pen or the pencil' (328),
     have too often elicited flattery rather than searching criticism, to the
     detriment of their subsequent efforts.
84. 22 (1870): 99.
85. 16 (1867): 49, 53. Misreading the essay in general and the conclusion in
     particular, Lynne Atkins has seen in Bodichon's article a significant link-
     age between 'the issues of women's oppression and slavery' and claims
     that Bodichon 'suggests that there are many other lives like' this dismal
     one she described ('Expanding the Limits of Domesticity: Nineteenth-
     Century Nonfiction by Women' [dissertation, Wayne State University,
     1984] 22). Atkins does not mention the article by Frances Power Cobbe
     discussed in my next paragraph, which might have better served her
     purposes; she does, however, reprint, annotate and treat very illuminat-
     ingly another 1860s *Macmillan's* article by a woman, Caroline Norton's
     September 1869 'Lady Duff-Gordon and Her Works' (174–89, 190–93
     and 15–21).
86. 6 (1862): 363.
87. 10 (1864): 219, 220. A frequent contributor to *Macmillan's Magazine*,
     Dinah Mulock Craik was anything but indifferent to the rights of women.
     As Sally Mitchell has pointed out in her *Dinah Mulock Craik* (Boston:
     Twayne, 1883), Craik's *A Brave Lady*, serialized in *Macmillan's* from
     May 1869 until April 1870, 'is propaganda for the Married Women's
     Property Act which was once more being debated in Parliament' (69) –
     one example of how fictional as well as nonfictional prose served to put
     forward women's concerns in the *Magazine* during the period discussed
     in this chapter.
88. 12 (1865): 495, 498.
89. *Saturday Review* 25 (1868): 339–40.
90. *The Saturday Review 1855–58: Representative Opinion in Victorian
     England* (New York: Columbia University Press, 1941) 110, 11–12.
     Also see Chapter 6, 'Eliza Lynn Linton and "The Girl of the Period"', in
     Elizabeth K. Helsinger, Robin Lauterbach Sheets and William Veeder,
     The Woman Question: Defining Voices (New York: Garland, 1983):

103–25; and Nana Rinehart, '"The Girl of the Period" Controversy', *VPR* 13 (1980): 3–9. Rinehart calls Penelope Holland's February 1869 article in *Macmillan's*, which is to be treated below, one of the two 'most thoughtful responses to Linton's attack on the fashionable woman' (5), the other being Anthony Trollope's *The Vicar of Bullhampton*.

91. Three weeks after the appearance of this pair of articles in *Macmillan's*, on 20 February 1869, *Punch* printed a full-page drawing also captioned 'Two Girls of the Period'. This showed a young nun on her hands and knees scrubbing a floor in a religious establishment, watched by a horrified 'Fashionable Convert' and a smug 'Ritualistic Priest'. The latter says to the former: 'THERE, MY CHILD, OBSERVE THAT EXAMPLE OF HUMILITY AND DEVOTION. HOW SWEET TO CHANGE THE VANITIES OF THE WORLD FOR A LOT SO HUMBLE!' She replies: 'OH, BUT THAT IS NOT AT ALL WHAT I EXPECTED! – AND WEAR SUCH AWFUL SHOES? AND – OH REALLY, ON SECOND THOUGHTS, I SHALL STICK TO BELGRAVIA.' *Punch*'s gibe may or may not have been inspired by the articles in *Macmillan's*, but it certainly echoed the public concern over convents to which Holland also reacted in her article in the April *Magazine*.

92. 19 (1869): 323.

93. 19 (1869): 323, 327, 331.

94. 19 (1869): 339.

95. 19 (1869): 451–2, 454.

96. Like Holland's earlier article in *Macmillan's*, this was one of a pair, headed 'Two Views of the Convent Question'. The second member of the pair, 'Nature and the Convent' (unsigned, and unattributed in *Wellesley*), does not require consideration here: it is a slight, half-hearted defense of the conventual system. As had been the case with 'Two Girls of the Period' two months earlier, the two articles were preceded by an editorial note, which drew readers' attention to the importance of '[t]he Convent Question': 'These papers ... will show that it may be treated with earnestness as well as with ability, and that it is not necessary always to deal with questions affecting women in the tone of alternate flippancy and patronage prevalent in some quarters' (19 [1869]: 534).

97. The case is described at great length in Part II of the *Annual Register* for 1869 under 'Remarkable Trials' as 'Saurin v. Star. The Convent Case'.

98. 19 (1869): 536, 537, 539.

99. However, indirectly – by marriage, as it were – Linton's association with *Macmillan's* predated its first number, for it was her husband, the engraver William James Linton, from whom she had long been separated by the time 'The Modern Revolt' was published, who had designed the *Magazine*'s cover. W.J. Linton did other work for Macmillan and Co.: he engraved Richard Doyle's illustrations for Thomas Hughes's *The Scouring of the White Horse* (1859 [1858]), prepared Dante Gabriel Rossetti's block for the title page of Christina Rossetti's *Goblin Market and Other Poems* (1862), and cut two blocks for her *The Prince's Progress and Other Poems* (1866). See G.A. Macmillan 279, 5; and *The Letters of Christina Rossetti* 1, ed. Antony Harrison (Charlottesville: University Press of Virginia, 1997) 158.

100. The authors of *The Woman Question: Defining Voices* prefer 'The Modern Revolt' to 'The Girl of the Period'; see Helsinger, Sheets and Veeder 107.

101. 23 (1870): 142, 143, 147, 149.
102. 'More Political Ethics: The Neapolitan Revolution, and the Fugitive Slave Law', 3 (1860): 68. Nine months earlier, in the February 1860 number, W.E. Forster, writing in the wake of John Brown's execution on 2 December 1859, had expressed profound sympathy for the cause in his 'Harper's Ferry and "Old Captain Brown"'.
103. 8 August 1863: 2348.

CHAPTER FOUR

Margaret Oliphant

As we saw in the first chapter of this study, Alexander Macmillan had a way of ingratiating himself with eminent writers, cultivating personal and professional relationships that led to the appearance of their work in *Macmillan's Magazine* and in Macmillan & Co. books. In this chapter, I hope to show how this process operated and how it evolved over time, concentrating on Margaret Oliphant, whose interactions with Macmillan and others affiliated with his firm during three and a half decades are especially richly, if not always quite clearly, documented. The abundance and the variety of her work – nonfiction as well as fiction, periodical writing, including serials, as well as books – and the different ways in which it moved from conception to execution make it possible to derive a remarkable picture of how one representative author accommodated herself to the requirements of *Macmillan's Magazine* and its parent company – and also of how those who paid her for what she produced often had to accommodate themselves to her demands.

During Oliphant's long career, from the publication of her novel *Passages in the Life of Mrs. Margaret Maitland* in 1849 until her death in 1897, she worked with a number of different publishing houses. Best known for her association with the firm of William Blackwood and Sons, she was nearly as closely connected with Macmillan and Co. Although she did not write for *Macmillan's Magazine* as prolifically as she did for *Blackwood's Edinburgh Magazine*, she serialized twice as many novels in *Macmillan's* as did her nearest rival, William Black; some 30 of her books bore the Macmillan and Co. imprint, and others were included in Macmillan's Colonial Library for sale in the Empire. As was also true in her relationship with Blackwood, her contributions to the company magazine often preceded books incorporating those materials; conversely, her writing of Macmillan and Co. books sometimes led to spin-off articles, at first in *Macmillan's Magazine* and later also in that firm's *English Illustrated Magazine*.

Because many, although by no means all, of the relevant documents have survived, it is possible, more than a century after Oliphant's death, to trace the vicissitudes of her long connection with Macmillan and Co. in general and *Macmillan's Magazine* in particular. This task does entail some difficulties. Although much of Oliphant's copious correspondence with Macmillan and Co. has nothing to do with *Macmillan's Magazine* and therefore no legitimate claim on space in this study, her work for the *Magazine* must be considered in the context of her exceedingly complicated relations with the firm and those who guided its fortunes, and so we often need to stray beyond those letters concerned specifically with her periodical contributions. Moreover, some crucial letters from Oliphant are missing, and the chronology of those that have been preserved is not always clear: she was rather cavalier about dating her letters, often supplying only the days of the week. (On many, dates are entered, usually in pencil, in handwriting that obviously is not hers; frequently those dates are conjectural, and sometimes they are plainly wrong.) Finally, some of the surviving letters to Oliphant, particularly those from George Lillie Craik, have become so faded or smeared since the second half of the nineteenth century as to be virtually or totally illegible. What we have to work with, then, is a record that is far from perfect. Nevertheless, it is most revealing.

Establishing contact

Not surprisingly, in view of what we have already noticed about the readiness with which Alexander Macmillan formed ties with authors, it seems clear that he was the initial link between Oliphant and both his firm and his *Magazine*. Oliphant's earliest letters to him in the Berg Collection of the New York Public Library leave no doubt that they were acquainted with each other and each other's spouses by the autumn of 1858, over a year before the inception of *Macmillan's Magazine*. In one of those letters, dated 11 September, Oliphant reminded Macmillan that they had 'once' discussed her doing 'a story for girls'; if he were prepared to pay her £100 for such a one-volume novel, she said, 'I should be pleased to put it into your hands'. Already sounding a rather peremptory note that would often recur in her later transactions with Macmillan and Co., she continued: 'You will understand that I dont mean to send it to you first for approval – but if you think it worth your while, and are willing to take it on the mere assurance of my name such as it is – I should be glad enough to have it published by you.'[1]

Alexander Macmillan accepted Oliphant's terms and agreed to pay her the amount she named for the book, which she decided to call *Agnes Hopetoun's Schools and Holidays: The Experiences of a Little Girl*. She sent him the opening chapters in late September 1858, again setting a precedent for her future dealings with the firm by urgently requesting an advance, for reasons that she did not hesitate to explain to Macmillan:

> I should like if you could send me – to reach me on Monday – the money for this book – or rather I should say the half of it – which will answer my purposes perfectly – fifty pounds – I want it because

we are leaving this house, and I have various little things to do –
the rest of the story you shall have very shortly ... [2]

On 29 October she signed a receipt indicating that she had been paid
£50 on 1 October and the remaining £50 on 'this day'.[3] Another way in
which Oliphant's work on this girls' story foreshadowed what would
often happen later in her association with Macmillan and Co. was that
she was distracted and slowed down by illness in her family, her husband's in this case, but persevered despite such difficulty and got the job
done more or less on schedule, in time to have the book come out for
the 1858 Christmas trade.

Macmillan's Magazine is first mentioned in the Margaret Oliphant–
Alexander Macmillan correspondence more than three years after the
publication of *Agnes Hopetoun*. In an undated letter, which Oliphant
must have written in the early spring of 1862, she referred to the
Magazine twice. She began by telling Macmillan that Henry Blackett, of
Hurst and Blackett, the publisher of her latest book, *The Life of Edward
Irving*, had asked her – her word was 'adjures' – to do what she could
to induce 'all the critical authorities I know' to review it. 'I hope I may
venture to believe that an old friend like yourself will not think any the
worse of me for obeying my publisher's orders in this respect – If you
feel disposed to say a good word for me of course I shall be much
obliged.' Leaving nothing to chance, Oliphant went on to recommend a
reviewer of her new work: Robert Herbert Story, a Scottish clergyman
with whom she had recently become acquainted, 'who knows the subject very thoroughly' and who 'would not object to act as critic, if you
are thus amiably inclined – and if you will pardon me making the
suggestion'.[4] The complaisant Macmillan did ask Story to review *The
Life of Edward Irving* in the *Magazine*, and Story's notice, which appeared in the May 1862 number, was as warmly favorable as Oliphant
and Blackett could have hoped.

Alexander Macmillan himself was also an admirer of Oliphant's *Life
of Edward Irving*, urging his wife, David Masson and Charles Kingsley
to read it,[5] and that may have been one reason why he tried to recruit
its author for his still-newish *Magazine* at about the time that biography was published. However, in the same letter in which she made her
overture to Macmillan she declined his, pleading her time-consuming
commitments to *Blackwood's* and her objection to what she calls 'your
nominal principle' – that is, the idea that contributions to *Macmillan's*
should ordinarily be signed, rather than unsigned as in *Blackwood's*:

> not feeling myself, as myself, to be a person of any great weight or
> authority I am always glad to take refuge under the mantle of
> Maga – Perhaps if I should (which I fear is rather unlikely) con-
> tinue to grow wiser up to the age of threescore I may then venture

to believe that the world will be interested about my opinions on things in general – a matter which I suspect, the said world is totally indifferent about at the present moment.[6]

That was not, however, her final answer. Oliphant had formed a kind of mutual admiration-and-aid society with Robert Story, some of whose work she persuaded both Macmillan and Co. and Hurst and Blackett to publish.[7] Story's first book, a biography of his father, had just been brought out by Macmillan and Co. when Story's review of her *Edward Irving* appeared in *Macmillan's Magazine*. Swallowing her stated objection to the 'nominal principle', she volunteered to reciprocate by reviewing his *Memoir of the Life of the Rev. Herbert Story* in the same periodical, but Alexander Macmillan declined her 'kind offer to do Mr Story's book in our magazine': it had already been assigned to J. Llewelyn Davies, he wrote to her on 14 May 1862, but went on to renew his invitation of a few weeks earlier. 'I should have been so glad to have you among us even for an occasional paper like this, and hope yet to accomplish it.'[8]

Just over a year later, Alexander Macmillan's hope was realized, as was Oliphant's wish to promote her younger friend's work. The July 1863 number of *Macmillan's Magazine* carried an unsigned article, called 'Clerical Life in Scotland', which was a joint review of Story's life of his father and a more recent book, *Life of the Rev. James Robertson* by A.H. Charteris, published by Blackwood. (For whatever reason, no review of the *Memoir* by Davies or anyone else had appeared in the *Magazine* since Macmillan had put off Oliphant 13 months earlier.) The *Wellesley Index* lists this piece as probably by Oliphant on the basis of both internal and external evidence, but there is good reason to remove the qualifying 'prob.' from the *Wellesley* entry. Not only did Macmillan send her a check, along with the complimentary note he normally enclosed with such payment, on 30 June 1863 'for your paper in the Magazine', which must have been 'Clerical Life in Scotland', but in an earlier letter dated only 'Friday' Oliphant wrote to Macmillan: 'I have just returned to your printer the proof of my paper – *no name* please – not even initials. This I particularly desire in respect of this article and trust you will be good enough to secure that it shall be *quite anonymous*.'[9]

Two things about this undated letter indicate that it was written in the late spring of 1863, when 'Clerical Life in Scotland' would have been going to the printer. First, Oliphant entered a half-amused protest about the bad review of a recent book of hers published by Hurst and Blackett: 'It is unkind of Mr. Masson tell him, to maul his country-woman.' Her fellow-Scot David Masson was then editing the *Reader* as well as *Macmillan's Magazine* and that short-lived weekly had dismissed her short novel *Heart and Cross* as 'devoid of plot, or character, or any other of the elements which we instinctively look for in a story' in its 9 May 1863 number. Second, she asked Macmillan, 'When do you remove?'[10], presumably referring to his impending relocation from Cambridge to Upper Tooting, which occurred at midsummer 1863.[11] The tone of Oliphant's letter, it is worth noting, shows that she felt quite comfortable about addressing Macmillan personally and even playfully.

'Clerical Life in Scotland' was the icebreaker. Work by Oliphant appeared in 93 more numbers of *Macmillan's Magazine* during the next 27 years and she went on putting out Macmillan and Co. books until her death in 1897; another, *That Little Cutty and Other Stories* (1898), was an *opus posthumus*. Characteristically, Oliphant took the initiative with Alexander Macmillan in maintaining the flow that had begun with her review of Story and Charteris.

A Son of the Soil

In a remarkably forthright letter written on 27 August 1863, less than two months after the publication of 'Clerical Life in Scotland', Oliphant informed Macmillan that she was thinking of going 'to Rome for the winter with my children' (her husband had died, in Rome, in 1859),

> and as you know a poor scribbler like myself is never rich. I mean you to pay my expenses if you are so disposed. I am willing if you wish it to undertake for you *anonymously* a short sketch of the story you once proposed to me – a sketch to be filled up perhaps at some future time – something that would run through three or four numbers of your Magazine – for which you could give me a hundred pounds ... Now please to let me know as soon as you have considered this, as there is not very much time to lose, and if you dont want my wares I must carry them to another market.

Macmillan immediately agreed to Oliphant's proposition. On the next day he replied: 'I shall be delighted. I hope you will make it four numbers and I am sure you will do it well. November begins a new volume, and I should like you to do it in time for that.'[12] Undeterred by the fact that she had another serial novel (*The Perpetual Curate*) coming out in another monthly periodical (*Blackwood's*), Oliphant set right to work but did not allow Macmillan to forget that she expected prompt payment. In an undated letter written a week before her departure for the Continent, she told him with typical directness: 'I want you to send me, please, *now*, the £100 which I told you I wanted for my journey and which is to stand for four numbers of the *Son of the Soil*.' Understandably concerned as she was about the money and busy as she must have been with preparations for her trip, Oliphant nevertheless included a dinner invitation to Macmillan in the same letter; she asked him to bring along David Masson, whom she had obviously not yet met: 'I should like to make acquaintance with the captain I am fighting under even though I am an anonymous private in the regiment and I should like to see you before going away.'[13]

The opening installment of *A Son of the Soil*, consisting of three chapters, appeared in the November 1863 number of the *Magazine*, as Macmillan had hoped. However, matters did not proceed altogether smoothly after that promising start.

In the first place, Oliphant's story stretched well beyond the limit that she and her publisher had had in mind. By January 1864, when he received the three chapters of Part IV, it was obvious to Macmillan that Oliphant's 'short sketch' was not yet finished. He raised no objection but did wonder how long *A Son of the Soil*, of which he had been thinking as a brief serial that would become a short book, might go on. 'I must tell you the story promises well and will make an admirable and very saleable little volume', he wrote her on the 6th. 'But wont it grow beyond the dimensions of six numbers?' When the fifth part reached Macmillan three weeks later, he told Oliphant that he was pleased that her novel was 'going to grow'.[14] Grow it did: by the time its run in *Macmillan's Magazine* was finished in April 1865 *A Son of the Soil* had extended to 17 installments, and when Macmillan and Co. published the book version the following year the 'very saleable' small book had turned into two rather hefty volumes.

There was no April 1864 installment; instead, the following terse notice was printed at the bottom of the last page of that issue: 'Through unavoidable causes, Part VI. of "A SON OF THE SOIL," which should have appeared in the present number, is deferred by the author till the next. – *Editor*.'[15] It is not difficult to surmise what the gravest of those 'causes' must have been: on 27 January, the very day Macmillan wrote Oliphant to acknowledge receipt of Part V, her ten-year-old daughter Maggie died in Rome after a short illness, and Oliphant was overwhelmed by grief. Yet, as someone who had learned to cope with bereavement, however shattering, Oliphant went back to her writing as soon as she recovered from the initial shock and did not miss another installment during the remaining year of the novel's serial run.[16] From Rome, from Capri, from Paris, Oliphant sent Macmillan sets of chapters, demands for further payments,[17] and complaints about proofreading;[18] from his firm's new headquarters in London, the forbearing Macmillan sent back encouraging words – for example, on 26 July 1864: 'The story is altogether admirable, and I think gets better as one gets on. David Masson is very warm in its praise.'[19]

As the serialization of *A Son of the Soil* in *Macmillan's Magazine* drew near its close, new questions came up in the correspondence Oliphant was conducting with Alexander Macmillan. When would the serial in fact end? How could the anonymity of its authorship be protected? When and by whom would the book version be published? What changes, if any, should be made in the periodical text? How much, beyond what she had already been paid for the *Magazine* version, would she receive for the book? The last question concerning *A Son of the Soil* continued to rankle for three decades, as we shall see, partly because there had never been a contract – at least none that I have been able to discover in the Macmillan Archive; however, as will also become apparent, even when there were written financial understandings between Oliphant and Macmillan and Co. regarding payment for later books, confusion would often arise as to which party was in debt to the other and for how much.

The matter of the serial's conclusion turned out to be relatively simple. When Oliphant sent Macmillan the February 1865 installment from Paris, she wrote to him: 'I think I may say now with confidence that two more will finish the story.' Because the projected four-part story had already reached Part XV, Macmillan may be forgiven for asking, in the most restrained way imaginable, for further assurance that Oliphant would indeed wind up in April: 'I have two novelists wanting to go into the new volume of the magazine, which begins in May. If you feel you can complete by then well – if not we must manage.'[20] In this case, Macmillan had no need to worry: 'Part XVII – Conclusion' of *A Son of the Soil* appeared in the April 1865 number.

In August 1863 Oliphant had written to Macmillan that she was prepared 'to undertake ... *anonymously* ... a short sketch of the story' that was to become *A Son of the Soil*. Although she changed her mind about its length, she remained adamant on the question of her anonymity.[21] When a reviewer of the fifteenth *Magazine* installment, in the *Spectator* of 4 February 1865, quite casually identified her as its author, she held Macmillan responsible. He protested his innocence:

> Indeed you are wrong. As far as the keeping of your secret was in my power, or in the circle of my influence it certainly has been kept. Very many in London & elsewhere, who know your writings have *guessed* you as the author, no one *knows* it from me, or from my house ... Your 'speech betrayed you' my dear friend – that is all.[22]

In that same letter of 20 February 1865, Macmillan promised that when the novel was published as a book – whether by his own firm or by Hurst and Blackett, a decision that had not yet been made – both he and Henry Blackett would do everything in their power to preserve her secret, '"for the love I bear to you", not as in the least believing myself to blame'. Oliphant stood her ground about not putting out the book under her name, which first appeared on the title page of the one-volume edition of 1871: 'Since people have decided it to be mine', she wrote Macmillan, 'let them have their own way but we need not give them any definite information on the subject.'[23]

Hurst and Blackett had published no fewer than 11 of Oliphant's novels, as well as her *Life of Edward Irving*, between 1853 and 1863 and were preparing to bring out a twelfth, *Agnes*, when *A Son of the Soil* was winding down in *Macmillan's Magazine* in the spring of 1865. Although it was at Oliphant's request that Macmillan had entered into discussion with Henry Blackett about which of their houses would issue the book version of *A Son of the Soil*, he nevertheless felt compelled to reassure her twice within five days in mid-April that he was reluctant to let the novel go. On the 12th he wrote to her that he was 'disinclined to part with a pet child, even though he has taken to private ways of his own', and on the 17th he declared that 'I have no sort of wish to part with the Son of the Soil', adding that 'I thought I was carrying out your wish in trying to please Mr Blackett'.[24]

In the end, Macmillan and Co. did publish *A Son of the Soil*, anonymously, but not until the following year. Both Alexander Macmillan and Blackett wanted to do what they could to keep that Oliphant novel from competing with another; and, because Blackett was planning to bring out her *Agnes* in time for Christmas 1865, Macmillan decided to put off *A Son of the Soil*. With an author as prolific as Oliphant, however, there was no way to keep her books from treading on one another's heels: *Miss Marjoribanks* had started in *Blackwood's* in February 1865, two months before *A Son of the Soil* ended in *Macmillan's*, and was published by Blackwood in 1866 as a book; 1866 was also the year *Madonna Mary* was serialized in *Good Words* and published by Hurst and Blackett at Christmas.

While *A Son of the Soil* was nearing the end of its run in *Macmillan's Magazine* and as the time arrived when it became necessary to think of the novel's conversion from a serial to a book, Alexander Macmillan did not hesitate to offer Oliphant suggestions as well as praise. After all, its subject, the travails of a rural Scottish clergyman, was of as much personal interest to him as to her; indeed, Oliphant's letter of 27 August 1863 to Macmillan implied that he 'proposed' it to her. Could she, he asked, engage in some 'judicious compression'? 'The Parish squabbles are too local ... The petty and passing should be as unconspicuous as possible, the permanent and eternal as full in flow as you can make it.' Could she also 'eliminate the *polemic* which is an artistic mistake, and dreadfully weakens the general interest'? Writing as her friend and her editor (the *Magazine*'s actual editor, David Masson, took no part in this correspondence) as well as her publisher, Macmillan put forward such suggestions with considerable diffidence:

> Of course you will only follow any hint I threw out so far, and no further than it becomes your *own way*. After the manner of my sex I am fond of seeing things done in my own way, but I am not masterful when its of no use. I tyrranize [sic] over my own household of course, but this does not warrant me in attempting it elsewhere, particularly when I know I could not carry it out![25]

For her part, Oliphant stuck to her guns and did not hesitate to deploy some of her artillery in the service of the gender warfare to which Macmillan had also alluded. 'We will not go into argument about the laws of fiction, but I fear the local particulars are more in my way than grand universals of any description – and I am dreadfully addicted to having things my own way like as (you men say) most women.'[26]

The picture of how much and when she was paid for *A Son of the Soil* yielded by the surviving Oliphant–Macmillan correspondence is not totally in focus. We know that she asked for £100 before she submitted the first four numbers of the *Macmillan's Magazine* serial in November 1863 and for £250 more in January and May of the following year. We also know that Macmillan wrote to her on 6 December 1864 that he would deposit £150 at her bank 'this week, and another £100 early in February, on account of the separate novel' – presumably the book edition of *A Son of the Soil*. In the same letter he added:

> I have been quite unable to decide what to offer you for this. I find opinions as to its chance of success vary very much. I have considerable hope myself. Mr Mudie, who likes it very much himself is doubtful. As we get towards a close we will be able to judge better.[27]

When February arrived and the two-volume edition was about to appear, Oliphant expressed some puzzlement as to what additional payment she might receive. 'I know you gave me £250 over and above the payments on account of the Magazine. But I dont suppose you will think this sufficient for the reprint.' Macmillan's reply, which was meant to set her straight, named £700 as the amount she had already received for *A Son of the Soil* and all but promised her another £50.

> £400 we put down to Magazine use, £300 for subsequent copyright. The sale as a two volume novel we have not calculated to be more than 1250 copies & this will not yield much above £300 & I was looking to its sale in our six shilling series for any profit we might make. As your revision has been extra work I think we ought perhaps to pay a little more ['say £50' is written above the line] than we have. Indeed I meant to do so if the first edition ran off pretty quickly. But I do not think on the whole that what we have paid is too little.[28]

As late as 1894, long after Alexander Macmillan had retired and when Oliphant was engaging in one of her periodic epistolary quarrels over money with Macmillan's long-time partner, George Lillie Craik, the matter of how much she had been paid for *A Son of the Soil* and how little revenue that novel had brought in was still festering. Craik saw fit to use *A Son of the Soil* as an example of how Macmillan and Co. had not taken advantage of Oliphant but rather had lost money on some of her books. Although Craik's figures do not quite coincide with those Alexander Macmillan had given Oliphant nearly three decades earlier, they do seem to show that Macmillan's misgivings about the likely sale of the book were borne out: 'We published the *Son of the Soil* in the Magazine first, & again in book form in 1866. We charged £318 of the money we paid you (£708) to the book – the rest to the Magazine. After 27 years we are out of pocket £125.7.7.'[29]

Interlude

Although nothing by Margaret Oliphant appeared in *Macmillan's Magazine* for nearly seven and a half years after the concluding installment of *A Son of the Soil* in April 1865, her absence from its pages during that interval was certainly not the result of any lack of effort on her part. In June of 1866, for instance, she offered to review *Felix Holt* for the *Magazine*, but Alexander Macmillan was nervous about the possibility that she would deal too harshly with George Eliot's new novel. As he wrote to her on 18 June, he regarded the *Saturday Review*'s warmly favorable notice, which was published on 16 June 1866, as 'just to my taste', 'the model of what a good article should be', and told her that 'if you agree generally with the manner & matter then I *should* like an article extremely'. 'But', he cautioned, 'I would not like to "go in" at the book. It is only baseness open and palpable that I would go in at.' Oliphant could not or would not give Macmillan the assurance he wanted, so that two days later he ended their brief negotiation on the matter of *Felix Holt*: 'I am excessively sorry to miss the chance of another article from you, but I really would not like to "pitch into" George Eliot in the Magazine.'[30]

Two years later, on 22 July 1868, Macmillan declined Oliphant's offer of some new fiction for the *Magazine* on the grounds that there was already plenty on hand but attempted to soothe her by adding that 'I have told Mr George Grove, our Editor now, of your wish to write occasionally, which I have no doubt he will be glad to avail himself of.' As happened throughout their long correspondence, however, Macmillan injected a mollifying personal note into what must have struck Oliphant as a disappointing business letter. Writing to Oliphant at Windsor, where she was then living, he mentioned that his son George was going 'down to Eton today to try for the scholarship. Should he be successful we shall be coming down to Windsor before long.' The boy was indeed 'successful', and Oliphant managed to look after him while he was at the nearby public school (where her son Cyril was one of his fellow-pupils), a fact that was not lost on his grateful father. On 6 November 1868, for example, Alexander Macmillan wrote Oliphant to thank her for her 'great kindness' to George. (Not surprisingly, when the son later joined the family firm Oliphant addressed her letters to him as 'George', not 'Mr Macmillan', which was the form she used in writing to his father and his cousin Frederick.) Macmillan was also gratified by Oliphant's favorable review in the August 1866 *Blackwood's* of one of the most important Macmillan and Co. books of the mid-1860s, Samuel White Baker's *The Albert N'Yanza, Great Basin of the Nile, and Explorations of the Nile Sources* (1866; frequently reprinted) and promptly wrote to thank her.[31]

Oliphant again approached Alexander Macmillan about writing for the *Magazine* in January 1870, 18 months after her most recent attempt, and was again gently rebuffed: 'I think our Story telling is arranged for till some time in 1871. But I wish you could arrange with Mr Grove for some really great story. Write him.' The real purpose of that portion of the Margaret Oliphant–Alexander Macmillan correspondence was to discuss her forthcoming *Francis of Assisi* (1870), a book she was then writing for Macmillan and Co.'s Sunday Library for Household Reading series; because it had no direct connection with *Macmillan's Magazine*, there is no need to say anything about it here, except to make two points that remind one of her financial disputes with Macmillan and Co. over *A Son of the Soil*. First, Oliphant again felt compelled to ask Macmillan for payment 'at your earliest convenience', and second, Craik was not above reminding Oliphant years later that *Francis of Assisi*, like *A Son of the Soil*, had ended up losing rather than earning money for Macmillan and Co., at least £70.[32]

Although it could hardly be called a 'really great story', a novella by Oliphant, *The Two Marys*, did appear in *Macmillan's Magazine* in four parts starting in September 1872 and ending in January 1873. (There was no October 1872 installment and no printed explanation of its absence, as there had been when the sixth part of *A Son of the Soil* had failed to appear on schedule in the *Magazine* eight and a half years earlier.) Unlike the evolution of that earlier *Magazine* serial, too, the publishing history of *The Two Marys* is skimpily documented. Indeed, I have been able to find only one reference to it, in a letter dated 24 October 1872 from Alexander Macmillan to Oliphant, admitting to some confusion about the terms on which she had been paid for the story: was the £100 she had received supposed to be for the copyright, he asked, and 'if not by paying you another £50 might we republish it in a separate form?' 'We wish to do what is fair to you', Macmillan assured her, but added that in his judgment republication would 'not bring in very much'.[33] (As it turned out, *The Two Marys* never did appear in book form under the Macmillan imprint; the volume by that title published as late as 1896 by Methuen is a curious amalgam of the first two parts of the *Macmillan's Magazine* version and a much longer novella, *No. 3, Grove Road, Hampstead*, that came out originally in *Good Cheer*, the Christmas 1880 number of another periodical, *Good Words*.)

A year and a half after the conclusion of *The Two Marys*, Oliphant began a string of publications in *Macmillan's Magazine* that was to remain virtually unbroken for the next 10 years, starting with *The Convent of San Marco* (July–September 1874 and January, June and September 1875) and continuing with *The Curate in Charge* (August 1875–January 1876), *Young Musgrave* (January–December 1877), *He That Will Not When He May* (November 1879–November 1880), and *The Wizard's Son* (November 1882–March 1884), as well as three shorter pieces: her essay on 'Thomas Carlyle' (April 1881) and two 'Little Pilgrim' stories (May and September 1882). All of these periodical publications, except 'Thomas Carlyle', later became Macmillan and Co. books, although not always without trouble or confusion.

The Convent of San Marco and *The Makers of Florence*

One bio-bibliographical problem confronting the often perplexed student of Margaret Oliphant's prodigious career concerns the relationship between her six *Macmillan's Magazine* essays on *The Convent of San Marco* and *The Makers of Florence* – or, more precisely, the third part, 'The Monks of San Marco', of that big book. An attempt to solve that problem must begin with her old friend Alexander Macmillan. Having lost his first wife in 1871, he married a woman named Emma Pignatel in the autumn of the following year, and it was she who persuaded him – 'and he needed persuasion, for he was no European traveller – to make his first journey to Italy'[34] in 'the early months of 1873'.[35] Among the places visited by the newlyweds was Florence, a city that made such a profound impression on Alexander Macmillan that he quickly turned himself into an amateur authority on its history, its artistic and architectural treasures, and the literature associated with it. It is not surprising, therefore, that shortly after his return to England, when he yet again found himself rejecting a 'scheme which [Oliphant] so kindly mentioned' to him, he told her of his infatuation with Florence and, aware of her first-hand knowledge of Italy, offered the counter-suggestion that she undertake 'a volume about the Italian Poets with portraits and other illustrations as a Christmas book'.[36]

Macmillan wrote that on 26 May 1873. By early summer he could hardly contain his enthusiasm about this project. He had 'been exercised a great deal about the book since I heard from you and since I last wrote', he told her in a letter dated 1 July; his visit to Florence had interested him 'immensely', but he had been disappointed by his subsequent reading of Thomas Adolphus Trollope's 'rather clumsy' *History of Florence* (1865), which he thought failed to do full justice to 'the marvellous life of poetry, art, and deep human emotion' that pulses through the city of Dante and Savonarola and its 'great artists and architects'. Macmillan now envisaged Oliphant's book as a treatment of Dante firmly set in the Florentine context: 'Everything in Florence seems full of poetry. Dante is inconceivable out of Florence.' An ambitious project of the sort he had in mind would take more than a year to complete, he conceded, particularly if appropriate illustrations were to be assembled; the 'literary part', however, 'might be done ... at intervals'.[37]

Macmillan continued to correspond with Oliphant about the subject of Florence throughout the remainder of 1873. 'Florence has amazingly affected him', Craik wrote to her on 7 August and informed her that Macmillan had agreed 'to give £300 for the book on Florence, which I should think would benefit by your going to take another look at the place'. Oliphant could not act on Craik's tempting advice until Easter 1874 but enjoyed herself so much when she did go that she felt free to ask Macmillan three years later, on 11 April 1877, to subsidize another such Italian journey: 'You should give me a commission for a companion volume on Venice. This is my only way of giving my boys foreign trips.'[38] That proposal also resulted in a Macmillan and Co. book, *The Makers of Venice*, but not until 1887.

When Alexander Macmillan referred to Oliphant's doing the 'literary part' of *The Makers of Florence* 'at intervals', he clearly had in mind printing sections of this work in progress in his *Magazine* and spelled out a procedure – a procedure in which he and the *Magazine*'s editor, George Grove, would be involved right along with Oliphant – in two letters he sent her after her return from Italy, on 27 May and 23 June 1874. In the first, written as her initial *San Marco* paper was being set in type for the July 1874 number of the *Magazine*, Macmillan told her that 'after I read your article I shall be able better to see the kind of illustrations suitable for your book'. In the second, Macmillan congratulated her on the 'excellent' first essay and went on to suggest that she

> go on writing your book according to the original scheme, and we will set it up in the magazine type. Mr Grove will use what he can, which I fancy will be a good deal, in the Magazine. The rest will be in type open to any modification you may think fit before it is sent to the printer as *copy* for the actual book.[39]

However, the work did not progress as smoothly as her publisher and she must have hoped it would. For one thing, Oliphant found herself with too much material – about Savonarola, for example. As she complained to Grove on 10 February 1875 while trying to boil it down for *Macmillan's*, 'My despairing attempts to cut it short, have only made it bad without making it short.' That work also dragged on much longer than anticipated. On 9 June 1875 Alexander Macmillan had to caution Oliphant not to produce more text than could be accommodated in one volume, even at the cost of giving Michelangelo less ample treatment than he deserved: a longer work 'would upset all our calculations and I fear would not sell as well as we would hope this to do ... We want the book out this year – that is in time for the Christmas sale.'[40]

He was not to get his way, however, for *The Makers of Florence*, although confined to one volume, was not published until late the following year. Letters from Alexander and George Macmillan written in the summer and early autumn of 1875 suggest that the book was in production and ready to be advertised as forthcoming, but as late as 20 June 1876 George Macmillan was still nagging Oliphant to return proofs because 'we want to get as much of the book printed off as possible before the press of autumn work comes upon us'.[41] Part of the delay was caused by the need to secure appropriate illustrations (there were, of course, none in *Macmillan's Magazine*); also, as usual, Oliphant was overextending herself, writing away at several tasks simultaneously; and once again she was slowed down by desperate family circumstances, the final illness and death in the summer of 1875 of her brother Frank, for whom and for whose children she had been caring.

In one sense, then, mining a book that Oliphant was writing (*The Makers of Florence*) for *Macmillan's Magazine* articles (*The Convent of San Marco*) did not turn out to be a good idea, because doing so did not significantly ease her labors or simplify her life; in another sense, however, the Florentine project became something of a cash cow for her. Not only did it lead to the writing of similar successful Macmillan and Co. books – *The Makers of Venice*, already mentioned, as well as the later *Royal Edinburgh* (1890), *Jerusalem* (1891) and *The Makers of Modern Rome* (1895) – but it also paid off almost immediately in the form of other, non-Macmillan and Co. publications. Even before she made her trip to Florence, presumably with the substantial help of the Macmillan advance, she offered to produce articles based on her on-site research for *Blackwood's*; as she wrote to John Blackwood on 9 February 1874, 'Dante, Michael Angelo, and Savonarola are my three chief points, and I should not like to lose any of my material.'[42]

Oliphant certainly did not 'lose' much of the material she gathered for *The Makers of Florence*. As ultimately published by Macmillan and Co., the book consisted of three parts: 'The Poet: – Dante', 'The Cathedral Builders' and 'The Monks of San Marco'. The six *Macmillan's Magazine* articles on *The Convent of San Marco* became the first seven chapters of the third part; though most of the changes Oliphant made were editorial rather than substantive, she did considerably expand the second *San Marco* paper, 'The Frate' (August 1874), into two book chapters, 'The Good Archbishop' (Antonino Pierozzo) and 'Girolamo Savonarola: His Probation'. Only one chapter of *The Makers of Florence* appeared originally in *Blackwood's*: the final one, 'Michel Angelo', was first presented to readers of that periodical as 'Michael Angelo' (October 1875).[43] However, Oliphant also reprinted the whole of the first part of *The Makers of Florence* in 1877 as *Dante*, a slim volume in a series of Foreign Classics for English Readers that she was editing for Blackwood; and in 1875, the year before *The Makers of Florence* and two years before *Dante*, she published versions of the first and the third Dante chapters in the *Cornhill Magazine* as 'The Early Years of Dante' in October and 'Dante in Exile' in December. Only Oliphant's three chapters on 'The Cathedral Builders' comprising the second part of *The Makers of Florence* and the chapter 'The Piagnoni Painters' in the third part did not do double or triple duty for her, but given the present state of Oliphant's bibliography it would not be surprising to find them turning up in some as-yet undiscovered book, periodical or newspaper.[44]

Just as it requires patient diligence to sort out the relationship between Oliphant's periodical articles, including *The Convent of San Marco*, and *The Makers of Florence*, so it is difficult to determine exactly how much Macmillan and Co. paid Oliphant for the *Magazine* articles and the book. As we have seen from Craik's letter of 7 August 1873 to Oliphant, Alexander Macmillan agreed to pay her £300 'for the book', and she seems to have received at least a portion of that sum in advance to enable her to go to Florence. On 31 December of that year, Macmillan promised her that 'Mr. Craik our "Finance Minister"' would 'be willing to pay you say £100 on account next week, if that will meet your requirements'; because Oliphant apparently had no other Macmillan and Co. project in hand at the time, this was probably meant to go toward *The Makers of Florence*, but it cannot be determined whether it was part of the £300 mentioned earlier or an addition to it. Nearly a year later, after three *San Marco* articles had appeared in *Macmillan's* and a fourth was due out the following month, Craik wrote her on 7 December 1874 that he was sending her a check (possibly for £40; much of this letter is almost impossible to decipher) 'in payment of the four papers', adding that 'Your papers have been exceedingly admired.' Only one portion of the financial dealings concerning *The Convent of San Marco/The Makers of Florence* is anything like fully documented in the surviving records. On 12 July 1875, Oliphant sent Craik 'the bulk of the remainder' of the *Florence* manuscript and assured him that she would 'immediately proceed to revise the San Marco papers for the press'; she was nursing her critically ill brother and needed money, she said, and asked for the remaining £200 that she was to be paid for the book. 'I am so sorry to have to ask it but you know my circumstances.' Craik replied on the 14th: 'Because you asked I am sending you the money for the Florence. I am very glad it is so far completed. I hope it will have the appreciation it deserves. The parts in the Magazine were admirable & we are trying to make pictures worthy of it.' The Macmillan Archive also contains a receipt, dated the 14th and signed by Oliphant, for that £200, indicating that this sum was the balance of the £360 due her for the copyright of *The Makers of Florence*. Finally a letter of 15 January 1876 from Craik to Oliphant refers rather cryptically to an enclosed check, amount unspecified, 'which I gladly send you ... for the June and September articles' – presumably the last two *San Marco* papers, which had appeared in the *Magazine's* 1875 numbers for those months.[45]

The Curate in Charge

Among the other writing that occupied Oliphant during the gestation and birth of *The Convent of San Marco* and *The Makers of Florence* was another *Macmillan's* serial novel, *The Curate in Charge*, which began its run in the *Magazine* a month before the final *San Marco* essay appeared there (so that the September 1875 number contained two pieces by Oliphant) and which was published in two volumes by Macmillan and Co. in 1876, the same year as *The Makers of Florence*. Alexander Macmillan did not participate directly in what remains of her correspondence with his firm regarding this novel – she dealt first with Grove and later with George Macmillan – but, given what we know about the relationship between Oliphant and Alexander Macmillan, it is likely that they had some early communication and almost certain that they later exchanged some now-missing letters about it. Grove's first letter to Oliphant concerning *The Curate in Charge*, dated 15 September 1874, clearly rests on a prior understanding, one that must have involved beginning the story in *Macmillan's* well before it actually started its run. Thanking her for her 'explicit' note, Grove wrote:

> I think I can defer the beginning of the story till June [1875; in the event this turned into August] – I certainly cannot give up having your name to it. So will you kindly tell me your terms for the use of the story in the Magazine – a story of the same length as the Rose in June [a reference to a six-installment novel, *A Rose in June*, by Oliphant that had just been completed in the August 1874 *Cornhill Magazine*]? I will then speak to Mr Macmillan on the subject and the probability is we shall be able to decide at once.

On the 18th, Oliphant proposed a payment of £500, to cover serialization in *Macmillan's* as well as book publication in England and the United States, and Grove replied three days later that 'Mr. Macmillan accepts your terms'.[46]

Grove began gently pressing Oliphant early in the new year. 'Have you thought about the title of your story for the Magazine?' he asked her on 5 January 1875. 'We ought to be beginning our American arrangements,[47] and time is getting on, so that I shall be glad if you can give me your idea.' We do not have Oliphant's reply, but two letters she sent Grove in February indicate that she was already hard at work on her 'story'. In the first, dated the 10th, she confessed that her work on *The Convent of San Marco* had caused her great fatigue but remarked that writing her new novel gave her some relief: 'I am so weary after this laborious piece of business that I have plunged into the "Curate in Charge" by way of refreshing myself, and will probably work it out at once'; she also asked for confirmation that what Grove wanted for the *Magazine* was a novel of about the same length as the six *Cornhill* parts of *A Rose in June*. On the 22nd she sent Grove a brief account of the subject of *The Curate in Charge* but refused to commit herself as to the outcome of the plot: 'Exactly what the people are going to do I cannot tell, as the story is not finished and my personages have an unaccountable liking for their own way, and never conduct themselves exactly as I intend them to do.'[48]

Oliphant did finish *The Curate in Charge* by the end of the following month, and on 31 March 1875 Craik informed her that the manuscript had arrived and that he was enclosing 'a cheque for it, with a form of receipt, all I believe in the way Mr Macmillan wrote about'. That receipt indicates that the £500 for the copyright of *The Curate in Charge* covered 'all rights at home and abroad appertaining thereto'; in addition to signing the receipt on 1 April, Oliphant inserted the words 'with the exception of the Continental Edition published by Baron Tauchnitz' between 'abroad' and 'appertaining'.[49]

Perhaps because, for the first time in the history of Oliphant's association with *Macmillan's Magazine*, she had finished a whole manuscript before its serialization began, there seem to have been no hitches connected with its periodical publication. George Macmillan did remind her on 9 December 1875 that the January number of the *Magazine* would come out before Christmas and that therefore she should return the corrected proofs of the final installment 'as soon as possible' – which she must have done, to judge by his letter of thanks dated five days later. He raised one awkward point in those two letters: for some reason Oliphant had stopped giving titles to her chapters beginning with the ninth in the October 1875 installment; could she now please supply them? The matter was urgent because – as he wrote to her on 21 December, obviously referring to the book rather than the serial version – 'We are anxious to publish the Curate in Charge at once, being specially advised to do so by Mr Mudie, who is of course an authority.'[50] Not only did Oliphant comply for purposes of the book version but she also mended her ways for the serial version: the last three chapters of *The Curate in Charge* as they appeared in the January 1876 *Macmillan's* once more bore titles.

Young Musgrave

As had been the case with *The Curate in Charge*, Alexander Macmillan was involved in the genesis of Oliphant's next *Macmillan's* serial, *Young Musgrave*, but took no part in the subsequent written negotiations concerning its appearance in the *Magazine* or its publication as a Macmillan and Co. book. Those pertaining to the former were again handled by Grove and those pertaining to the latter by Craik, George Macmillan and Frederick Macmillan – not always, as we shall see, working in concert.

It was George Grove, clearly thinking of a serial for the *Magazine*, who officially broached the question of this project to Oliphant. In a letter dated 10 June 1876 he alluded to a conversation that Alexander Macmillan had had with her 'about a story to follow Mr Black's now running in the Magazine' (William Black's *Madcap Violet*, January to December) and asked her for

> a thorough good grand story – one of your first rate achievements[.] The Curate in Charge was a lovely story, but I am somewhat ambitious, and want a bigger canvas & brighter colours; something that will make every one talk, and say 'By Jove Mrs Oliphant has surpassed herself.'[51]

Some time during the summer of that year Oliphant must have accepted Grove's invitation, for on 28 August he asked her to let him know 'the title of your story which is to follow Madcap Violet in Macmillan' and to confirm his understanding 'that the story is to be a 3 volume novel and the price £750 for the entire copyright'. From a letter Grove wrote her on 7 October it is apparent that Oliphant had asked for more money and that Craik, who had 'come home' to the office after an absence, was willing to pay a higher price: 'We agree to your proposal, and will give you £1000 for the whole property in the book excepting the Tauchnitz Edition, which is yours.' Grove further stipulated that the £1000 would be paid in two equal installments, the first on 1 January 1877 and the second 'on the delivery of the last portion of the MS.' and that 'The novel is to begin on January 1st and to run for 12 months, and to be called "Young Musgrave".'[52]

That sounds straightforward enough, and Oliphant certainly kept her part of the bargain, at least as far as delivery of copy was concerned. Young Musgrave began its 12-month run in Macmillan's in January, as planned, and came out as a three-volume Macmillan and Co. novel before the end of 1877. However, the financial part of her arrangement with the firm, as often happened, turned out to be more complicated than it initially sounded. There was no problem about the first payment of £500: Craik deposited it into her bank account on 1 January, and on the same day she signed a receipt for that sum 'on account of "Young Musgrave"'. On 8 June, Oliphant received a further £200, in the form of a two-month bill, again 'on account of Young Musgrave', but if this was a loan rather than an advance it was not repaid, for after she sent the rest of the manuscript in August Frederick Macmillan wrote her on the 23rd that he had paid into her account 'the £300 that remained due to you for "Young Musgrave"'.[53]

The figures do add up (£500 + £200 + £300 = £1000), and so it is tempting to regard the matter of her remuneration for Young Musgrave as settled and go on to something else. Yet there seems to have been more to it. As late as 31 October 1878 – the year following the publication of Young Musgrave in Macmillan's and in book form, and shortly after Craik had negotiated an agreement for her next serial novel, He That Will Not When He May – Craik rather sheepishly wrote Oliphant that one of his clerks had pointed out to him that she had been inadvertently overpaid by £100 for Young Musgrave. He apologized for the error and proposed that the amount be deducted from the next payment she was to receive for her new novel. Characteristically, Oliphant did not care for Craik's suggestion. Confessing that she had thought her final payment for Young Musgrave to have been too high but never got around to mentioning it, she pleaded with Craik 'not to deduct [the £100] from my next payment ... as I really want the money badly' and requested that, instead, 'it represent the final payment' for He That Will

Not When He May, which would not be due until that novel was published as a book, 'or I will do my magazine work for it during the year'.[54] The fact that Craik and Oliphant agreed that her last £300 for *Young Musgrave* was an overpayment confuses our arithmetic, calls into question both Oliphant's honesty[55] and Macmillan and Co.'s efficiency, and raises the possibility that she received another, unrecorded, advance of £100 while working on that novel.

Barely five weeks after Oliphant accepted Grove's (and Craik's) offer of £1000 for *Young Musgrave*, the editor of *Macmillan's Magazine* was getting nervous about her failure to send him any chapters. 'December is fast approaching and you begin in January', he reminded her on 13 November 1876. She came through almost immediately, for on the 18th he wrote her again to inform her that the first two parts had already gone 'to the Printers'. Not until the following month, on 13 December, was Grove – possibly prompted by an inquiry from Oliphant – relaxed enough about the manuscript to remember that he had not let her know that he liked what she had submitted. 'Forgive me for not having written to you sooner about "Young Musgrave". I hope it pleases you for I think it extremely good, as good an opening as you have perhaps ever made. I hope it will go on in the same vein to the end.' Grove's little compliment hardly turned Oliphant's head: enclosing a letter to him with the manuscript of Parts III and IV, she wrote on 8 January 1877: 'I am glad you like the beginning – I mean to try for a stronger interest and story than ordinary, but most likely in this I shall break down.' Although we do not have all the covering letters that accompanied the material she sent Grove, it seems clear from those that have survived that she generally provided two installments of *Young Musgrave* at a time, at least during the early stages of its composition, for on 7 April 1877 she asked him to pardon her for sending only one part, something of which she said she felt 'rather ashamed'; the fact was, she explained, that she had been spending 'a great deal of time' on the *Dante* she was writing for Blackwood.[56]

By May 1877 something else was making Grove nervous: how long would the *Macmillan's Magazine* version of *Young Musgrave* 'last', he asked Oliphant on the 31st: 'just 12 months'? That was, he thought (correctly), 'our understanding at the beginning'. On the previous day, George Macmillan had raised his own queries about the three-volume version. Macmillan and Co. planned 'to begin setting up "Young Musgrave" in book-form before long', he informed her, 'so that it might be quite ready when it is wanted. May we print from the magazine as it stands', he wanted to know, 'or shall you want to correct it further?' Like Grove, but for his own rather different purposes,

Macmillan needed to get some idea of the novel's intended length because that would 'of course guide us in our choice of type'.[57]

Oliphant must have reassured Grove, as on 2 June 1877 he thanked her for her answer to the letter he had written her two days earlier. Her reply of 1 June to George Macmillan, unlike that answer to Grove, can still be found in the Macmillan Archive. In it, she told him essentially what she had told the editor of *Macmillan's Magazine*, that *Young Musgrave* 'will be twice the length of the Curate in Charge or perhaps [and this did not turn out to be as ominous as the men at Macmillan and Co. may well have feared] even more'. She was 'working busily at' the novel, she wrote, and hoped 'to get on towards the end soon'. 'Pray suspend the revising of Young Musgrave a little', Oliphant requested; 'I think I shall want to make alterations.'[58]

Nevertheless, Oliphant must have felt herself to be under considerable pressure in mid-1877, as she had been before and would be again during her long and productive career. The serial version of *Young Musgrave* had another six months to run in *Macmillan's*, but she was already being required to make decisions about a novel she had not yet completed. By this time Oliphant was no longer turning out manuscript much ahead of the *Magazine*'s publication schedule: she did not send Grove Part VIII, which was to appear in the August number, until 4 July but hoped 'to forward the remaining numbers within this month or early in next'.[59] In the event, it took her nearly seven more weeks to finish.

Even before Oliphant mailed the rest of her manuscript on 20 or 21 August, however, the Macmillans started to badger her about the 'alterations' she had said she wanted to make in the serial version of *Young Musgrave* before it became a book. George Macmillan's question of 4 August is typical: 'We are rather anxious to begin to print off "Young Musgrave". When can you send us some revised copy?' On the 23rd, when Frederick Macmillan informed Oliphant about that mistaken final payment of £300, he reminded her that 'We shall be glad to begin printing in book-form as soon as you can send us the corrected copy.' She complied immediately: one batch of revisions came in on the 25th and another on the 28th.[60]

After August turned into September, the nature of the demands from Macmillan and Co. changed. Now Oliphant was being asked, constantly and insistently, for corrected proofs of what was to become the three-volume edition. That she was dilatory about returning them is indicated several times in her correspondence with George Macmillan right into November. As early as 24 September he wrote to her that 'Of course if you don't wish to correct any more, we are only too glad to be allowed to go ahead. You shall therefore be troubled with no more proofs unless you actually ask for them.' One letter from Oliphant, dated only 'Saturday', indicates that she had 'mislaid some proofs' and, because she had gone 'over the Magazine slips so carefully', she 'scarcely thought it worth while to correct these proofs again'. She did promise to 'go over' the third volume, though, 'as that has only once been corrected for the Magazine'. She asked for those proofs to be sent to her in a letter of 2 October to George Macmillan, and Frederick Macmillan did so the following day. However, Oliphant still had to be prodded into correcting them promptly: Macmillan and Co. wanted to publish the three-volume edition 'early in November', George Macmillan wrote to her on 20 October, and would 'feel extremely obliged if you will help us to that end'. On 9 November he had to write her again:

> A grumble comes to us from the printer that they are waiting for return of proofs – the latter half of Vol III, I think. This grumble it is my unpleasant duty to report to you. Can you soothe their minds, & ours?[61]

There is much more to this correspondence regarding *Young Musgrave* than I have thought it necessary to mention here, but we should be mindful of this one point: during the months of August to November 1877 when Oliphant and her publisher were wrangling about the book version of the novel, the serial version continued to appear in *Macmillan's Magazine*, and Oliphant was free to make changes in her text. These, however, turned out to be less significant toward the end of the novel's run in *Macmillan's*, when Oliphant was under such pressure from her publisher, than the alterations she had seen fit to make in the first eight parts had been. A probably more important point is this: as the preceding brief account of *Young Musgrave* has shown, converting a *Macmillan's Magazine* serial into a Macmillan and Co. novel was not as easy as it might sound, particularly when it seemed important to start planning the production of the book before the serial had been finished.

He That Will Not When He May

The serial publication of *He That Will Not When He May*, which ran in *Macmillan's Magazine* from November 1879 until November 1880 and was printed as a three-volume novel in September of the latter year, raised a different set of issues from those that had surrounded the appearance of its immediate predecessor. Unlike *Young Musgrave*, *He That Will Not When He May* was completed well before the start of its serialization; Craik acknowledged the arrival of 'the last of the copy' on 11 December 1878.[62] There were other difficulties, however.

As Grove had done when he began negotiating for *Young Musgrave* in August 1876, Craik offered Oliphant £750 for her new novel 26 months later. 'We will gladly take your novel for the magazine or otherwise as we may decide', he wrote her on 22 October 1878, adding that this payment would cover 'the whole copyright, excluding Tauchnitz which I remember you like to keep in your own hands' and that it would be divided into three installments: '£350 now[,] £200 when the manuscript is in our hands & the rest when the whole book is published'. Again Oliphant objected, this time not to the total amount of her stipend but rather to the size of the second installment. The memorandum of agreement which she accepted on the 24th stipulated payments of £350 immediately, £300 'on delivery of the manuscript', and £100 'when the publication is completed' – terms she preferred to those originally proposed by Craik. She also asked about the feasibility of getting her copyright back at some future time, and again Craik did his best to accommodate her, writing, also on 24 October, that

> if you find at any time after we have had the fair use of it that you can make a collected edition of your books, we will not stand in the way of your acquiring this one or the others that we have. It must depend on circumstances whether we ask anything for them, but I think you can trust us that we shan't pose [?] any obstacle that will prevent you in such an enterprise.[63]

Shifting £100 from the third installment to the second was a minor adjustment, although as we have seen it did bring to light the overpayment in this amount that Oliphant had received for *Young Musgrave*. The timing of that second £300, however, turned into a more serious issue. On 5 December 1878, a Thursday, Oliphant wrote to Craik that she would send off '[t]he rest of my novel ... either on Saturday or Monday' and asked him to 'do me the favour to have the three hundred pounds paid on Saturday to my bankers'. Craik's answer, dated that Saturday, the 7th, consisted of one sentence: 'I will pay the three hundred pounds into your account when the rest of the manuscript comes.' His curt reply offended Oliphant. Ignoring the previous advances she had received from Macmillan and Co., most of which Craik himself had authorized, she took exception to his insistence on sticking to the letter of their agreement by requiring receipt of the manuscript before making the second payment and accused him of not trusting her. She wrote right back, also on the 7th, 'that you may see I had no intention of deceiving you, I send by this same post in a registered packet ... the second half of "He that will not when he may" – with the exception of the very end which shall be sent on Monday'. Craik acknowledged receiving 'the last of the copy' on 11 December, but before that, on the 9th, he apologized for his letter of the 7th, claiming that he had misunderstood hers of the 5th (which is hard to believe) but sidestepping the matter of trust that she had raised. That letter of 9 December was almost as terse as the one he wrote her on the 7th.[64]

Craik's letter of the 11th brought up another question that was to cause trouble between him and Oliphant: when to begin *He That Will Not When He May* in *Macmillan's*. Craik was aware that two novels were then being serialized in the *Magazine*: Annie Keary's *A Doubting Heart*, which had begun in June 1878, and Frances Hodgson Burnett's *Haworth's*, which had started in October of that year. 'I speak without referring to the Magazine', he wrote Oliphant, 'but I think Miss Keary's story ends about June [1879] & we should begin yours in July'. If Craik had consulted Grove before writing that letter, he might have been able to predict more accurately when *A Doubting Heart* would end, which turned out to be December, not June, 1879; having finally spoken to him, Craik wrote to Oliphant on 27 January 1879 that Grove 'proposes to begin your story after Haworths, which will finish in October'. Perhaps as a sop, Craik went on to express his 'hope [that] this is satisfactory to you, for it will begin our new volume which dates from November'.[65] It all happened as Craik had said: Burnett's novel did indeed 'finish in October', and the first four chapters of Oliphant's were given prominence by leading off Volume 41 of *Macmillan's* the following month.

Oliphant was not appeased by this revised arrangement, however, believing that Craik had been taking advantage of her. On 15 February 1879 she wrote to him that she would prefer to have *He That Will Not When He May* start 'in July as you originally intended'; 'I should not have offered it to you at so cheap a rate', she continued, using rather elusive logic, 'had I had the slightest idea that you were likely to require it so soon'. Disregarding the question of her fee, Craik replied two days later to thank her for the 'opportunity of publishing the story sooner, but we have now arranged for the later date & it would not be a convenience to us to change it'.[66]

Evidently Oliphant was not willing to let the matter rest there, for Craik pointed out to her on 17 May that they had agreed on a fair price for the novel and that, if she was having second thoughts,

> we are quite willing to give you it back for the £750 we paid you. Free to deal with another house you may make a more advantageous arrangement, & I assure you, while we should be pleased & proud to have the book, we shall all be glad for your sake that you get more.

In a later letter to Oliphant, dated 4 June, Craik told her much the same thing. Oliphant's resigned response to this offer to sell back the copyright of *He That Will Not When He May* for the £750 she had received, and most likely no longer had, was negative. She did not want to 'haggle', she said in a letter dated 5 June; 'a thing that is done is done … One must pay the penalty of one's weaknesses – of all kinds.'[67]

Thus *He That Will Not When He May* began appearing in the *Magazine* in November 1879 as Craik and Grove had stipulated. George Macmillan asked her at least twice during its 13-month run whether she wished to make any changes in the serial version before the printers began putting it into 'book form';[68] apparently she did not, for there are no substantive alterations in the three-volume version.

As this brief account of the publishing history of *He That Will Not When He May* has shown again, there were difficulties in the relations between Oliphant and members of the House of Macmillan, and these were to grow more serious after her old friend Alexander Macmillan withdrew from the business in the 1880s. However, although such disagreements and misunderstandings may occasionally have frayed the ties that she and her publisher had formed more than two decades before 1880, those bonds were not severed until Oliphant's death in 1897.

Difficult negotiations

On the Macmillan and Co. side, there was generous praise for the work Oliphant produced as well as a willingness to have her do more, for book as well as periodical publication. Alexander Macmillan approached her about writing the volume on *Dress* for the Art at Home series issued by his firm between 1876 and 1883; she gladly accepted – 'I think I should be rather entertained by doing it', she wrote to him on 13 October 1877 – and her little book, which sold for a half-crown, came out the next year. Craik offered her £50 for the copyright, implying that he was extending himself in so doing: he pointed out that the normal payment for each Art at Home volume was £40, but he feared that such a fee would not adequately 'repay' her for her work, so that 'we would not grudge you £50', and that was the amount she received. It was Craik, too, who corresponded with Oliphant about turning 'A Beleaguered City', a story that had appeared in the *New Quarterly Magazine* in January 1879, into a Macmillan and Co. book. He had read it 'with great pleasure', he wrote to her on 4 September 1879. 'I scarcely think I could name anything of yours so fine', he added, but worried lest its relative brevity might be a problem. 'There is too little for a volume, but if you have the original manuscript, which you say contains more than was printed, we might make a book of it all.'[69] Twelve days later, Craik informed Oliphant that he and his colleagues at Macmillan and Co.

were so enthusiastic about her novella that '[w]e thought of printing it in a more careful way & with better paper than usual. This will give it an exceptional look as we think it an exceptional book.'[70] As published for the 1879 Christmas trade (although dated 1880) with an expanded title, *A Beleaguered City: Being a Narrative of Certain Recent Events in the City of Semur, in the Department of the Haute Bourgogne*, it contained one chapter that had not appeared in the *New Quarterly Magazine* as well as other new material.

On her side, Oliphant did not hesitate to ask Alexander Macmillan and Craik for advances and loans or to propose new projects to them and to Grove. Although she endured some rebuffs, she never stopped trying. In February 1873, for example, she offered to write a review of a work by her friend John Tulloch – probably his *Rational Theology and Christian Philosophy in England in the Seventeenth Century* (1872) – for *Macmillan's*. Alexander Macmillan, to whom her letter had been addressed, replied encouragingly; he felt sure that Tulloch's book was 'of interest' and referred the matter to the *Magazine*'s editor: 'I have told Mr. Grove that if he can make room for your article – which I earnestly hope he can – I shall be gratified.' Ten years earlier, under Masson's editorship, such an intervention by Macmillan would most likely have been decisive; in 1873, however, no 'article' on Tulloch, by Oliphant or anyone else, appeared. Four and a half years later, on 4 July 1877, Oliphant wrote directly to Grove about a different project: could he give her *Magazine* space for an article on new methods of teaching the deaf?[71] Again Oliphant's overture led to nothing.

Other initiatives taken by Oliphant were more ambitious. In addition to contributing to *Macmillan's* and other periodicals, she badly wanted to edit a magazine herself but got nowhere in her efforts to enlist the support of Macmillan and Co. Her first attempt came in July 1878. On the 3rd she outlined to Craik her idea for a weekly to be called *The Three Kingdoms*, which would treat the 'spiritual side of Literature, Science, and history and would embrace serious criticism of all kinds and biographical essays, with the necessary sweetening in the way of fiction'. On the 15th she wrote to Craik again on the same subject, informing him that she had given Alexander Macmillan 'a kind of prospectus' the day before, but on the 18th Craik sent her a disappointing answer: 'We have all carefully considered the idea – but I am sorry to say it does not strike us as likely to take.' Oliphant tried again near the end of 1880, turning to Alexander Macmillan himself this time. Having just seen a copy of the American *St. Nicholas*, she was struck by the fact that there was no such periodical in England – and presumably she felt qualified to edit one. 'Do you ever think of the idea you once had of a child's magazine?' she asked him on 23 December. Yes,

Macmillan replied the next day, he and his associates had been considering such a venture, 'but we have been much occupied of late & the starting of any periodical is a serious matter',[72] and so she was rejected once more. Yet, as we shall see, Oliphant did not abandon her desire to edit her own magazine, the tone she took when she raised the subject turning more strident later in the 1880s as her relations with Macmillan and Co. and Grove's editorial successors grew increasingly turbulent.

Two other proposals from Oliphant during the years preceding the serial publication of *He That Will Not When He May* remain to be considered here. Although the first led to nothing, both indicate to what lengths Oliphant was willing to go when her chronic need for money became acute. Moreover, her raising these ideas so candidly with Craik, who by the late 1870s had replaced Alexander Macmillan as her principal correspondent at Macmillan and Co., demonstrates her confidence that, despite the differences that occasionally arose between her and Craik, he would give them serious attention. Although Oliphant could be difficult and demanding, she was not totally cut off from reality.

A letter she wrote to Craik on 27 April 1878 is most peculiar. She told him that the house in Windsor in which she had been living had been put on the market and that she would like to buy it. 'I have a story, finished some time ago, the same length as the Curate in Charge, which if sold for the same price would enable me to do this' – that is, make a down payment. The trouble was that 'this story is … in the office of the Blackwoods, from whom I wish to get it back, giving them a longer one in exchange'. However Oliphant was not offering the novel to Craik, nor was she exactly asking him to extract it from the hands of her Edinburgh publisher. As she put it, 'You will see clearly that I am not proposing a regular business transaction but that you should do me a great favour – and yet having asked you to do it I may not want it after all.' After more such obfuscation, Oliphant appealed to Craik's friendship and good will, much as she had been in the habit of doing with Alexander Macmillan a decade or two earlier: 'you have always been so kind and friendly that you will not mind I am sure the trouble of trying to understand this rigmarole'.[73]

Responding to this remarkable letter (which could not have been easy) two days later, Craik regretted that he could not 'answer it as you would like'. There would be no space in *Macmillan's Magazine* in the foreseeable future for a serialized story: Katharine Cooper's *Sebastian* was concluding in the May number and Annie Keary's *A Doubting Heart* was set to begin in June. He would, however, be prepared to offer £350 for the copyright of a two-volume novel of the same length as *The Curate in Charge* – sight unseen, as usual – 'if we published it as a library book at once, & if you are willing to agree to this we will gladly arrange it so'.[74] For whatever reason, there was no agreement and no book.[75]

Oliphant's second overture came on 24 December 1879. Could Craik help her find 'something to do of a permanent character, which would relieve me a little from the necessity of perpetual writing'? She went on to explain that 'as I am growing old I have more and more desire for a regular quarter day, a regular occupation, and so much money certainly coming in'.[76] Craik's reply, dated 2 January 1880, suggested that Macmillan and Co. might be willing to accommodate her:

> The question you raise about regular work is a very important one, equally so for you and for us. I feel that capacities like yours, that can do almost anything, ought to be remuneratively employed & we wish you would let us think over the matter for a short time. All I propose to say just now is that we understand your wish & we should be as glad as you if we can arrange anything. I will write again soon.[77]

Some of the ensuing negotiations appear to have been oral rather than epistolary, but other January 1880 correspondence provides some hint as to the shape they took. On the 19th Craik invited Oliphant to 'Come & see us & you shall hear what we have been thinking of and discussing.'[78] During that meeting someone (no doubt Oliphant herself) seems to have revived the idea of her taking on an editorship, for on the 29th she sent Craik a number of suggestions regarding the possible nature and contents of a paper or magazine to be published by Macmillan and Co. under her direction.[79] However, Craik's response the next day once again dashed cold water on the idea: he informed Oliphant that he and his colleagues had considered the idea further but had decided that it would not work out at that time.[80] In the same letter, Craik did encourage her to proceed with a literary history that she had mentioned to him, made suggestions about its scope and contents, and offered her £1000 for a three-volume work; it came out in 1882 as *The Literary History of England in the End of the Eighteenth and Beginning of the Nineteenth Century*. Also, perhaps as an outgrowth of these exchanges, Oliphant was engaged to read manuscripts for Macmillan and Co. during the early 1880s.[81] At any rate, the question of regular payment for more or less 'regular work' was to come up again soon, in connection with the publication of her next *Macmillan's Magazine* serial novel, *The Wizard's Son*, which began in November 1882.

Short pieces

Prior to that, the *Magazine* printed three shorter pieces by Oliphant. After her old friend Thomas Carlyle died on 4 February 1881, Oliphant asked Craik if she could write an article about him for *Macmillan's*. Craik had someone else in mind, but when he was turned down Grove wrote to her on 7 March urging her to do it after all, 'if possible for inclusion in the April number'.[82] Oliphant came through; her 'Thomas Carlyle' (part obituary, part disappointed review of J.A. Froude's recently published edition of Carlyle's *Reminiscences*, part Oliphant's own recollections of the Carlyles)[83] did appear in that number, and Craik was gracious enough to compliment her on its 'insight and eloquence' after he saw the manuscript.[84]

During the 10 years or so following the publication of 'A Beleaguered City' in the *New Quarterly Magazine*, Oliphant published a good deal of short supernatural fiction in various periodicals, including two stories in *Macmillan's*: 'A Little Pilgrim: In the Unseen' in May 1882 and 'The Little Pilgrim Goes Up Higher' in September of the same year. Oliphant sent Craik the manuscript of the former on 12 April 1882 along with a letter in which she made light of the story and mentioned the original of its protagonist, a Windsor neighbor named Nelly Clifford who had recently died in her sleep:

> I have been wasting my time upon the enclosed when I ought to have been working – and send it to you now as much to keep myself from doing more to it as for any other reason. I dont know if you will like it. It has given myself a little pleasure to follow my own little friend into the unseen and in this way it may please others too.

Craik was delighted by it ('I like & we all like "The Little Pilgrim" exceedingly & I feel sure a large number will be touched as we have been'), he wrote to her on 17 April, adding that he was enclosing 'a cheque with the amount of which I hope you will be satisfied'. Thanking Craik for the check two days later ('surely it satisfies me'), Oliphant claimed that 'I had no thought of pay at all'.[85]

Public response to this 'Little Pilgrim' story in *Macmillan's* was so favorable that Craik asked Oliphant on 23 May what she would think about bringing it out 'separately', either by itself at a shilling or with other stories; on the 25th he suggested waiting until she wrote 'a final chapter' and then deciding whether that should also appear in the *Magazine* before joining the two stories in book form. As it turned out, 'The Little Pilgrim Goes Up Higher' was published in *Macmillan's* in September 1882 and both stories were printed the following month in a Macmillan and Co. volume under the title *A Little Pilgrim in the*

Unseen, dedicated to the memory of Nelly Clifford and selling at 2s. 6d. Frequently reprinted, the little book sold extremely well – more than 20,000 copies by December 1885 – and so Craik was naturally receptive to Oliphant's idea for 'a second series of the little Pilgrim',[86] which came out in 1888 as *The Land of Darkness Along with Some Further Chapters in the Experiences of the Little Pilgrim*.

The Wizard's Son

There are three noteworthy features associated with the serialization in *Macmillan's Magazine* of Oliphant's *The Wizard's Son*. First, it was part of a package deal that brought her very close to the goal of regular payment for her work at which she had been aiming for the previous two or three years. Second, however, that same creative financial arrangement contributed to heightened misunderstanding and even ill will between her and Macmillan and Co. and, third, it involved her in a quarrel with the *Magazine's* editor that caused her to rely even more than formerly on Craik and members of the Macmillan family to act as her intermediaries when she submitted work for periodical publication.

On 28 July 1881,[87] Oliphant proposed to Craik that Macmillan and Co. pay her £1000 per annum for two years in return for which she would produce 'three novels – one for use in the magazine[,] the others to be published in the usual way'. She suggested quarterly payments but preferred to view them as a consolidation of her 'earnings into regular income' rather than as advances, pledging 'to publish nothing else during the time that would in the least interfere with them'. Such an arrangement, she believed, would 'relieve me of the uncertainties and negotiations which always annoy me, and it would divide my money into regular payments'.[88]

There is no written record of the negotiations that took place over the next few months, but it is clear that at some point the flourishing newspaper syndicate run by W.F. Tillotson in Bolton entered the picture, since on 25 November Oliphant and Craik agreed on an arrangement that called for one novel (*The Wizard's Son*) to be serialized in *Macmillan's*, a second (*Sir Tom*) to appear in several English and Welsh newspapers under the auspices of Tillotson's Fiction Bureau, and a third (*Hester*) to be published 'in library form', that is, in three volumes.[89] In a letter of 19 December 1881 Craik spelled out more fully the terms of the agreement: briefly, in addition to £300 from Tillotson, Oliphant would receive £1700 from Macmillan and Co.; *The Wizard's Son* would start in *Macmillan's Magazine* 'at the end of next year'; Macmillan and Co. would retain 'the copy right & entire rights of the three books ... with the exception of what we get from Tauchnitz or for translations, which belong to you'; and

> We are to pay you £250 a quarter beginning 1 January 1882 & the same each quarter till the whole is paid. The first payment in order to arrange for a recent advance is to be £150 but on your side it is understood that you are always to be advance of the payment in furnishing us with copy.[90]

Craik's reference to a 'recent advance' serves as a reminder that Oliphant continued to draw on Macmillan and Co. before the contractually stipulated dates on which she was to be paid for her work, a practice that was to go on until her death. The whole story is too complicated and often too remote from our concern with *Macmillan's Magazine* to rehearse here, but we should note that Tillotson's entry into Oliphant's professional life confused still further her already tangled financial affairs, for she took to borrowing from Macmillan and Co. against payments from Tillotson that were due her.[91] On the one hand, Craik and his colleagues did what they could to help Oliphant, at least once even advising her on how best to deal with that Lancashire magnate,[92] and there is no record of any missed payments from Tillotson via Oliphant to Macmillan and Co. However, on the other hand, their willingness to yield to Oliphant's repeated pleas for money made them progressively less patient in the face of her periodic complaints that they had not been dealing honestly with her.

In July 1884 Oliphant asked Craik for an explanation of the status of her account. The tone of her request may be inferred from his reply. *The Makers of Florence* and *A Little Pilgrim in the Unseen*, Craik informed her, 'are almost the only books of yours that have paid their expenses'; four others – *A Son of the Soil*, *Agnes Hopetoun's Schools and Holidays*, *A Beleaguered City* and *The Literary History of England in the End of the Eighteenth and Beginning of the Nineteenth Century* – were loss-makers to the tune of £1200. He then went on to lecture Oliphant about the issue of gender as it applied to her case – an issue that she herself had brought up.

> I have written all this to let you know matters connected with publishing that may guide you afterwards & above all not to let you suppose that we deal less liberally with you than we would with a man. You rather thought this when we were talking the other day. I assure you it is quite a mistake & on the contrary I believe we should all like to take your side because you are a woman – or rather yourself.[93]

This was not an isolated incident. Oliphant and Craik were often at odds about who owed how much to whom, and their exchanges designed to straighten things out were sometimes marked by asperity. The most prolonged and bitter episode of this kind occurred in June and July of 1894. Acknowledging receipt of Oliphant's *Historical Sketches of the Reign of Queen Anne* in 'typewritten' form on 26 June and responding to her dissatisfaction about what she had been paid for it, Craik observed that

> It is now a good many years since we paid for this book & the receipt from you [which I have been unable to locate] is for the copyright. We shall lose the interest on our outlay, which is as positive as the loss of an actual payment, but I wish you to make the best you can out of your book & I therefore make this offer to resign it at the actual cost price of some years ago.[94]

Writing to Oliphant again two days later, Craik tried to explain that Macmillan and Co. was not trying to take advantage of her and insisted that the money she was offered for her work must be commensurate with the sales history of her previous efforts.

> If I refer to the results of our publishing with you it is in all friendship but you have referred yourself to the idea of our profit compared with our payments to you & knowing the facts as I do I cannot allow you to believe that you are right in your conjectures. ... I may say that the one successful book which has helped to balance many losses is *The Makers of Florence*, & but for the profit on this book we should have been losers on the total of our publishing ventures with you. When I tell you this I cannot believe that you will be surprised that we hesitate to make payments that we see no hope of getting back. You must always remember that what I do in business arrangements is not personal – I am only one in the firm & I must act in the interest & with the concurrence of my partners. I offered to resign the Queen Anne book as you were not satisfied with the payment – a payment I believe considerably more than we can hope to get back.[95]

Macmillan and Co. did in fact publish the *Historical Sketches of the Reign of Queen Anne* before the end of 1894, but Oliphant's unwilling-ness to avail herself of Craik's offer did not put a stop to the dispute that its late delivery had occasioned. In two more letters, dated 5 July and 12 July, Craik continued to press his case; Oliphant's contibutions to this portion of their long correspondence are unfortunately missing. The first of those two letters from Craik was relatively moderate in tone,[96] but in the second he seemed very close to the end of his tether. Again he protested that Macmillan and Co. had not been cheating her; on the contrary, he claimed, his firm did not make money 'from fiction & modern literature',[97] and her books in particular had certainly not en-riched it. The tone of this letter is weary, almost despairing: it is 'useless', Craik wrote, 'for me to argue this point with you'. 'It is unfortunate & a distress to me', he added, 'that, after many years of effort to do the best I could for you, in the end you are disappointed ... I hope with all sincerity that you will find others to undertake to do what has long been a pride and pleasure to me.' To judge by Craik's answer to her response, he had not succeeded in enlightening or appeasing her. His letter, dated 18 July, is badly faded and mostly illegible, but a reference to Oliphant's 'offensive insinuations' does jump out at the straining reader, as does this sentence: 'I am unaccustomed to treatment of this kind & no one would be surprised that I resent it & protest against it.'[98] What is surprising is neither the injured tone of Craik's letters of the 5th and the 12th nor the anger expressed in the one of the 18th but rather that, despite such hostility on both sides, Oliphant continued to write for Macmillan and Co. and that the subsequent correspondence between her and Craik resumed the civility of their earlier exchanges.

One final element of the circumstances surrounding the serialization of *The Wizard's Son* in *Macmillan's Magazine* remains to be considered. When it began appearing in November 1882, the *Magazine*'s editor was George Grove, with whom Oliphant's relations were correct if not exactly cordial. In May 1883, after six of the novel's 17 periodical installments had been published, Grove was succeeded by John Morley, and he was decidedly no friend to Oliphant. They had crossed swords even before Morley became editor of *Macmillan's*. While he was at the helm of the *Pall Mall Gazette*, Morley had declined to accept Oliphant's services as a reviewer – a slight that Oliphant continued to resent for years.[99] An added source of strain between them was the unfortunate fact that Morley in his capacity as the initiator and first editor of Macmillan and Co.'s English Men of Letters series had strong objections to Oliphant's contribution, a volume on Richard Brinsley Sheridan, which came to him in January 1883, four months before he became editor of *Macmillan's Magazine*.

Craik took it upon himself to act as intermediary in the matter of her *Sheridan*. To Morley he pointed out on the 25th that too much had been invested in her book 'to throw it aside if we can help it'; it would be preferable, Craik cautioned Morley, not to send 'your letter to Mrs. Oliphant' until Craik had had an opportunity 'to tell her what you propose to do to the book – & that it is all in her interest & in a field that you specially know'. To Oliphant Craik tried to explain the following day that Morley was an authority on 'the political aspects of Sheridan's time', the feature of the book 'to which he takes exception', and that therefore it would behoove her to accept the changes that Morley was proposing. Oliphant took no more kindly to Craik's intercession than she did to Morley's criticism, complaining bitterly about Morley in several letters she wrote to Craik during the spring of 1883, both before and after Morley took charge of *Macmillan's*: she objected to Morley's changing the text of *Sheridan* without consulting her and while disregarding her own corrections; she refused to engage in face-to-face discussion with Morley, 10 years her junior and lacking her 'literary reputation', for fear that she might lose her temper; she even offered to withdraw the book, with which she herself was not satisfied, and repay the £100 she had been advanced. A bit later, when she wanted to write a *Macmillan's* review of a book on Fiji by Sir Arthur Gordon (a politic task for her to undertake, because Gordon was about hire her son Cyril as his private secretary), she asked Craik on 23 May 1883 to see 'if Mr Morley would have it? I don't like suggesting anything to him myself'.[100] Morley would not, although he did express some interest to Craik, and the review, expanded into a substantial article, appeared instead in the October *Blackwood's*.

Oliphant's correspondence about the serialization of *The Wizard's Son* began quietly enough. By that stage of her relationship with Macmillan and Co., Craik had become the member of the firm who normally dealt with her, and it was to him that she sent the first installment of her new novel on 4 October 1882 – in case, she said, Grove should be away from the office when it arrived.[101] That part, consisting of three chapters and 20 printed pages, came out in the November number of the *Magazine*, given prominence by virtue of leading off a new volume, and publication of subsequent installments continued at the same clip throughout the short remainder of Grove's editorship, each consisting of three chapters averaging about 22 pages.

The trouble started in May 1883, after Morley was installed in the editor's chair. The most visible change he introduced in the contents of the *Magazine* was the inclusion of a 'Review of the Month' with which each number ended until July 1885. Brief though this new feature was, seldom running to more than 10 pages, its inclusion meant that something else in *Macmillan's* would have to go; Oliphant, as the author of the only serial appearing when Morley took over, was an obvious target. To banish *The Wizard's Son* from the pages of *Macmillan's* would have been impossible, but to shrink it was an option, one that Morley chose to exercise. Once more it fell to Craik to break the news to Oliphant. On 22 May he wrote to her as follows:

> Mr. Morley tells me that after this you are to have shorter instalments of *The Wizard's Son* in the Magazine – In arranging this he does not of course intend to interfere with the story & we should be sorry if you injured the book by curtailment. It really does not signify how long the story continues in the Magazine but it is convenient that the instalments should not be longer than about 16 pages.[102]

Oliphant had other concerns just then, as she explained in the answer she wrote to Craik the following day: she was finishing her corrections of *Sheridan* and falling behind in her writing of the two other novels for which she was under contract to Macmillan and Co., *Hester* and *Sir Tom*. 'I begin for the first time to get muddled about my work, and to feel overwhelmed by various requirements'; moreover, she was 'under the grip of a miserable cold'. So Morley's diktat regarding the fourth book on which she was working simultaneously was a relatively minor matter: 'About the Wizard's Son, as long as I have room enough to work out my story the length of the numbers is nothing to me.' Although the June installment, which Oliphant had already completed, came to 24 pages, the last nine parts of this serial averaged just under 17 pages each, considerably shorter than those she had written while Grove was still in charge. However, by October, and again in December, Oliphant let Craik know in no uncertain terms that she had been chafing under the space restrictions laid down by Morley.[103] By the time the last three chapters of *The Wizard's Son* were printed in the March 1884 number of the *Magazine*, Oliphant was already revising the text of the serial version for book publication[104] and reading proofs,[105] and the three-volume edition of the novel was published by Macmillan and Co. in June.

More friction

By then another source of friction between Oliphant and the firm had arisen. Having asked repeatedly and fruitlessly during the previous four and a half years to be entrusted with the editorship of a Macmillan and Co. periodical, Oliphant could not have been pleased to learn in February 1883 that a new one would be launched in the autumn and that there were no plans to involve her in its direction. Informing her on the 23rd that the *English Illustrated Magazine* was to begin publication in October, Craik felt compelled to add that

> We thought of asking your assistance in the editing, but the care of
> the illustrations will be of first importance & after full considera-
> tion we resolved to entrust the whole conduct to one familiar with
> engraving & acquainted with many artists [J.W. Comyns Carr]. We
> feel that the success of the venture largely depends on the illustra-
> tions.[106]

Oliphant's reaction to this news can only be imagined. Perhaps it was in an effort to mollify her that, exactly one month later, Craik raised the possibility of printing 'some part of the book on Venice' – *The Makers of Venice*, on which she had been working intermittently since 1881 – in the *English Illustrated*. Oliphant was interested, and two weeks later Craik wrote to her that 'I will find out from Mr. Comyns Carr when he would like your article for the Illustrated Magazine & get him to settle it all with you.' However, during the month after that there must have been second thoughts, since on 27 April 1883 Craik assured Oliphant that no text or illustrations from 'the Venice book' would appear in that periodical if she thought that anticipating its publication in volume form 'would injuriously affect' sales.[107] Regardless of what Oliphant did think, nothing from *The Makers of Venice* was ever published in the *English Illustrated Magazine*, and – as we shall see shortly – she was not really happy about its exclusion.

She did eventually contribute five pieces to the *English Illustrated*, although her relations with its editors were no smoother than her dealings with John Morley. Comyns Carr ignored her suggestion about a possible article on Marco Polo, first made seven months before the first number of the new magazine appeared,[108] and when he ran her 'Heidelberg' in October 1884 Oliphant was displeased by the form in which it was printed. Craik apologized to her, twice, on 29 September and 8 October 1884.[109] In the second of those letters, Craik laid it on thick. 'I hope there will never again be any difficulty between our Editors & you. I am sure they are both very desirous to satisfy you & do always what will please you.' Comyns Carr, Craik told her, had evidently misunderstood her wishes regarding 'Heidelberg'; as to Morley, he 'would like it very much' if she submitted another 'Little Pilgrim' story to *Macmillan's*. He ended with a compliment, neither the first nor the last in his long correspondence with Oliphant:

> What a desperately busy person you are! There is no end to the books you write & never a bad one. The Longman story [*Madam*, which ran in *Longman's Magazine* from January 1884 to January 1885] is admirable & when I consider it is one of many I am amazed at the strength & the quantity of it all.

A letter of 10 October 1885 from Oliphant to Craik, which ostensibly concerns her next contribution to the *English Illustrated Magazine*, 'Dr. Barrère' (December 1885), deserves extended mention here not only because it demonstrates her feelings toward Comyns Carr but also, and especially, because it brings to the surface once again a fixed idea that she had been harboring for at least a half-dozen years. She wrote that she was sending her story, which Comyns Carr had requested for the Christmas number, to Craik rather than directly to the editor of the *Magazine* because 'it has run to greater length than he wished and he may not therefore be able to use it. I have written to him to say so, but having no answer prefer to send it to you. Your editors seem to have a proclivity towards misunderstanding with me or I with them.' That she was still not on good terms with Comyns Carr is also clear from a reference in this letter to her progress on *The Makers of Venice*: several chapters were done, and she had hoped to get them into the *English Illustrated Magazine* 'with their appropriate pictures, but Mr. Comyns Carr is not of my opinion either on that point'. Moving from her differences with one editor to the old question of a similar position for herself, she also included in the same letter a renewed plea that Craik 'find me something like an editorship where there would be steady income without perpetual strain – such as his friends have found more than once for Leslie Stephen, but then he is a man'.[110]

Things went no better after Clement Kinloch Cooke succeeded Comyns Carr as editor of the *English Illustrated Magazine*. Writing to Craik from Beaulieu on 23 January 1889, Oliphant suggested that a series of articles about the French Riviera would be appropriate for that periodical; Craik wrote back on the 25th that there would be no space for them and suggested that she try to place them elsewhere. On 7 April 1892, Oliphant complained to Frederick Macmillan about Kinloch Cooke's treatment of her: he had asked her for 'a story in three parts for the Illustrated Magazine', she had laid aside some other work in order to write it, and then he had refused to print it. Replying on the 13th and choosing his words very carefully, Macmillan explained that, although he believed that 'there could be no "impropriety" in anything coming from your pen', he did agree with Kinloch Cooke that her novella, *A Widow's Tale*, was unsuitable for the 'peculiar audience' to which the *English Illustrated* was addressed. 'You have no idea how careful we have to be and how we are inundated with letters if anything appears in its pages to which the "British Matron" finds it possible to take exception', and there would certainly be strong objections from that prudish readership to 'a story the principal interest in which was the attempt of a man to force his way into a woman's room which although unsuccessful was followed by the flight of the woman as the man's mistress'. Although conceding that 'this is an unfair description of the story', Macmillan insisted that 'it is near enough to give colour to such complaints'.[111]

Neither Macmillan's defense of Kinloch Cooke's decision nor his offer to help Oliphant place her novella 'in some less peculiarly situated periodical' did much to calm her, for a week later he had to write to her that he was unwilling to discuss any further the appropriateness of *A Widow's Tale* for the *English Illustrated Magazine* or to second-guess the editor's judgment. He did, however, express his willingness to pay her 'any reasonable sum of money in consideration of the inconvenience to which you have been put, or, if you prefer it, we will purchase the manuscript with the right of publishing it or disposing of it as we think right'.[112]

It will be clear, then, that John Morley was not the only periodical editor with whom Oliphant found it difficult to work harmoniously.

Nor did she get on much better with Mowbray Morris, Morley's successor at *Macmillan's*. Just as Oliphant seems not to have corresponded directly with Morley, preferring to use Craik as her intermediary, so there are no surviving letters from her to Morris or from Morris to her; again Craik played the go-between, to little avail. Having failed, despite his encouraging words to Oliphant in October 1884, to persuade Morley to print another of the 'Little Pilgrim' stories in *Macmillan's*, he was equally unsuccessful with Morris. Craik wrote to Morris on 4 October 1886, at Oliphant's request, to ask if he would like to have her 'The Land of Darkness' 'for your new year number. It is a sequel to "The Little Pilgrim" which originally came out in the Magazine & whc is still popular.'[113] Morris declined to take 'The Land of Darkness', and it appeared instead in the January 1887 number of *Blackwood's*.[114] Nor could Craik induce Morris to print excerpts from her *The Makers of Venice* in *Macmillan's Magazine* before the book was published in 1887. In the spring of 1890 Oliphant, despite Craik's intercession, also failed to place an article on Robert Henryson in the *Magazine*; it was Craik who wrote to her on 5 June that 'as you will see by the enclosed note from Mowbray Morris he does not think it suitable for Macmillans. I am very sorry that this is his view but I can do nothing else than to let you know.'[115]

Final contributions

It is hardly surprising, therefore, that very little from Oliphant's pen was published in *Macmillan's Magazine* during the last dozen years of her life. The spate of Oliphant books brought out by Macmillan and Co. did continue unabated: 11 works of fiction from 1886 on (12 if we count the posthumously published *That Little Cutty and Other Stories* [1898]), as well as *The Makers of Venice* (1887), *Royal Edinburgh* (1890), *Jerusalem* (1891), *Historical Sketches of the Reign of Queen Anne* (1894) and *The Makers of Modern Rome* (1895); but the flow of her contributions to *Macmillan's* had slowed down to a trickle by contrast with what she had produced for the *Magazine* during the editorships of David Masson and George Grove, who were more amenable to suggestions from Alexander Macmillan than John Morley and Mowbray Morris were to recommendations by George Lillie Craik. Nevertheless, those final pieces, although they amount to just two items in the long list of Oliphant's published works, are of particular interest.

An old acquaintance of Oliphant's, the novelist and poet Dinah Mulock Craik, died unexpectedly on 12 October 1887. As a long-time Macmillan and Co. author and *Macmillan's Magazine* contributor, whose novel

John Halifax, Gentleman (1856) had made her something of a household name, she was a natural subject for an obituary essay in the *Magazine*; as it happened, she was also the wife of George Lillie Craik, and Oliphant, who had known her since both of them were young women, was that article's natural author.

For once, and for understandable reasons, Oliphant approached Frederick Macmillan rather than George Lillie Craik about doing this particular piece. After speaking with Morris, Macmillan wrote to Oliphant on 9 November 'that Mr Morris will be able to give you 5 pages for the paper on Mrs Craik'. Haste was necessary, though: Morris needed copy 'this week as he is making up the December number & wants to put your article first'. Oliphant came through promptly; it was only a day later that Macmillan sent her this two-sentence note: 'I am much obliged to you for the article. You shall have a proof immediately.'[116] As promised, 'Mrs. Craik' led off the December 1887 number of *Macmillan's*.

Even more than Oliphant's 'Thomas Carlyle' six and a half years earlier, 'Mrs. Craik' was a highly personal statement. 'We were contemporaries in every sense of the word', Oliphant wrote, referring not only to Craik's age (she was born two years before Oliphant) and to the difficulties that Craik, like Oliphant, had surmounted in launching her career at about the same time as Oliphant, but also to the fact that both of them had lived long enough to perceive mortality as an increasingly pressing concern:

> The slow disappearance one by one of contemporaries and companions, the tendency towards the grave which has set in drawing us with it, the growing solitude in which we move, make us realise better than anything else that our cycle of life is rounding to its close.

Packed with biographical information, much of it obviously acquired at first hand, this brief article served – along with Oliphant's *Autobiography and Letters* – as a source for the standard modern treatment of Craik's career, Sally Mitchell's *Dinah Mulock Craik*.[117] It is likely that one of Oliphant's own sources was Craik's widower. Referring to the charitable uses to which her subject had put the pension that Queen Victoria had granted her when she was still Dinah Maria Mulock, which 'at least one ungracious commentator' claimed was 'unnecessary' after she married and had a husband to support her, Oliphant wrote that 'I am asked to say that ... it was, from the period of her marriage, religiously set aside for those in her own walk of literature who needed it more than herself.'[118] Who other than George Lillie Craik himself would have asked her to say that?

The last of Oliphant's novels to be serialized in *Macmillan's Magazine*, *Kirsteen*, turned out to be not only a great success in the early

1890s – much admired by J.M. Barrie and W.E. Henley, among others, although not by Henry James, to whom Henley had recommended it[119] – but also a work that critics and scholars have singled out from her prodigious output for serious attention a century later. Merryn Williams in 1986 called *Kirsteen* 'arguably her masterpiece', Margarete Rubik in 1994 put it on her not-so-short list of Oliphant's 'best works', and Linda Peterson in an essay published in 1995 treated it respectfully as a particularly significant female *Bildungsroman*.[120]

Yet *Kirsteen's* path to publication was not a smooth one. In October 1888, Oliphant tried to get the novel serialized in *Blackwood's*, asking £400 for it, but was turned down[121] and then almost immediately offered it to Craik, who warned her that, because 'we fail to get the same result from your later [novels] that we once got', he would have to pay her significantly less for it 'than you have been used to'. 'I say this now', his letter went on, 'for you might like to go elsewhere. I am sincerely anxious that you should do the best for yourself.'[122] Having already tried and failed to 'go elsewhere' and in need of money as usual, Oliphant did not take time to bargain but accepted £300 'for the entire copyright' and signed a receipt for a payment in that amount the day after Craik wrote to her.[123]

It came as something of a shock to Oliphant when Craik informed her on 15 April 1889 that 'We propose to begin "Kirstine" [sic] in the Magazine in July'. Two days later she protested that

> our bargain was solely for its publication in book form. Dont you think this is a little *brusque* on your part? I shall have great pleasure in preparing it for the Magazine and it is what I should have desired – but at the same time not a word on this subject has been said to me. ... Have I done anything rude or disagreeable that your tone towards me is so dry and peremptory?[124]

In his reply of 24 April, it was Craik's turn to protest. He insisted that there had been nothing 'dry or peremptory' about his letter of the 15th and reminded Oliphant that she had sold Macmillan and Co. the 'entire copyright' of *Kirsteen* six months earlier. 'It happens that we could have it in the Magazine, but rather than that you should feel that you have been wronged we will give this up and publish it in the regular form.' He then lapsed into the lecturing mode that he sometimes adopted in dealing with Oliphant:

> I must, however, say that you have no right to interfere & I feel the inconvenience of our right being questioned. Had I ever thought of this, I should have hesitated to buy a book which we did not see our way to publish at the time. We kept it waiting for such an opportunity as the Magazine offers. The terms of this agreement are so explicit that I could not conceive our right being stated in any more embracing way.[125]

In another letter written six days later on the same vexed subject of *Kirsteen* and its possible appearance in *Macmillan's Magazine*, Craik was more conciliatory, giving voice to some hurt ('It is a pain to me to feel that you have any idea that our relations are not in every way satisfactory'), proclaiming his good intentions ('I have always striven to do the best I could for you & have no reflection that I forgot your interest at any time'), and, not least, sweetening the pot ('That there may be no feeling of dissatisfaction on your part I propose to pay you a further £100 for the book. Will that be in all ways satisfactory to you?').[126]

In the end, *Kirsteen* was serialized in *Macmillan's*, beginning not in July but in August 1889 and running until August 1890. There was the usual fretting from Macmillan and Co. about the timely submission of copy for the *Magazine* and the prompt return of corrections for the book, but otherwise matters proceeded without any further unpleasantness, and the three-volume version, dedicated to Oliphant's friend Christina Rogerson, came out in September 1890.

Making peace

It would be inappropriate to close this account of Margaret Oliphant's long association with *Macmillan's Magazine* on an even mildly sour note. To be sure, there were unpleasantnesses surrounding the serialization of *Kirsteen*, as there had been disagreements earlier. However, although *Kirsteen* was the last of Oliphant's works to be published in the *Magazine*, she went on producing Macmillan and Co. books until the end of her life. Moreover, most of the letters she exchanged with Craik and his associates during the 1890s, especially before but also after the crisis of June to July 1894, were businesslike at worst and personally friendly at best. Craik's often-expressed respect for Oliphant also outlasted their quarrels and outlived Oliphant herself. Money – in the form of advances and loans requested and received, as well as payment rendered for work performed – remained a major issue in their correspondence, and Craik continued to show his readiness to bend or break house rules in order to satisfy Oliphant's needs. On 10 December 1891, for instance, Craik sent Oliphant £15 for preparing the index for her *Jerusalem*, which was about to be published; this was not the normal fee, he wrote her, 'but you are different from others & I like to make it a larger payment'. In January 1893, Oliphant asked for a £300 advance toward the £800 she was to be paid for *The Makers of Modern Rome*; Craik complied promptly, as he did two months later when she requested another. On 15 March 1893, he explained himself to her as follows:

> It is a rather serious matter to advance three quarters of the price of a book before any part of the MS is in our hands, but we are anxious to meet your convenience so that under the circumstances you mention we are today paying a further £300 into your bankers.

Two months after that, on 15 May 1893, Craik loaned Oliphant £150, assuring her of his 'interest in all the domestic things you tell me ... I may soon see you & speak what I might have written but believe in my continued sympathy in all that concerns you.'[127]

Just what these particular 'domestic things' were we have no way of knowing, but there is much evidence in Craik's letters to Oliphant of his concern over her family's troubles and his solicitude for her own health and well-being. Within days after Oliphant's death on 25 June 1897, Craik initiated a movement to establish a public memorial to honor her, inducing a reluctant William Blackwood to assume the honorary secretaryship of the committee that raised the necessary funds and made the necessary arrangements. All this took time, but on 16 July 1908 a handsome plaque bearing Oliphant's likeness and attesting to 'her genius and power as a novelist, biographer, essayist and historian' was unveiled by J.M. Barrie in St Giles' Cathedral, Edinburgh.[128] A different sort of memorial to Oliphant appeared much sooner, as the opening piece of the August 1897 *Macmillan's*, the first number to go to press after she died: a three-stanza elegiac poem by John Huntley Skrine, 'In Memoriam Margaret Oliphant, Died June 25th, 1897'.

On balance, Craik's admiration for Oliphant's many accomplishments powerfully outweighed and ultimately negated the irritation she had often caused him. As for Oliphant, she brought her voluminous and often tempestuous correspondence with Craik to a poignant close in a letter written just nine days before she died. From what she knew was her deathbed, she made one last effort to square both her financial account with Macmillan and Co. and her personal standing with Craik, concluding as follows: 'I am dying but not suffering much. I am sorry there has been a cloud on the end of our long friendship – but no unkind feeling on my part. Goodbye.'[129]

Notes

1. Berg ALS.
2. Berg ALS.
3. Add MSS 54919, fol. 1.
4. For an account of Story and his friendship with Oliphant, see Vineta Colby and Robert A. Colby, *The Equivocal Virtue: Mrs. Oliphant and the Victorian Literary Market Place* (Hamden, CT: Archon, 1966) 77–

81. The Colbys drew much of their information from the *Memoir of Robert Herbert Story* (1909) by his daughters Elma and Helen Constance.

5. Add MSS 55380, fols 99 and 107.
6. Berg ALS.
7. Colby and Colby 79.
8. Add MSS 55380, fol. 122.
9. Add MSS 55381, fol. 263; Add MSS 54919, fol. 301.
10. Add MSS 54919, fol. 302.
11. Graves 200.
12. Add MSS 54919, fols 313–14; Add MSS 55381, fol. 422.
13. Add MSS 54919, fols 299–300.
14. Add MSS 55382, fols 14 and 28.
15. 9 (1864): 536.
16. Merryn Williams sees a drastic change in the two-thirds of *A Son of the Soil* written after Maggie's death: having 'begun as a novel about social mobility', it 'abruptly became a novel about death'. Williams considers this Oliphant novel 'the most powerful she had written yet' (*Margaret Oliphant: A Critical Biography* [New York: St Martin's, 1986] 47).
17. On 20 January 1864, she asked Macmillan to deposit another £100 in her bank account as soon as possible (Add MSS 54919, fol. 303); a similar request on 12 May was followed by the underlined phrase '*on receiving this*' and a reference to 'another £50 about the beginning of June' (Add MSS 54919, fol. 305).
18. 'I am overwhelmed with work and proofs drive me frantic. They are the one thing intolerable in literature' (Add MSS 54919, fol. 317).
19. Add MSS 55383, fol. 208.
20. Add MSS 54919, fol. 307; Add MSS 55384, fols 158–9.
21. Oliphant was not normally named as author on the title pages of her novels until later in the 1860s. Of her first 28 novels, only four – *Zaidee* (1854–55, 1856), *The Athelings* (1856–57, 1857), *Agnes Hopetoun's Schools and Holidays*, and *Agnes* (1866) – were explicitly identified as hers at the times of their publication.
22. Add MSS 55834, fol. 158.
23. Add MSS 54919, fol. 328.
24. Add MSS 55384, fols 363 and 372.
25. Add MSS 55384, fols 159, 363 and 532.
26. Add MSS 54919, fol. 322.
27. Add MSS 55383, fol. 692. 'Mr Mudie' was Charles Edward Mudie, proprietor of the powerful Mudie's Select Library.
28. Add MSS 54919, fol. 320; Add MSS 55842, fol. 34.
29. Add MSS 55843, fol. 504.
30. Add MSS 55386, fols 173 and 189. No real review of *Felix Holt* appeared in *Macmillan's Magazine*, but a more general survey of 'George Eliot's Novels' by John Morley in the August 1866 number pleased Eliot so much that 'she had GHL [George Henry Lewes] call upon [Alexander] Macmillan to thank him for it, and an introduction to GE followed' (*The George Eliot Letters*, ed. Gordon S. Haight [New Haven: Yale University Press, 1955] 3: 309). Eliot subsequently published three poems in *Macmillan's*, but Alexander Macmillan's efforts to recruit her as the author of the Shakespeare volume in Macmillan and Co.'s English Men of Letters series were unavailing (Morgan 116–17).

31. Add MSS 55388, fols 582 and 914; Add MSS 55386, fol. 321.
32. Add MSS 55390, fol. 594; Add MSS 54919, fols 9–10; Add MSS 55408, fol. 603. Craik's letter of 31 March 1879 raises one of several tantalizing questions left unanswered by the incomplete state of the Macmillan Archive: what became of a book on St Margaret of Scotland that Oliphant proposed to write and for which she received payment from Macmillan and Co. in 1879? It was in an ultimately successful effort to get her to accept £150 rather than £300 against half the profits for this book that Craik mentioned the loss the firm had incurred with *Francis of Assisi* (Add MSS 55408, fol. 603; also see Add MSS 54919, fols 104–105 and 106–107; Add MSS 55408, fol. 570–71; Add MSS 55410, fol. 1048). It seems clear that the St Margaret book never appeared and it is likely that Oliphant eventually used some of the material it would have contained in two other Macmillan and Co. publications: a November 1889 article, 'Margaret of Scotland', in the *English Illustrated Magazine* and the first chapter, 'Margaret of Scotland, Atheling – Queen and Saint', of *Royal Edinburgh* (1890).
33. Add MSS 55393, fol. 328.
34. Morgan 108.
35. Graves 316.
36. Add MSS 55393, fol. 967.
37. Add MSS 55394, fols 88–9.
38. Add MSS 55394, fols 228–9; Add MSS 54919, fols 51–2.
39. Add MSS 55395, fols 676 and 799–800.
40. Add MSS 54919, fol. 19; Add MSS 55397, fol. 516.
41. Add MSS 55397, fols 743, 824, 963 and 697; Add MSS 55399, fol. 700.
42. *The Autobiography and Letters of Mrs. M.O.W. Oliphant Arranged and Edited by Mrs. Harry Coghill* (Edinburgh: Blackwood, 1899) 243. The Colbys usefully summarize Oliphant's protracted dealings with the Blackwood family (139–70). As they point out, Macmillan was not the first publisher to finance Oliphant's Continental travels: the Blackwoods 'subsidized her trip to Italy with her dying husband in 1859, paying for articles they did not even use' (154). Could Oliphant have conceived of this offer 15 years later as a kind of payback?
43. Among Oliphant's alterations, mostly minor, was a revised opening: the *Blackwood's* version commented on the fact that 1875 marked the 400th anniversary of Michelangelo's birth, but by the time *The Makers of Florence* was published the following year that reference had lost its topicality and was dropped. Evidently Blackwood did not object to Oliphant's including in the periodical article a puff for a Macmillan and Co. book published in 1875 to commemorate the occasion, Charles Christopher Black's *Michel Angelo Buonarroti: Sculptor, Painter, Architect*; not surprisingly, that reference was *not* dropped from *The Makers of Florence*. In devoting one chapter of her book to Michelangelo as against three to Dante and five to Savonarola, Oliphant did accept Alexander Macmillan's advice regarding its length and shape.
44. They are not mentioned in the second of John Stock Clarke's two Oliphant bibliographies, *Margaret Oliphant (1828–1897): Non-fictional Writings: A Bibliography* (St Lucia, Australia: Department of English, University of Queensland, Victorian Fiction Guides 26, 1997). For refer-

ences to the earlier of those bibliographies, which deals with her fictional writings, see notes 49, 89, 91 and 123 below.

45. Add MSS 55394, fol. 888; Add MSS 55396, fol. 580; Add MSS 54919, fols 26–7; Add MSS 55397, fol. 643; Add MSS 54919, fol. 28; Add MSS 55398, fol. 699. One of the numerous tables in Gaye Tuchman and Nina Fortin's *Edging Women Out: Victorian Novelists, Publishers, and Social Change* (New Haven: Yale University Press, 1989) purports to list 'Macmillan's payments to Margaret Oliphant … ' (195–6). According to that table, she received £360 on 14 July 1875 for her 'Book on Florence', but – not unusually in *Edging Women Out* – this entry captures only a portion of a complicated and sometimes obscure series of transactions.

46. Add MSS 55396, fols 111 and 147.

47. *The Curate in Charge* was published in the United States by Harper in 1876.

48. Add MSS 54919, fols 20 and 21–2.

49. Add MSS 55397, fol. 211; Add MSS 54919, fol. 5. Although *The Curate in Charge* was the first of Oliphant's Macmillan and Co. novels to be brought out in Leipzig by Bernhard Tauchnitz, her *The Last of the Mortimers* had appeared under that imprint 14 years earlier, almost simultaneously with its publication in England by Hurst and Blackett, and there were to be 44 Oliphant novels in Tauchnitz editions before the end of the century. For her Macmillan and Co. books at any rate, Oliphant preferred to make her own arrangements with Williams and Norgate, Tauchnitz's London agent. See John Stock Clarke, *Margaret Oliphant (1828–1897): A Bibliography* (St Lucia, Australia: Department of English, University of Queensland, Victorian Fiction Research Guides 11, 1986) *passim*; and William B. Todd and Ann Bowden, *Tauchnitz International Editions in English 1841–1955* (New York: Bibliographical Society of America, 1988) 1003 and *passim*.

50. Add MSS 55398, fols 499, 531 and 567.

51. Add MSS 55399, fol. 654.

52. Add MSS 55400, fols 199 and 442.

53. Add MSS 55401, fol. 266: Add MSS 54919, fols 42 and 56; Add MSS 55403, fol. 503.

54. Add MSS 55407, fol. 366; Add MSS 54919, fol. 93.

55. In writing to Craik on 20 August 1877 that the remainder of the manuscript was on its way and asking him to pay in at her bankers' the balance due her, 'if possible on the 23d', the amount she had stated was £200 rather than £300 (Add MSS 54919, fol. 150).

56. Add MSS 55400, fol. 755; Add MSS 55401, fol. 120; Add MSS 54919, fols 43 and 50.

57. Add MSS 55402, fols 728 and 714.

58. Add MSS 55402, fol. 745; Add MSS 54919, fol. 55.

59. Add MSS 54919, fol. 58.

60. Add MSS 55403, fols 347, 503, 518 and 536.

61. Add MSS 55403, fol. 702; Add MSS 54919, fols 69–70 and 61–2; Add MSS 55043, fols 785 and 950; Add MSS 55404, fol. 164.

62. Add MSS 55407, fol. 790.

63. Add MSS 55407, fol. 292; Add MSS 54919, fol. 91; Add MSS 55407, fol. 314.

64. Add MSS 54919, fol. 314; Add MSS 55407, fol. 745; Add MSS 54919, fols 97–8; Add MSS 55407, fol. 757.
65. Add MSS 55407, fols 790 and 1274.
66. Add MSS 54919, fols 102–103; Add MSS 55408, fol. 53.
67. Add MSS 55408, fol. 1053; Add MSS 54919, fols 108–109.
68. Add MSS 55410, fols 482 and 911.
69. Add MSS 54919, fol. 63; Add MSS 55401, fol. 734; Add MSS 54919, fol. 90; Add MSS 55409, fol. 90. Craik was apparently replying to a letter from Oliphant – reprinted in Coghill 286–7, where it is mistakenly included in her correspondence for 1880 – in which she asked him if he had seen the story and would be interested in publishing it in book form.
70. Add MSS 55409, fol. 478.
71. Add MSS 55393, fol. 603; Add MSS 54919, fols 58–9.
72. Add MSS 54919, fols 87 and 88–9; Add MSS 55406, fol. 454; Add MSS 54919, fol. 112; Add MSS 55411, fol. 998.
73. Add MSS 54919, fols. 79–81.
74. Add MSS 55405, fols 884–5.
75. The 'story' in question was very likely *Diana Trelawny: The History of a Great Mistake*, which was ultimately published in *Blackwood's* as *Diana: The History of a Great Mistake* from February through July 1892 and as a two-volume Blackwood novel in the latter month. For an account of the Blackwood side of its publishing history, see Colby and Colby 150–52.
76. I did not find this letter in the Macmillan Archive. Part or all of it is printed in Coghill 291–2 but erroneously dated 1880.
77. Add MSS 55409, fol. 1397. The following month Oliphant also wrote to William Blackwood of her desire 'to get regular work which I can arrange beforehand and which will bring in regular payment' (Blackwood MSS 4410, quoted in Colby and Colby 146).
78. Add MSS 55410, fol. 52.
79. Coghill 294–5.
80. Add MSS 55410, fol. 153.
81. See, for example, Add MSS 55412, fols 801–802, 822, 982, 1076, 1142, 1221 and 1414; and Add MSS 55415, fols 248, 273 and 619.
82. Add MSS 55385, fol. 566.
83. D.J. Trela usefully contextualizes this article in 'Margaret Oliphant, James Anthony Froude and the Carlyles' Reputations: Defending the Dead', *VPR* 29 (1996): 199–215. Also see J.A. Haythornthwaite, '"That False and Odious Impression": Mrs. Oliphant, Froude and the Carlyles', *Carlyle Newsletter* 3 (1982): 25–32.
84. Add MSS 55412, fol. 167.
85. Add MSS 54919, fol. 121; Add MSS 55413, fol. 1412; and Add MSS 54919, fol. 123.
86. Add MSS 55414, fols 171–2 and 188; Add MSS 55420, fol. 1393; Add MSS 54919, fol. 167.
87. Oliphant included no year in the date at the head of this letter in the Macmillan Archive; some unknown hand, not hers, penciled in '1882', but that conjectural date, like a number of others in the British Library's collection, must be wrong.
88. Add MSS 54919, fols 125–6.
89. Add MSS 55413, fol. 363; Add MSS 54919, fol. 34. Each of the three

was ultimately published by Macmillan and Co. as a 'three-decker': *Hester* (1883) was followed by *The Wizard's Son* and *Sir Tom* the next year. For a concise bibliographical overview see Clarke 62–3.
90. Add MSS 55413, fols 528–9.
91. These were not always for Macmillan and Co. books: in 1892, for instance, she received loans in the amount of £500 'on account of' what she was to get from Tillotson for the novel *The Sorceress* (Add MSS 54919, fols 256 and 267), which would be published in three volumes by F.V. White early the following year, after its serialization under Tillotson's auspices (Clarke 75).
92. Add MSS 55430, fol. 473.
93. Add MSS 55843, fols 84–5.
94. Add MSS 55444, fol. 1055.
95. Add MSS 55444, fols 1103–1104.
96. Add MSS 55843, fols 496–7.
97. Oliphant was by no means singled out for this kind of fiscal truth-telling. For example, Henry James, whose connection with Macmillan and Co., like hers, lasted for nearly four decades, was periodically reminded by Frederick Macmillan that his works of fiction were money-losers. See Moore *passim*, especially 146–7 and 159–60.
98. Add MSS 55843, fols 504–505 and 507–508.
99. Add MSS 54919, fols 160–61.
100. Add MSS 55415, fols 485 and 495–6; Add MSS 54919, fols 139–40 and 141–2.
101. Add MSS 54919, fol. 131.
102. Add MSS 55415, fols 1338–9.
103. Add MSS 54919, fols 142–3, 152 and 153–4. She was still anxious over this question of length as the final *Macmillan's* installment of *The Wizard's Son* was going to press; on 21 February 1884 Craik had to reassure her, in response to a telegram she had sent him, that this last part was 'not too long' (Add MSS 55417, fol. 554).
104. If she restored material that she had been forced to cut, this is not apparent from a comparison between the two published versions; she did make some additions but also some cuts.
105. Add MSS 55417, fol. 674.
106. Add MSS 55415, fol. 631. It is possible that Craik was not telling Oliphant the whole truth. Comyns Carr had indeed been offered the editorship, at an annual salary of £400, on 18 January 1883 (Add MSS 55843, fols 52–3), but six months earlier, on 6 July 1882, Craik had mentioned a 'new magazine' to John Morley, who was not notably 'familiar with engraving' or 'acquainted with many artists', which Morley would edit at the same salary (Add MSS 55843, fol. 47). Could Craik have been referring to the *English Illustrated*, which would have meant that Comyns Carr was a second choice? Comyns Carr himself discussed the circumstances under which he accepted the position, as well as what he regarded as the strengths and weaknesses of the periodical, in *Some Eminent Victorians: Personal Recollections in the World of Art and Letters* (London: Duckworth, 1908) 158–9.
107. Add MSS 55411, fol. 1485; Add MSS 55415, fols 861, 934 and 1161.
108. Add MSS 54919, fol. 140. Oliphant tried again three and a half years later. On 23 July 1886, Craik wrote to her that he had given the

manuscript of 'Marco Polo' to Comyns Carr (Add MSS 55422, fol. 576), who still did not choose to print it in the *English Illustrated Magazine*. It was, however, published in the September 1887 number of *Blackwood's*.

109. Add MSS 55418, fols 716 and 823–4.
110. Add MSS 54919, fols 160–1. Did Oliphant remember that two of her rival female novelists had become editors of literary monthlies two decades earlier? Mary Elizabeth Braddon was the first editor of *Belgravia*, founded in 1866; and Ellen Price (Mrs Henry) Wood assumed the editorship of the *Argosy* the following year.
111. Add MSS 54919, fols 203–204; Add MSS 55427, fols 1135–6; Add MSS 54919, fols 265–6; Add MSS 55436, fol. 810.
112. Add MSS 55436, fol. 843. With or without Macmillan's help, *A Widow's Tale* appeared in the *Cornhill Magazine* in July, August and September 1893.
113. Add MSS 55422, fol. 1069.
114. Having made a down payment of £75 toward 'a second series of "The Little Pilgrim"' in June 1886 (Add MSS 55422, fol. 146), Macmillan and Co. did publish *The Land of Darkness along with Some Further Chapters in the Experiences of the Little Pilgrim* in 1888. None of the three stories in this collection had appeared originally in *Macmillan's Magazine*. In addition to 'The Land of Darkness', the volume contained 'The Little Pilgrim in the Seen and Unseen' (*Scottish Church*, July 1885) and 'On the Dark Mountain' (*Blackwood's*, November 1888).
115. Add MSS 55421, fols 167, 316, 375, 497 and 1048; Add MSS 55430, fol. 1368.
116. Add MSS 55425, fols 303 and 314.
117. Boston: Twayne, 1983.
118. 57 (1887): 82, 81, 82.
119. Colby and Colby 133.
120. Merryn Williams, *Margaret Oliphant: A Critical Biography* (Basingstoke: Macmillan, 1986) 159; Rubik, *The Novels of Mrs. Oliphant: A Subversive View of Traditional Themes* (New York: Peter Lang, 1994) 307; and Peterson, 'The Female *Bildungsroman*: Tradition and Subversion in Oliphant's Fiction', *Margaret Oliphant: Critical Essays on a Gentle Subversive*, ed. D.J. Trela (Selingsgrove, PA: Susquehanna University Press, 1995) 81–7.
121. Blackwood MSS 4523, quoted in Colby and Colby 145.
122. Add MSS 55427, fol. 212.
123. Add MSS 55427, fol. 212; Add MSS 54919, fol. 197. Craik's offer of £300 for *Kirsteen* was considerably lower than the amounts Oliphant had received for most of her earlier Macmillan and Co. novels. That decline continued in the payments for the four post-*Kirsteen* novels she published with his firm: £250 each for *The Railway Man and His Children* (1891) (Add MSS 54919, fol. 251), *The Heir Presumptive and the Heir Apparent* (1892) (Add MSS 54919, fol. 229), *The Marriage of Elinor* (1892) (Add MSS 54919, fol. 250) and *Lady William* (1893) (Add MSS 54919, fol. 282). All of these 'three-deckers', however, had been serialized in, and presumably paid for by, non-Macmillan and Co. periodicals and newspapers prior to their appearance in book form (Clarke 72–3). And she was compensated rather better for her Macmillan

and Co. nonfictional books during the 1890s: £600 for *Royal Edinburgh* (Add MSS 54919, fol. 210), £1200 for *Jerusalem* (Add MSS 54919, fols 226, 243, 244 and 249), and £800 for *The Makers of Modern Rome* (Add MSS 54919, fols 279, 280 and 284). This discrepancy is consistent with Craik's remark to Oliphant in 1894 that her fiction had generally lost money whereas *The Makers of Florence* had been her one Macmillan and Co. book to enjoy commercial success.

124. Add MSS 54919, fols 211–12.
125. Add MSS 55428, fol. 528; Add MSS 54919, fols 211–12; Add MSS 55428, fol. 577.
126. Add MSS 55428, fol. 629.
127. Add MSS 55435, fol. 473; Add MSS 54919, fols 279 and 280; Add MSS 55439, fol. 1450; Add MSS 55440, fol. 938.
128. Colby and Colby 243–4. Shortly after Oliphant died, Craik was also instrumental, along with Blackwood, in securing a Civil List pension of £75 per annum for Oliphant's niece Denny, who had been financially and emotionally dependent on her aunt (Colby and Colby 268).
129. Blackwood MSS 4664, quoted in Colby and Colby 241.

CHAPTER FIVE

John Morley and Mowbray Morris

By the end of 1882, Alexander Macmillan and George Lillie Craik had decided that it was time to bring to a close George Grove's long tenure as editor of *Macmillan's Magazine*. On 8 December, while Macmillan was indisposed with a cold, Craik sent Grove what was in effect a three-page letter of dismissal. Sales had been declining, Craik wrote, owing in part to 'energetic competition' from other periodicals, intensified the previous month by the successful launch of the sixpenny *Longman's Magazine*, while 'our payment for authorship was considerably increased'. It was therefore necessary for Macmillan and Co. 'to consider our position'. Besides, because Grove was about to assume the directorship of the new Royal College of Music, 'an office which must take up much of your time & energy', it seemed appropriate 'to make some other arrangement about the editing'. Craik reminded Grove, not quite accurately, that his predecessor, David Masson, had resigned his post 'when he went to Edinburgh' because he felt that his new duties were incompatible with his continuing as editor of *Macmillan's*; but Craik did go on to suggest that Grove carry on until the end of the current volume, in April 1883.[1]

John Morley

John Morley succeeded Grove as editor of *Macmillan's Magazine* in May 1883, with the start of Volume 48. He had been working for the House of Macmillan as a trusted publisher's reader since the mid-1860s, about the same time that he began contributing to the *Magazine*, when he was not yet 30. In 1877 it was Morley who had proposed to Craik the inception of what was to become the English Men of Letters series, which would reach 39 volumes under his supervision;[2] he himself had written the one on Edmund Burke (1879). Not only had Morley proved his value to Macmillan and Co. in these ways, but he had already served with considerable distinction as the editor of another highly respected periodical, the *Fortnightly Review*, from 1867 to 1882, and of an equally admired evening newspaper, the *Pall Mall Gazette*, from 1880 to 1883. The additional fact that Morley was on excellent terms with both Alexander Macmillan and Craik must have made him seem to them Grove's ideal successor.[3]

A good deal has been written, by Morley and others, about his long editorship of the *Fortnightly Review*,[4] but there is almost nothing in print about his much shorter tenure at the helm of *Macmillan's*. Morley himself is silent about the *Magazine* in his *Recollections*, and Charles Morgan barely mentions it in his chapter on 'John Morley's Influence' in *The House of Macmillan*.[5] The reason for this contrast with what is so widely known about Morley's connection with the *Fortnightly* surely owes less to the brevity of his editorship of *Macmillan's* than it does to the relative lack of distinction of the *Magazine* under his guidance; certainly no one would say of it, as William Haley did of the *Fortnightly Review* while Morley was in charge, that it was 'a brilliant leader of thought',[6] articulating as it did the Liberal position in politics and the Positivist position in philosophy and providing an outlet for a number of the more exciting newer voices in English literature.

As editor of the *Fortnightly*, Morley had been able to attract or retain an outstanding array of writers. It would be unfair to cite as an example Morley's frequent publication in the *Fortnightly* of work by such eminent contributors as John Stuart Mill, George Henry Lewes, Walter Bagehot and Dante Gabriel Rossetti, all of whom died before Morley took over *Macmillan's*; yet neither did the *Magazine* under his editorship feature writing by surviving luminaries like Algernon Charles Swinburne, William Morris, Leslie Stephen, Sidney Colvin, Robert Louis Stevenson, Andrew Lang, George Saintsbury, John Addington Symonds, John Tyndall and Herbert Spencer, who had given Morley's *Fortnightly* much of its luster. Frederic Harrison, one of the founders of the *Fortnightly*, made dozens of appearances in the *Review* while Morley was in charge, but only one in *Macmillan's* between May 1883 and October 1885; so did George Meredith and Walter Pater, who had also been frequent contributors to the *Fortnightly*. Thomas Henry Huxley and James Bryce, who had written for both *Macmillan's* and the *Fortnightly* before May 1883, contributed to the first number of the *Macmillan's* for which Morley was responsible and then never again.

It is difficult to resist the suspicion that Morley, an exceptionally energetic and versatile man, did not put the same effort into *Macmillan's* that had gone into his editing of the *Fortnightly*. He continued to devote much of his time after May 1883 to evaluating book manuscripts and carrying out other duties for Macmillan and Co., and with his by-election victory at Newcastle-upon-Tyne in February 1883 he had finally launched his Parliamentary career after a decade and a half of unavailing efforts to win a seat in the House of Commons. D.A. Hamer has suggested that Morley took on the editorship of *Macmillan's* in order to improve his precarious financial position,[7] perhaps basing his judgment on what Stuart Rendel wrote to Sir M.E. Grant-Duff on 6 April 1883: 'I understand that Morley gives up the P[all] M[all] G[azette] very shortly, and that he takes up the editorship of *Macmillan*, so as to secure a modest income and adequate leisure for his political life.'[8]

Always productive, Morley did contribute more often than anyone else to *Macmillan's Magazine* during his editorship. As mentioned in Chapter 4, he concluded each number of the *Magazine* with a 'Review of the Month'[9] (stealing space from the serialization of Margaret Oliphant's *The Wizard's Son* in the process), continuing a tradition he had begun with his monthly surveys of 'Home and Foreign Affairs' in the *Fortnightly Review* from January 1876 onward. The first five of the 'Reviews' in *Macmillan's* were the work of W.T. Stead, who had been Morley's assistant at the *Pall Mall Gazette*, but Morley himself began doing them in October 1883, after Stead had succeeded him as editor of the *Gazette*, carrying on for the next 21 months.

Reading Morley's 'Reviews of the Month' more than a century after they were published in *Macmillan's Magazine* gives one a sharp and absorbing sense of the often dangerous complexities of British public affairs at the time. Not only was this the period when what was to become the 1884 Reform Bill was inching its painful way to enactment, but the protracted debates about this further extension of the franchise were also bringing to the surface other vexing political and constitutional questions. Relations with Victoria's Irish subjects were a source of constant concern and acrimony, and on the European Continent the often inexplicable and sometimes menacing behavior of foreign nations – especially Germany and Russia – and their leaders bore close watching. Farther overseas, there were worrying developments in various parts of the Empire and other regions actually or potentially in the British sphere of influence, most notably in Egypt and the Sudan.

Some of the important issues addressed in Morley's 'Reviews of the Month' were also raised in articles written by others during his editorship, for example Willliam O'Connor Morris's on 'Irish Local Government' (August 1883), F. Barham Zincke's on 'The Labourer and the Franchise' (November 1883), John Smith Moffat's on 'Intervention at the Cape' (November 1884), two pieces by T.W. Fowle on the redistribution of Parliamentary seats (August 1884 and January 1885) and papers by Edward A. Freeman and Bernhard Wise on the future organization of the British Empire (April and July 1885). However, these appeared too seldom and too irregularly to confer on the *Macmillan's Magazine* of the 1880s a distinctive political point of view.

One recurring topic in Morley's 'Reviews of the Month', his account of General Gordon's doomed mission in a besieged Khartoum culminating in his death on 26 January 1885, can be read as a 14-month serial narrative whose tragic outcome was unknown but not unforeseeen from its outset. No one, Morley wrote in the February 1884 number, shortly after Gordon had been dispatched 'to the scenes of his former heroic exploits in the cause of humanity', had any clear sense of what that 'brave and heroic' general who 'has gone on his hazardous errand without extra military support' was supposed to be doing in Khartoum or what would happen in the event of his failure;[10] throughout the ensuing months, characterizing it as 'the most foolish, random, improvident, and ineffectual mission that was ever imposed or accepted by statesmen in their senses'[11] and describing the futile military and political moves devised to relieve Gordon and his beleaguered forces, Morley repeatedly warned that an unhappy issue could not be ruled out; and in March 1885, after the disastrous termination of this 'wretched episode of miscalculation and disaster' ('A more cruel blow has seldom fallen, nor has the death of a brave soldier ever been more untimely'), Morley had every right to claim that its horrifying conclusion had been predicted 'in these pages'.[12]

Neither in assessing what he took to be the reasons for that debacle nor in analyzing the causes of other grave difficulties confronting the government of the day, especially in its handling of Irish affairs, did Morley minimize the weakness, indecisiveness and lack of competence of the Liberal leadership with which he had been, and would again be, closely aligned. After Prime Minister Gladstone resigned on 9 June 1885, Morley blamed 'the most marked mishaps of his late administration' on 'his backwardness in insisting on his own views', but did give him credit for the skill with which he had handled recent developments on the Continent, like the ascendancy of a Germany manifesting undisguised imperial ambitions: 'if any statesman of less moderation, equity, and credit for desiring peace than Mr. Gladstone had presided over our affairs, the process would have ended in disaster'.[13]

In addition to his 22 'Reviews of the Month', Morley also contributed a number of other essays, mostly substantial notices of new publications, to *Macmillan's* during the two and a half years of his editorship. Like other reviewers in the *Magazine*, Morley did not see it as his mission to promote new Macmillan and Co. titles: indeed, of the 10 books on which he wrote, only three had been brought out by that firm, which also served as the British publisher of a fourth, Francis Parkman's *Montcalm and Wolfe*, originally issued in Boston under the Little, Brown imprint. Nor was Morley's treatment of these new books unduly favorable. For example, although he devoted more space to J. Mackenzie Wallace's *Egypt and the Egyptian Question* (Macmillan) than to an English translation of Gabriel Charmes's *Five Months at Cairo and in Lower Egypt* (Bentley) in reviewing 'Two Books on Egypt' in the December 1883 *Magazine*, he did express some reservations about Wallace's argument and style. The second of these Macmillan and Co. books, J.R. Seeley's *The Expansion of England*, occasioned a lengthy historiographical essay in the February 1884 *Macmillan's*, in the course of which Morley took issue with some of Seeley's positions. In reviewing the third, Mark Pattison's *Memoirs* (April 1885), Morley called attention to the autobiographer's personal limitations while conceding that the late rector of Lincoln College, Oxford, had produced 'an instructive account of a curious character' that 'contains valuable hints for more than one important chapter in the mental history of the century'.[14] Two points about this last review are of special interest: it was obviously written from personal knowledge of Pattison, and it contains a spirited denial of the belief already widespread at the time, a little more than a dozen years after the publication of *Middlemarch*, that he had been the prototype of George Eliot's dessicated Edward Casaubon in that novel.

As widely read in *belles-lettres* as he was in political history, Morley had long been a great admirer of Eliot, none of whose books was published by Macmillan and Co., although as we have noticed she was also a favorite of Alexander Macmillan and had contributed poetry to his *Magazine* in the 1870s, during George Grove's regime. Eliot was the subject of three of Morley's literary essays in *Macmillan's*. The earliest of these – in the August 1866 number, long before he himself became editor – had lavished high praise on the Arnoldian criticism of life in 'George Eliot's Novels'. Yet Morley's high regard for Eliot fell considerably short of uncritical adulation. Nearly two years later, in July 1868, he had expressed respectful disappointment with *The Spanish Gypsy* because, in his view, Eliot's talents and the theme of the work did not lend themselves comfortably to the form of a dramatic poem: it 'will be loved not by the crowd but by a select few, and this not for its general structure but on the strength of select passages'.[15] Later still, during his editorship of *Macmillan's*, Morley reviewed J.W. Cross's *George Eliot's Life as Related in Her Letters and Journals* in February 1885, shortly after its publication by Blackwood, and took the opportunity to set down a detailed and warmly appreciative appraisal not only of her widower's book – 'a striking success' – but also of Eliot's life work. Although he held that the greatness of her achievement could not be questioned, he did call attention to what he believed to be Eliot's weaknesses as a writer, which he attributed to her isolation from ordinary human intercourse and her melancholy nature; Eliot's poetry he called 'magnificent but unreadable'.[16]

Next to Morley, the critic whose work appeared most often in *Macmillan's* during his editorship was a gifted young woman who had contributed to both the *Fortnightly Review* and the *Pall Mall Gazette*

while he was at the helm of those publications and whom he had recruited in March 1883, shortly before he took charge of the *Magazine*, to
write a monthly '*compte rendu* of some new books, English or French',
which 'should be as lively and readable as possible – not erudite and
academic, but literary, or socioliterary, as Ste Beuve was'.[17] This was
Mary Augusta Ward, Matthew Arnold's niece, who had signed herself
Mary Arnold before her marriage to Thomas Humphry Ward in 1872
and whose name appears in traditional histories of Victorian literature as
Mrs Humphry Ward. However, by the time she was approached for this
assignment by Morley she had already contributed three essays on Spanish literature and history to *Macmillan's* in 1871, 1872 and 1882 and had
become a Macmillan and Co. author with her children's novel *Milly and
Olly* (1881).[18] Therefore Morley, although he obviously admired Ward's
considerable talents, cannot be given sole credit for attracting her to the
Macmillan's, or the Macmillan and Co., fold.

Ward's contributions to the *Magazine* were not quite so frequent as
Morley had originally hoped – there were 15 of them between June
1883 and September 1885, and she also collaborated with Morley on a
review of Anthony Trollope's *Autobiography* (November 1883) – and
some of them strayed beyond book reviewing into wider fields. In all of
this writing, however, Ward showed herself to be an alert critic, responsive to what struck her as noteworthy in European, especially French,
as well as English literature and culture. Thus, for instance, she wrote
an appreciation of the French artist Jean-Louis-Ernest Meissonier (June
1884), an account of the 'Swiss Peasant Novelist' Albert Bitzius (whose
pen name was Jeremias Gotthelf; October 1883) and a description of
the new Amsterdam Rijksmuseum (September 1885), as well as reviews
of Tennyson's *Becket* (February 1885) and of new editions of Keats's
Poetical Works and Other Writings (March 1884) and Jane Austen's
Letters (December 1884).

Ward had a particular interest in memoirs and autobiographies, especially by French authors, contributing perceptive pieces on the significance
of such examples of what she called 'the literature of introspection' as
Maxime du Camp's *Souvenirs littéraires* (June 1883), Ernest Renan's
Souvenirs d'enfance et de jeunesse (July 1883), Xavier Thiriat's *Journal
d'un solitaire* (January 1884) and Henri Frédéric Amiel's *Fragments
d'un journal intime* (February 1884).[19] It is not surprising, then, that
her warmly favorable review of her old friend Walter Pater's historical
novel *Marius the Epicurean* emphasized its personal, autobiographical
elements as they bore witness to the spirit of the age in which it was
written:

> It is in books like *Sartor Resartus*, or *The Nemesis of Faith*, *Alton
> Locke*, or *Marius*, rather than in the avowed specimens of self-

revelation which the time has produced, that the future student of the nineteenth century will have to look for what is deepest, most intimate, and most real in its personal experience.[20]

This review appeared in the *Magazine* in June 1885, shortly after the two-volume edition of Pater's book was published by Macmillan and Co.

Perhaps the most interesting of Ward's *Macmillan's* essays are two exercises in cross-cultural criticism: 'Recent Fiction in England and France' and 'French Views on English Writers'. In the first, published in August 1884, she pointed to the not altogether healthy influence that she saw American and especially French novels as having on native productions. Dismissing Emile Zola as inconsequential at best, she discussed in generally unfavorable terms three recent French novels – Victor Cherbuliez's *La ferme du Choquard* (1883), Georges Ohnet's *Lise Fleuron* (1884) and Alphonse Daudet's *Sapho* (1884), the last of which she regarded as particularly noxious – and predicted that the English novel would manage to resist the powerfully seductive influence of the French and that before long the tradition of Eliot, Thackeray, Gaskell and Charlotte Brontë would be revived. In the second, which appeared nine months later and in which she repeated her strictures on what she called 'the strange and bastard forms of the *roman expérimentale et scientifique*',[21] Ward challenged the chauvinistic notion that the French mind is incapable of appreciating the work of English authors, citing some recent criticism by Edmond Scherer, James Darmesteter and Gabriel Sarrazin; Sarrazin she viewed as a well-meaning but humdrum and sometimes eccentric amateur, but she praised, not without reservations, the *aperçus* of Scherer and Darmesteter.

Aside from such work by Mary Augusta Ward, Morley's *Magazine* was not particularly notable for its literary essays, although George Birkbeck Hill did write interestingly on Samuel Johnson's *Rambler* (September 1883) and on creative 'Genius' (October 1883), and Matthew Arnold did choose to print two of his speeches from the 1880s in *Macmillan's*: his brief 'Address to the Wordsworth Society: May 2nd, 1883' (June 1883) added little to his earlier utterances on that poet; and his 'Emerson' (May 1884), subsequently incorporated in his *Discourses in America* (Macmillan, 1885), although longer and more original than the 'Address', could not by itself compare in importance to the body of criticism Arnold had done for the *Magazine* during the eras of David Masson and George Grove. Joining Ward as a writer on the visual arts was the thirtyish Edmund Gosse with his only two contributions to *Macmillan's*: 'The Pulse of English Art in 1883' (August 1883) and 'The Winter Exhibitions' (February 1884). The even younger William Archer made his sole appearance in Morley's *Magazine* with an unflattering review of Henry Irving's production of *Twelfth Night* at the Lyceum Theatre (August 1884).

There was considerably less poetry published in *Macmillan's* during the two and a half years of Morley's stewardship than had appeared under his two predecessors: eight poems in all, or about one in every four numbers.[22] None of these had any particular claim to distinction, and in at least two cases involving poetry by well-known authors the intervention of Alexander Macmillan played a role in their publication in the *Magazine*: Charles Kingsley's posthumous 'Juventus Mundi' (June 1884) and Tennyson's 'Freedom' (December 1884).[23]

Although in his mid-sixties and semi-retired, Macmillan continued to take an interest in the periodical he had founded a quarter of a century earlier. He was in touch with Morley much less frequently than he had corresponded with Masson and Grove, but did not hesitate to refer material to him or occasionally to give him advice. For example, it was apparently Macmillan who was instrumental in inducing Morley to serialize Anne Thackeray Ritchie's novel *Mrs. Dymond* starting in March 1885; he also urged on Morley a manuscript by his late friend the Cambridge mathematician Isaac Todhunter, which was given to him by Todhunter's widow. The author of these 'Notes on Popular English', Macmillan explained to Morley in a letter of 22 October 1884, 'was for many years our most profitable author [of mathematical textbooks] besides being a very worthy friend'. Assuring Morley that there was no hurry, he added: 'If you think you can insert them as an article I shall be very glad to gratify the good lady.' Macmillan and Mrs Todhunter did not have long to wait: the article appeared in the December number. Seven months later, on 18 May 1885, Macmillan cautioned Morley to print the forthcoming 'From Montevideo to Paraguay' by another old friend and Macmillan and Co. (and *Macmillan's Magazine*) author, William Gifford Palgrave, without a signature or initials because, Macmillan wrote, Palgrave did not want his name associated with whatever offense this pair of articles might give rise to, although Macmillan doubted that anyone who really cared would find it difficult to work out who wrote them.[24] As Palgrave had requested via Macmillan, they were published anonymously, in June and July.

One other intercession by Alexander Macmillan on behalf of a former close associate yielded less immediate results. As we have noted, John Malcolm Ludlow, one of the more irascible of the original Christian Socialists, had become estranged from Macmillan during the 1860s; a prolific contributor to *Macmillan's Magazine* in its early years, Ludlow had ceased appearing there after 1865. On 28 May 1883, Macmillan wrote to Morley to ask if he knew Ludlow, 'a very old friend of mine', describing the breach in their friendship and explaining how he was attempting to repair it:

> Some not uncharacteristic ways he has of looking at things have rather dislocated the foundations of our love – not on my part – I think, and we have seen very little of each other of late. But as we were driving round by Wimbledon on Whitmonday I passed his house & left my card.

In response, Ludlow must have sent Macmillan a note in which he brought up the possibility of resuming his relationship with the *Magazine*, for Macmillan, in a letter of the same date to Ludlow, pointed out that 'John Morley now edits our Magazine since our dear Grove has risen to knighthood & high Musical progress' and told Ludlow that he was forwarding his note to Morley 'and asking him to write to you direct'.[25]

The recoverable facts are that (a) Morley must already have known Ludlow, two of whose articles had appeared in the *Fortnightly* early during Morley's time as editor of that periodical, and (b) one more piece by Ludlow did appear in *Macmillan's*, although not until July 1885. Its title, 'International Co-operation in Scandinavia', might suggest that the *Magazine* was reverting to its early interest in Christian Socialism and the Cooperative movement it had engendered, but this was not the case, for Ludlow's essay dealt with cooperation as embodied in a proposed Danish–Swedish–Norwegian Commission – cooperation *among* the Scandinavian nations rather than among the classes *within* one or more of them.

It is also a fact that Christian Socialism and cooperation were no longer issues with which the *Magazine* under Morley could be identified. Edward Stuart Talbot's May 1884 review of *The Life of Frederick Denison Maurice*, edited by his son Frederick and published by Macmillan and Co. in March of that year, did pay tribute to the 'prophet' of both those movements, but this was an isolated case. Another voice from the *Magazine*'s past, Henry Fawcett's, was heard in 'State Socialism and the Nationalisation of the Land' (July 1883), his first contribution to the *Magazine* in nearly 15 years, but about the only respect in which Fawcett's article resembled the credo of Christian Socialism was in its skepticism about the efficacy of what both Fawcett and the Christian Socialists referred to as 'state socialism'.[26] Fawcett's position was also quickly contradicted by Alfred Russel Wallace's two-part 'The "Why" and "How" of Land Nationalisation' in September and October.

Perhaps understandably, musical topics, which had been accorded a fair amount of space under Grove, by now ensconced at the Royal College, received none at all under Morley. There were other breaks with what might be called the traditions of *Macmillan's Magazine*. Only one article on women's issues was printed by Morley: Frances Martin's 'Holidays for Working Women' in March 1884. Although pieces dealing with the United States continued to appear, these generally tended to deal with local color and social history rather than with the weightier, often life-and-death matters featured under Masson and Grove: Arthur H. Paterson on the then still Wild West (August 1883 and January 1884), Charles Edwards on Florida (August 1884) and Arthur Granville Bradley on Virginia (March and April 1884). Himself a Virginia gentleman farmer, Bradley did offer a bit of serious political analysis in his March 1885 'The Southern View of the Election of Cleveland', but his rather benign view of race relations in the post-Reconstruction South would probably have given pause to the Abolitionists who had written for the early *Macmillan's*, just as it would probably give offense to most readers today who take the trouble to look it up.

Never *Macmillan's Magazine*'s chief claim to fame, serial fiction certainly did not flourish under Morley. Two novels begun during Grove's editorship, Margaret Oliphant's *The Wizard's Son* and Julian Hawthorne's *Fortune's Fool*, were completed during Morley's two and a half years; a third, Anne Ritchie's *Mrs. Dymond*, started under Morley and finished under his successor, Mowbray Morris. Margaret Veley's *Mitchelhurst Place*, which ran in the *Magazine* from May through October 1884, was the closest thing to a full-length novel appearing in its entirety during Morley's 30 months; now virtually forgotten, it must have achieved some popularity in its day, as the two-volume Macmillan and Co. edition put out in September 1884 was reprinted two months later and issued in a one-volume second edition the following year. *Unexplained*, a novella by another Macmillan and Co. author, Louisa Molesworth, appeared in the *Magazine* in May and June of 1885; it was subsequently included in *Four Ghost Stories* (Macmillan, 1888). A third dimly remembered woman writer also contributed short fiction to the *Magazine* in this period: Emily Lawless, author of *A Renegade* (March and April 1884), *Borroughdale of Borroughdale* (November and December 1884) and *A Millionaire's Cousin* (January to March 1885). The last of these novellas was published by Macmillan and Co. as a slender sixpenny volume later that year.

Apparently Morley had been rather slow to let Lawless know whether or not the first of these stories was acceptable, as George Macmillan wrote to him twice in October 1883 to tell him that she was anxiously awaiting his verdict. It was George Macmillan, too, who had sent Morley a translation from Turgenev the previous month because 'we thought you might possibly care to consider [it] for the Magazine if it is well done'. Four days later, on 1 October, Macmillan wrote again to say that 'I am glad to find that you think the Turgenieff stories would suit the Magazine, for that was what struck me.'[27] Morley acted with more alacrity in dealing with the Turgenev material than he was to show in his handling of Lawless's novella: 'Senilia: Prose Poems by Ivan Turgenief' was published in *Macmillan's* in two parts, in November and December 1883.[28]

Transition: John Morley, Thomas Hardy and Mowbray Morris

Morley did play a role in the appearance of one arguably major novel, Thomas Hardy's *The Woodlanders*, in *Macmillan's*, although it did not begin its run in the *Magazine* until he was no longer editor. There is a double irony here: posterity has granted Morley little credit for acquiring this story, which overshadowed in importance all the serial fiction actually published during the Morley years, for the *Magazine* (and for Macmillan and Co., which published the three-volume version in 1887); and – as we shall see shortly – the editor under whose aegis *The Woodlanders* did appear, Mowbray Morris, was less than sympathetic to Hardy's work.

As mentioned in Chapter 2, Morley in his capacity as a reader for Macmillan and Co. had been involved in the rejection of Hardy's *The Poor Man and the Lady* and had not shown appreciably more partiality toward its successors, *Desperate Remedies* and *Under the Greenwood Tree*. However, it was apparently he who approached Hardy in 1884 about writing a new novel for *Macmillan's Magazine*. In October of that year Morley set up a meeting with him and Alexander and George Macmillan in Macmillan and Co.'s office during which the matter was discussed, but five months later Frederick Macmillan, who had taken charge of this project on returning from a trip to America, had to confess to Hardy that there seemed to be no record of what had been decided.

> Unfortunately as you called in person no letter was written you & my partners cannot find any memorandum made at the time as to the date at which the publication of the story was to begin & the price to be paid for it. Perhaps you will kindly let me know what was arranged.[29]

After this embarrassment, negotiations concerning what was to become *The Woodlanders* proceeded smoothly and courteously, apparently without any further participation by Morley, and Hardy's story began its 12–month run in *Macmillan's* in May 1886 – six months after Mowbray Morris had succeeded Morley as editor.

There is almost no clear evidence that Morris interfered with the substantive text of *The Woodlanders* as it appeared in *Macmillan's*

Magazine.[30] What we know of Morris's direct involvement with the serial version indicates that it was largely limited to two matters. First, Morris, along with Frederick Macmillan, opted for *The Woodlanders* rather than *Fitzpiers at Hintock* as the nascent novel's title, Hardy having offered them the choice between the two.[31] Second, as Dale Kramer points out in Appendix VII of his Clarendon edition of *The Woodlanders*, Morris did alter somewhat Hardy's original division of the novel into 12 installments; however, Kramer adds, it cannot now be determined whether these changes were the result of 'space requirements' or of 'editorial opinion' regarding 'the best place to stop the action one month and to begin it the next'.[32]

More indirectly, Morris did apparently have some inhibiting effect on the nature of Hardy's emerging text. Writing to Hardy on 19 September 1886, Morris gave Hardy a 'gentle hint on one small matter – the affair between Miss Damson and the Doctor' (that is, Suke Damson and Fitzpiers), which seemed to Morris to show unmistakable signs of heating up in the fifth installment of *The Woodlanders*, recently published in the September number of *Macmillan's*:

> I am not afraid (as you may imagine) for my own morals: but we have, I fancy, rather a queer public: pious Scottish souls who take offence wondrous easily. ... Of course, it is very annoying to have to reckon for such asses: still, I can't help it: an editor must be commercial as well as literary; and the magazine has scarcely so abundant a sale that I can afford to disregard any section of its readers.[33]

However, possibly anticipating what Morris called this 'gentle hint', Hardy had already marked for excision from his serial text the final sentence of the novel's twentieth chapter: 'It was daybreak before Fitzpiers & Suke Damson re-entered Little Hintock', after their haycock dalliance. In the manuscript of *The Woodlanders*, now at the Dorset County Museum, Hardy had entered the words 'Omit for mag.' next to that sentence,[34] and it does not appear in the September *Macmillan's* installment.

In the absence of more specific evidence of editorial tampering, we can only surmise that, having been cautioned by Morris, Hardy exercised a kind of self-restraint amounting to self-censorship in preparing *The Woodlanders* for *Macmillan's Magazine*. This was not the first time, nor would it be the last, that he chafed under what he perceived as the restrictiveness of serial publication, and it happened that Mowbray Morris and *Macmillan's Magazine* were also involved in his next such unhappy experience.

Having endured rejections of *Tess of the d'Urbervilles* by W.F. Tillotson's newspaper syndicate and *Murray's Magazine* during the summer and autumn of 1889 on account of its sexual explicitness, Hardy then submitted the manuscript to Morris for possible publication in *Macmillan's* – an act suggesting that Hardy's previous experience with *The Woodlanders* had not enabled him to plumb the depths of Morris's nervousness about such material in fiction. Morris, too, turned down the novel, although he praised its 'rural scenes' and voiced no objection to what some might have called the 'theological offence' of Tess's 'amateur baptism' of her baby. He did take exception to 'some passages in your manuscript where neither the thought nor the language is very clear to me', but obviously it was the nature of Tess's involvements with Alec and Angel that really bothered him. 'Of course', Morris told Hardy in a revealing letter of 25 November 1889,

> you will understand that I write only of the fitness of the story for my magazine, beyond which I have neither the right nor the wish to go. My objection is of the same nature as I found myself obliged, you may remember, to make occasionally to the Woodlanders. It is not easy for me to frame it in precise words, as it is general rather than particular. ... [Tess's] capacity for stirring & by implication for gratifying ['purely sensuous'] feelings for others is pressed rather more frequently & elaborately than strikes me as altogether convenient, at any rate for my magazine. You use the word *succulent* more than once to describe the general appearance & condition of the Frome Valley. Perhaps I might say that the general impression left on me by reading your story ... is one of rather too much succulence. All this, I know, makes the story 'entirely modern', & will therefore, I have no doubt, bring it plenty of praise. I must confess, however, to being rather too old-fashioned – as I suppose I must call it – to quite relish the modern style of fiction ... I make no doubt that your story will find many admirers, & certainly noone can deny its cleverness; but I have also no doubt that it would be unwise for me to publish it in my magazine.[35]

Mowbray Morris

Tess of course was ultimately published, in 1891 – as a bowdlerized magazine serial by the *Graphic* in England and by *Harper's Bazar* in America, and in three volumes by Osgood, McIlvaine. It was a popular success, but the critical response to Hardy's tale of 'A Pure Woman Faithfully Presented' was mixed.[36] Not surprisingly, one of the most hostile reviews, snide rather than savage, was the work of Mowbray Morris.[37]

Morris had already attacked Hardy in print, more than two years before that piece appeared in the *Quarterly*, and on that occasion his own *Macmillan's Magazine* had served as the forum for Morris's objections – not to any particular novel of Hardy's this time but rather to what might be called Hardy's theory of novel-writing, as stated in his now well-known 'Candour in English Fiction' in the *New Review* of January 1890.[38] The following month, in a *Macmillan's* article also called 'Candour in English Fiction', Morris ridiculed Hardy for calling 'the magazines, or at least their editors', the principal obstacles standing in the way of those conscientious writers who tried to depict real life in all its aspects, including sex. However laudable such honesty might be in the abstract, Morris argued, it was 'a little unreasonable' to demand it under existing commercial and societal circumstances.

> Mr. Hardy seems doubtful as to the future of our magazines. If he is really serious, and would wish to see an explicit *King Oedipus* published in an English magazine, he need be doubtful no longer. The future of that magazine would be the police-court.[39]

Although less genial and more pointed than his dicta concerning *The Woodlanders* and *Tess of the d'Urbervilles*, both Morris's 'Candour in English Fiction' and his *Quarterly* review of *Tess* raise similar questions about Hardy, as a practitioner as well as a theorist of fiction. Yet these utterances also provoke other questions, about the fitness of someone like Morris – who was, in his own words, 'rather too old-fashioned … to quite relish the entirely modern style of fiction' – to serve as the editor of a serious periodical at the *fin de siècle*.[40] Taken along with the fact that *Macmillan's Magazine*, presided over by Morris, lasted a mere seven years beyond the turn of the century, Morris's presumably accurate self-characterization makes one wonder about the extent of his responsibility for its demise after the October 1907 number.

As usual with such matters, the truth is elusive and complex. There is, on the one hand, considerable evidence to suggest that Morris was self-consciously and even proudly behind the times. One of his associates at Macmillan and Co., Charles Whibley, remembered him as something of a belated Regency buck:[41]

> A dandy of the true breed, he was punctilious in the matter of coats and cravats. In his club or at a dinner-party, he refused to be separated from his hat, and marked by a hundred small divergences his dislike of modern ease and modern uniformity.[42]

Widely read in classical and modern literature, Morris was nevertheless hemmed in by very limited geographical horizons:

> He had little knowledge, save from books, of the countries of Europe, familiar to most men. France and Germany were as remote from his experience as the South Pole. His noble insularity saw in America a land which no gentleman should visit.[43]

As a young man, Morris did spend four years, 1869–73, in the Antipodes as assistant to Sir James Fergusson, the governor of South Australia, but that was an experience he probably preferred to forget: while there he ran up large debts for which his father – also named Mowbray Morris, who served as manager of the *Times* from 1847 to 1873 – was held responsible, occasioning grave consequences for the senior Morris's physical and mental health.[44] On his return to England young Morris joined the staff of his father's paper and became its dramatic critic in 1877; because of the forthrightness of his articles and reviews he did not last long in that position.[45]

On the other hand, the management of Macmillan and Co., unlike his superiors at the *Times*, held Morris in high esteem, recognizing and rewarding his accomplishments throughout a professional relationship that endured for nearly three decades, until his death in 1911. He began contributing to *Macmillan's Magazine* in February 1882 and was offered the editorship three and a half years later. Frederick Macmillan wrote him on 6 August 1885, proposing that he assume the position 'from the beginning of the next volume i.e. the number to be published on November 1st 1885' at a salary of '£300 per annum', it being 'further understood that your own contributions are to be paid for at the ordinary rate of £1 per printed page'. Morris carried on for the next 22 years, much longer than any of his three predecessors, and was assigned other responsibilities for the House of Macmillan during that period and beyond, after the closure of the *Magazine*: the editorship of the English Men of Action series from 1887 and the rendering of 'general literary assistance including the reading of MSS & seeing books through the press when necessary' from 1892, at an annual salary of £100, which was raised to £300 in 1892 and £500 a year later, and to £1000 'for everything' – presumably including the *Magazine* – in 1902. Macmillan and Co. also paid Morris royalties for his work on the English Men of Action series and fees for various other editorial and writing jobs he took on from time to time; during a nearly seven-month sick leave in 1903 he continued to draw his full salary.[46]

Moreover, there were contemporaries who believed that Morris brought to his editorial duties what his friend James Rennell Rodd termed 'a fine and discriminating judgment in literature',[47] and his rigorous vetting of manuscripts earned him a reputation as 'a resolute foe to any slovenliness of style or speech'.[48] Such strictness could not have endeared him to some of those who contributed to the *Magazine*, but others were grateful for the care he devoted to their submissions. Rudyard Kipling, for one, recorded his appreciation for Morris's 'wisely' editing some of his early work 'a little'.[49]

The example of Kipling, a brilliant rising young star in the English literary firmament during the last dozen years of the nineteenth century, further complicates any attempt to dismiss Morris as simply an eccentric reactionary. In *Something of Myself* Kipling made it quite clear that it was Morris who approached him about writing for *Macmillan's* and not vice versa, and once they had made contact 12 of Kipling's stories and poems appeared in the *Magazine* in rapid succession between November 1889 and January 1893.[50] Unusually for *Macmillan's*, the December 1889 and January 1890 numbers each carried two pieces by the same author, one story and one poem of Kipling's, the former signed with his own name and the latter 'Yussuf'. This outpouring of work in *Macmillan's Magazine* did much to establish Kipling's reputation in England; Charles Carrington has written of one of the earliest *Macmillan's* poems, 'A Ballad of East and West', that it 'at once raised its author into the first rank of contemporary writers'.[51]

Aside from Morris himself, the author whose work appeared most often in *Macmillan's* during Morris's editorship was the military historian John William Fortescue. Although Fortescue never become so widely celebrated as Kipling, there are some remarkable parallels between the role Morris played in his professional life and what he did for Kipling's. Kipling returned to England in October 1889 after nearly seven years in India; Fortescue came back a year later following an almost four-year stint in New Zealand as private secretary to the governor.[52] Each young man – Kipling was 24 in 1889, Fortescue 31 in 1890 – was befriended by Morris shortly after his arrival in London and encouraged to contribute to the *Magazine*. And both Kipling and Fortescue used their association with Morris and *Macmillan's* as an entrée to a long-term relationship with the *Magazine's* parent publishing house. In Fortescue's case this began with a commission from Morris to write a book in his English Men of Action series: Fortescue's *Dundonald* appeared in 1895, as did another Macmillan and Co. book by him, *A History of the 17th Lancers*, Fortescue's elder brother's regiment. It was Morris, too, who persuaded Macmillan and Co. to invite Fortescue to write a history of the British army; originally conceived of as a one-volume study, this grew into two volumes by 1899, three by 1903, four by 1906 and eventually, by 1930, into 13.

Morris related his enthusiasm about Kipling to a young friend he had made while on a visit to Cambridge in 1885, Albert Victor Baillie, later Rector of Rugby from 1898 to 1912 and Dean of Windsor from 1917 to 1945.[53] 'I hope', he wrote to him on 10 November 1889,[54] 'you read the "Ballad of the King's Mercy" in my last number, and thought it good; if you did not, you will never come to any.' 'The writer', Morris continued, is a young fellow by name Rudyard Kipling – queer name, is it not? He is only twenty-four, and has been six years writing on a newspaper in India. Now he has come home to carve out a career with his pen in England. He ought to succeed. It is too early yet to say how much backbone he has, but he is wonderfully smart and has a real gift of writing, both in verse and prose ... He will do, I hope, a lot of work for me.

A characteristic note of caution does creep into Morris's appraisal of Kipling – 'He wants looking after, as he is apt to be unnecessarily frank, rather what the French call brutal' – and his letter concludes with a typical touch of Morrisian venom: 'Unfortunately [Kipling] is nephew to Burne-Jones – not by blood, however, so there is hope for him.'[55]

Morris's assessment of another distinguished contributor to *Macmillan's*, Henry James, was rather more mixed. On 4 March 1886 he wrote to Baillie that he had had dinner with James, and it was 'extremely amusing: what a pity that he cannot be as amusing when he writes'.[56] Although Morris considered him, unlike Kipling, hardly 'full of life and fun',[57] James did resume writing for *Macmillan's* under Morris's editorship.[58] As for James, he got on well personally and professionally with Morris but preferred to deal directly with Frederick Macmillan regarding payment for his work in the *Magazine*.[59] It was also James, again working through Macmillan, who prevailed on Morris to print 'The Gordon Boys' Home' (August 1886) by Arthur Collins, an acquaintance of James's, a paper describing the work of a charitable institution in which Collins was interested.[60]

A third major late-Victorian literary figure mentioned favorably by Morris in his letters to Baillie was Walter Pater. Like James, Pater had been publishing books with Macmillan and Co. and writing for *Macmillan's Magazine* before Morris became editor, but what had been a trickle of contributions under Grove and Morley turned into a stream under Morris.[61] Although Morris had begun printing work by Pater in December 1885, he met him for the first time at a dinner party in April of the next year and found him, he wrote to Baillie, 'particularly clever', calling him, proudly, 'a contributor of mine': 'there is a capital article by him on Sir Thomas Browne in the new number'.[62]

Like all but one of the essays Pater contributed to *Macmillan's* while Morris was editor,[63] 'Sir Thomas Browne' (May 1886) was later included in an influential Macmillan and Co. volume of his critical writings, in this case *Appreciations* (1889).[64] The *Magazine* also serialized the first five chapters of Pater's second novel, *Gaston de Latour*, from June to October 1888; like its better-known predecessor, *Marius the Epicurean*, it was published, although in fragmentary form, by Macmillan and Co., in 1896, two years after Pater's death.[65]

To have been instrumental in giving Rudyard Kipling his start in England and in bringing out new periodical work by Henry James and Walter Pater were not inconsiderable achievements, but Morris also scored other successes as editor of *Macmillan's*, especially before the turn of the century, in attracting notable writers. His old friend George Saintsbury, a series of whose articles on Dryden George Grove had earlier rejected, was a frequent contributor, writing on 'topics mostly proposed by' Morris;[66] such other men of letters as Andrew Lang, Augustine Birrell,[67] Alfred Ainger and A.C. Benson also made appearances, although less often than Saintsbury. Morris printed short fiction by H. Rider Haggard, Joseph Henry Shorthouse and Arthur Morrison, as well as prose by such 1890s icons as Ernest Dowson and Arthur Symons and writers who were to make their distinctive marks during the twentieth century: W.H. Hudson, John Buchan, Percy Lubbock, Ford Madox Hueffer (later Ford), Havelock Ellis and John Masefield.

These, however, were the bright spots in a generally and increasingly drab picture. For example, the fiction serialized in *Macmillan's* during its last 22 years was on the whole quite undistinguished. In addition to *The Woodlanders*, *Gaston de Latour* and two of Henry James's lesser novellas, Morris did bring out in the *Magazine* what Max Keith Sutton has referred to as R.D. Blackmore's 'possibly ... next-to-best novel',[68] *Perlycross* (June 1893 to July 1894),[69] as well as two titles each by a couple of American novelists whose reputations near the end of the nineteenth century stood higher in England than in the United States: Bret Harte's *Cressy* (August to December 1888) and *A First Family of Tasajara* (August to December 1891), and Francis Marion Crawford's *With the Immortals* (May to October 1888) and *Don Orsino* (January to December 1892). There was also the rather curious episode of young Winston Churchill's 'romance' *Savrola* (May to December 1899), which involved a good deal of correspondence among Morris, members of the Macmillan family and the literary agency A.P. Watt & Son, with Lady Randolph Churchill hovering in the background during her son's absence overseas. The whole story is too complex and tangential to rehearse here; suffice it to say that Churchill received £100 for the serial after some hesitation and a near-withdrawal of the offered fee by Macmillan and Co., and that Morris considered Watt to be 'beyond all question the greatest scoundrel unhanged'.[70]

The other novels and novellas serialized in *Macmillan's* in those final two decades were, however, the run-of-the-mill productions of totally or virtually forgotten authors like William Edward Norris, W. Clark Russell, D. Christie Murray, Henry Herman, Flora A. Steel, Helen Shipton, Mrs H.D. Everett, Agnes Marion Haggard, William Lorimer Watson, Mary Crawford Fraser, Cecil Lowis, Daisy Hugh Price, W. Beckford Long,

Eric Parker, Una Lucy Silberrad, 'K.L. Montgomery' (really a pair of sisters, Kathleen and Letitia Montgomery[71]), Stephen Gwynn, Hugh Sheringham and Neville Meakin, Eleanor Price, William Satchell and Margaret Hartley. All but a few of these serials were also brought out as Macmillan and Co. books.

Morris was somewhat more hospitable to poets than Morley had been, but aside from Kipling's he printed very little significant poetical work comparable to that by Tennyson, Christina Rossetti, Matthew Arnold, George Meredith and George Eliot in the *Magazine* of Masson and Grove. Tennyson and Meredith did have a total of three poems in *Macmillan's Magazine* during the Morris years – Tennyson's 'Vastness' (November 1885) and 'Carmen Saeculare: An Ode in Honour of the Jubilee of Queen Victoria' (April 1887) and Meredith's 'The Appeasement of Demeter' (September 1887) – but their presence there almost certainly owed less to Morris's exertions than to the Macmillans' wish to have two of their major house poets represented in the *Magazine*.[72] 'Vastness' had been accepted by Alexander Macmillan and Craik and set in type in October 1885, the month before Morris assumed the editorship, and the publication of 'The Appeasement of Demeter' was the result of a decision taken by George Macmillan and his associates in the family firm rather than by Morris. On 3 August 1887 Macmillan wrote to Morris:

> We have discussed the matter carefully and have come to the conclusion that we cannot well refuse George Meredith's poem and if we take it it must be at his price. So we have written to accept ... I do not say that if the offer were made frequently we should not cry Hold! Enough. But it is some years since he appeared last in 'Macmillan' & it will probably be some years more before he knocks at the door again.[73]

By the beginning of 1892, when Meredith did come knocking again, matters proceeded differently. He sent a poem – either 'The Empty Purse' or 'Night of Frost in May' – to Frederick Macmillan, asking 15 guineas for it and assuring the publisher that 'Your editor will be fully excused by me if he has no taste for my verse.'[74] Apparently Meredith's verse was not to Morris's taste, any more than Tennyson's was,[75] for the poem never appeared in *Macmillan's*, and neither did any other by Meredith after 'The Appeasement of Demeter'.

Apart from those by Kipling, Tennyson and Meredith, *Macmillan's* printed some 85 poems between November 1885 and October 1907. Nearly half of them appeared anonymously or pseudonymously, and all but a few of the rest – by William Allingham, Hallam Tennyson, Aubrey de Vere, Richard Le Galliene, Ernest Rhys and A.C. Benson – were the work of versifiers whose names have eluded the attentions of the period's literary historians.

Nor did the bulk of the nonfictional prose published in the *Magazine* during the last 22 years of its existence rise to the standard set by Pater, Saintsbury, Lang and the others previously mentioned. Morley's most exciting discovery, Mary Augusta Ward, refused to submit work to Morris, 'whom she disliked',[76] although a few authors who had written for *Macmillan's* under Morley and even earlier continued to appear. The most durable of these was A.G. Bradley, whose two-part account of 'Virginia and the Gentleman Emigrant' had come out as early as June 1875 and March 1876; between Bradley's 'Quail-Shooting in America', published at the end of Morris's first year (October 1886) and his 'Flodden Field', the last article in the final number of the *Magazine* (October 1907), he contributed some 40 papers. Other *Macmillan's* veterans included T.E. Kebbel, Goldwin Smith, Flora Steel, Anne Ritchie and Charles Edwardes. They were joined in the 1890s and beyond by the likes of David Hannay, Charles Whibley, C.B. Roylance-Kent, Stephen Gwynn, Hugh Sheringham, William Price James, L.J. Jennings and H.C. Macdowell.

As John Morley had done before him, Mowbray Morris himself wrote more diligently than anyone else for the *Magazine* while he was in charge – at least through the late 1890s, when for some reason he slowed down, finally stopping after the February 1900 number. Before then, however, he had produced more than 60 pieces, only a few of which were signed with his own name. They took a variety of forms: a series of *obiter dicta* called 'Leaves from a Notebook', book reviews, dramatic and art criticism, familiar essays, comments on writing and writers, and semifictional or outrightly fictional sketches. Not infrequently marked by irony and playfulness, they gave Morris ample opportunity to parade his predilections and prejudices, such as his interest in Scottish history, his fondness for Sir Walter Scott, his love of cricket, his knowledge of the Spanish Main,[77] his opposition to women's suffrage and his aversion to a great deal of modern literature. Although most of the books Morris reviewed were not issued by his employers, he nevertheless took the opportunity to promote Macmillan and Co. publications whenever possible, more vigorously than Morley or his first two predecessors had done. In an essay characteristically titled 'Some Random Reflections' (February 1886), for instance, Morris took as his point of departure a 'golden sentence' in Alfred Ainger's introduction to a new volume of Charles Lamb's works that the firm had recently brought out – Mrs. Leicester's School *and Other Writings in Prose and Verse* (1885) – to the effect that it was a mistake to publish 'every scrap of writing' that a deceased author might have left behind;[78] and 13 months later, in setting down 'Some Thoughts about Novels' (March 1887), Morris began with a favorable reference to James Russell

Lowell's *Democracy and Other Essays*, which Macmillan and Co. had just published. These were not the only cases of such mild puffery.

Not surprisingly for a man who thought of the United States as 'a land which no gentleman should visit', Morris occasionally allowed his anti-Americanism to creep into his writing for *Macmillan's*. In his 'How History is Written in America' (July 1896), for instance, he not only gave a harsh review to William Elleroy Curtis's *Venezuela: A Land Where It's Always Summer* (London: Osgood, McIlvaine, 1896), but also held Curtis's work up to scorn as an example of the ignorance and prejudice of American historians in general. After David Hannay, in his 'An American Historian of the British Navy' (May 1898), objected to Theodore Roosevelt's having been asked to assist in the writing of William Laird Clowes's *The Royal Navy from the Earliest Times to the Present* (2 vols, London: Sampson Low, Marston, 1897–98), Morris returned to the attack, supporting Hannay when Clowes defended his choice of Roosevelt in 'A Letter to the Editor' published in July 1898; Morris appended a note to Clowes's letter agreeing with Hannay that it had been inappropriate for Clowes to enlist the help of this American who had already shown some anti-British bias in his earlier *The Naval War of 1812* (New York: Putnam, 1882). Frederick Macmillan had suggested that Hannay be allowed to answer Clowes in the *Magazine*,[79] but Morris obviously preferred to take on the job himself. There was a more widespread protest against an earlier article of Morris's, 'American Diplomacy' (November 1897), in which he denounced what he considered the double-dealing of the United States in disputes with Britain throughout the nineteenth century right up to the then-ongoing negotiations about seal-fishing rights in the Bering Sea. Not without some pride, Morris reminisced nearly a decade later that the result of its publication 'was that eighty of our American subscribers immediately withdrew their names – the greatest, indeed I may say the only, compliment ever paid to my writing'. However, Morris, who was well aware of the commercial realities of periodical publication, also added, 'That way insolvency lies.'[80]

Mowbray Morris was not the only *Macmillan's* writer who subjected American individuals, practices and institutions to a degree of critical scrutiny that they would not have undergone in the earliest volumes of the *Magazine*. Some of this was friendly, or at least balanced: for example, L.J. Jennings's appraisal of 'General Grant' (January 1886), based on the English publication of Ulysses S. Grant's *Personal Memoirs* (London: Sampson Low, 1885), or Frederick Dixon's 'John Brown' (October 1888), which drew a generally sympathetic although not always historically accurate picture of the abolitionist. Reviewing James Bryce's three-volume *The American Commonwealth* (Macmillan, 1888) in the February 1889 number, Goldwin Smith could have been writing a century later when he deplored the 'saturnalia of passion, intrigue, corruption, calumny, and rhetorical mendacity' associated with presidential elections in the United States.[81] Nor was A. Maurice Low being unreasonable in either his 'A Mistaken Admiration' (May 1899), which argued that the American form of government by legislative committees is less effective than the British form of government by parliamentary ministries, or in his 'The Future of the Negro' (April 1900), which tried to account for the recent rise in anti-black feeling in the American South on demographic, political and psychological grounds.

The South Carolinian H.E. Belin's 'A Southern View of the Negro Problem' (July 1901), however, was something else again. Purportedly a review of William Hannibal Thomas's *The American Negro: What He Was, What He Is, and What He May Become*, which was published by Macmillan and Co. 1901, it barely mentioned either the author or his book but was in fact a virulent argument for white supremacy. To turn from Belin's article to Thomas's book offers no comfort: the latter is just as racist as the former, although superficially more rational in its tone, despite (or because of?) the fact that Thomas's own racial position was ambiguous. Of mixed blood, Thomas – as his introduction to *The American Negro* made clear – was nevertheless considered by others, and somewhat regretfully considered himself, to be a Negro.[82] A counterpart to what Belin wrote about the Southern United States in the wake of the Civil War and Reconstruction may be found in what one Stanley P. Hyatt had to say about 'The Black Peril in South Africa' (March 1906) following the Boer War, a textbook argument in favor of apartheid long before the term was anglicized.[83]

My selection of the above examples must not be taken to mean that *Macmillan's* had turned into a reactionary periodical in its last decades. It would be equally unjust and even more wrong-headed to take Carlyle's 1863 'Ilias (Americana) in Nuce' as proof that the *Magazine* had been racist even in its prime. The truth is that under Morris, as under Masson, it gave a voice to divergent viewpoints even without Alexander Macmillan, who had died in 1896 after years of professional inactivity, to articulate the principles that underlay such diversity.

There are also some pleasant surprises for the contemporary reader who harbors dark suspicions about the course that the *Magazine* was taking under Morris's editorship. On the matter of women's issues, for example, although the glory days of the 1860s were long since over, *Macmillan's* did print at least three highly laudatory articles about remarkable women who had flourished in earlier ages.[84] William Minto's 'A Champion of Her Sex' (February 1886) dealt with the Italian-born French writer Christine de Pisan (c. 1364–c. 1430), a pioneer in upholding the rights of women, whose works, Minto observed, 'anticipated most of the arguments familiar to the present generation'.[85] Lewis Bostock Radford's 'Lady Margaret Tudor' (October 1896) paid tribute to the life and works of the inexhaustible woman (1441–1509) who not only gave birth to the future Henry VII and acted as his dowager queen in all but name, but also conferred enduring benefactions on both Cambridge and Oxford Universities; as Radford put it, she lived in an eventful period during which, 'while men battled, women built'.[86] Mrs Arthur E. Quekett's 'Rachel Levin and Her Times' (August 1896), finally, held up for admiration the Jewish Berliner (1771–1833) who ran a distinguished literary salon, mingled with such notables as the Mendelssohn family, Mirabeau, Tieck, Madame de Staël, Beethoven, Goethe and Heine, cared for German victims of the war against Napoleon, and attended the Congress of Vienna with her husband, Karl August Varnhagen von Ense.[87]

One does often get the feeling in perusing Mowbray Morris's *Magazine* that his contributors tended to look back rather than forward: not only centuries back, as in the articles by Minto, Radford and Quekett, but also decades back. During the 1890s in particular, although there was nothing resembling what we think of as a *fin de siècle* mood pervading *Macmillan's*, it is impossible for any knowledgeable person looking over those volumes today to escape the inference that something irrecoverable was perceived to be drawing to its close – not so much the century as something intimately connected with the history of the *Magazine* itself.

For one thing, death took a heavy toll of those who had made *Macmillan's* what it was, and their passing was duly noted in its pages. Within three months in 1896, for instance, it ran obituaries of the two men who had been chiefly instrumental in its founding: Alfred Ainger's 'Alexander Macmillan (A Personal Reminiscence)' in March and J.F. Cornish's 'Thomas Hughes' in May. Also, as noted at the end of the previous chapter, the demise of Margaret Oliphant, who had been writing for *Macmillan's* for 35 years, occasioned a poem by John Huntly Skrine in the August 1897 number. The Tennysonian echo conveyed by Skrine's title, 'In Memoriam', may have been inadvertent, but the fact remains that, earlier in the decade, Alfred Ainger's 'The Death of Tennyson' (November 1892) had sounded an elegiac note that reverberated well beyond its immediate subject, the *Magazine*'s most eminent long-time contributor: the Laureate's death, Ainger wrote, 'dispirits and discourages us, because we feel that the last of a long line has departed, and we are anxious and uneasy as to the possibilities of the future'.[88] Such misgivings must have been reinforced by the termination of Queen Victoria's 64-year reign when she died a little more than eight years later. The March 1901 number contained no fewer than three tributes to her: A.C. Benson's prose 'Queen Victoria' at the beginning, his verse 'Victoria: February 2nd, 1901' at the end, and L.I. Lumsden's poem 'The Passing of the Queen' in between. Individually and cumulatively, the three pieces, for all their conventional praise of the deceased and attempted consolation of the bereaved, yield a sense of irreparable loss.[89]

The end

By the early years of the new century there were unmistakable signs that *Macmillan's* had entered a period of terminal decline. As we have noted, its quality had diminished, and the surviving records, although sketchy, indicate that its financial position was becoming increasingly precarious. The two factors were, of course, closely connected: the *Magazine* was now unable to attract the kind of writers who might have boosted its sagging circulation.

The normal fee for contributors had been £1 per page for decades; by 1897 it had been cut to 15 shillings,[90] and in 1905 it was cut again, to 25 shillings per 1000 words. If the average page contained 450 words, that would have reduced the usual payment to little more than 10 shillings per page.[91] These downward adjustments caused misunderstandings and hard feelings, especially when veteran contributors were affected, although George Macmillan and Mowbray Morris, working in concert, generally resolved any disputes in favor of the aggrieved authors.[92] In view of these tightening financial constraints, it is also not surprising that Morris took to complaining of a scarcity of suitable material, especially fiction, for the *Magazine*.[93]

Clearly, the periodical market was undergoing significant changes. In October 1905, one of *Macmillan's Magazine*'s chief rivals, *Longman's Magazine*, announced that it was ceasing publication, for reasons that must have been equally applicable to *Macmillan's*:

> Since the date of the first appearance of this Magazine, the times have changed in many respects, but in none more perhaps than in regard to periodical literature. The great advance made in cheap processes for the reproduction of drawings and photographs has called into existence a number of magazines and papers depending largely upon their illustrations. Competition for the patronage of the sixpenny public has become very severe, and the mere endeavour to keep up a high literary standard is nowadays not sufficient.[94]

However, *Macmillan's* under Morris soldiered on for two more years. The month after *Longman's* went under, in November 1905, a 'New

Series' of the *Magazine* was launched in what was obviously an attempt to increase its eye-appeal and boost its sales. Its format was spruced up: the stodgy double-columned page that had lasted for 46 years and 92 volumes was abandoned in favor of a single-columned page in larger print. The price was cut in half, to sixpence per number,[95] but *Macmillan's* still carried no illustrations, and its contents underwent no discernible change.

Morris seemed untroubled by the idea that any change might be called for. One sign of his complacency was the reply he prepared for a Frenchman, Bernard Henri Gausseron, who had inquired about the history of *Macmillan's* in April 1906, 18 months before it went out of business. It was difficult to answer Gausseron's 'question about the *general line* of the magazine in politics &c', Morris wrote:

> It would be simplest, I think, to say that the magazine has never taken a very pronounced line in any subject, but has always striven to be catholic, moderate, and, above all things, sensible: or one might say that the line it has always travelled has been the line of common sense.

Morris drew up a list of 'the most notable contributions' for Gausseron but was reluctant to send it to him.

> I should myself prefer to stop at the list of contributors. With the exception of two or three of Kipling's stories, and perhaps [Oliphant's] Kirsteen, no one of the contributions represents the best of the writer's work. Indeed, after such a notable list of authors, the list of titles is rather shabby. The best writers rarely send their best work to magazines, & I should doubt whether our titles would convey much meaning to foreign ears.[96]

What are we to conclude about Morris's state of mind as he wrote those sentences? Was he discouraged, or cynical, or merely realistic about *Macmillan's* as it had become in his hands during the last years of the old century and the first years of the new? Certainly any passionate sense of mission of the kind that had animated Alexander Macmillan and the others who had been involved with him in the early history of the *Magazine* is absent from what Morris wrote.

If there was any appreciable regret at Macmillan and Co. over its impending death, no evidence of such an emotion is to be found in the Archive. Morris must have known that the end was near by 3 July 1907, when he wrote to George Macmillan that he had received a novel from one Mrs Jamieson for possible use in the *Magazine*. 'Were it the best novel ever written', he added, 'it would of course be useless to me.' On 15 September Morris announced to Maurice Macmillan, 'Actum est – I have sent the last number to Clay' (the printing firm of Richard Clay and Sons). Macmillan's answer, dated 17 September, was equally laconic and dry-eyed: 'I got your letter about the Magazine. The way in which you have come to an end, leaving practically nothing outstanding, moves my admiration.'[97]

The October 1907 number of the *Magazine* was the last. It contained no announcement like that which had appeared in *Longman's* exactly two years earlier – not a word, not even a hint – to the effect that there would be no more in the future, let alone any reference to its past. The closest approach to a public epitaph for *Macmillan's* did not appear until more than two years later: in a short *Notes and Queries* piece called '"Macmillan's Magazine"', John Collins Francis summarized its achievements and expressed 'regret that a magazine with such a history, and bearing such a name, should not have received sufficient support to enable it to continue' but went on to say that 'the volumes on our shelves form a permanent record, and bear testimony to its honourable and useful life'.[98] More than nine decades later, we must agree.

Notes

1. Add MSS 55843, fols 49–51.
2. Morgan 115–18.
3. Although not generally noted for warmth, Morley praised Macmillan extravagantly in his *Recollections* (New York: Macmillan, 1917) 1: 34–5; earlier, he told Charles Graves that Macmillan was 'his "earliest and his greatest benefactor"' (Graves 408). Twenty years' worth (1874–94) of letters from Morley to Craik preserved in the first of three volumes of Supplementary Macmillan Papers in the British Library's Macmillan Archive (Add MSS 61894) are most cordial. Certainly Morley did not hesitate to take Craik into his confidence regarding his frequent financial embarrassments, and on one such occasion, six years before he assumed the editorship of the *Magazine*, he made it clear that there was no love lost between him and the man who then occupied that position: George Grove had refused to accept Morley's 'An Address to Some Miners' because he believed 'that it sets class against class'. Writing to Craik on 30 January 1877, Morley conceded that the article as submitted was probably inappropriate for 'your respectable public', 'and of course I would not allow Grove to alter a syllable of it, the more especially as the criticism with which he was good enough to favour me on the matter was childishly absurd' (fols 5–6). In the same letter Morley told Craik that he needed, almost immediately, the £75 that the 'Address' would have brought in, and Craik came through within a day, eliciting Morley's effusive thanks. 'You treat me a hundred times better than I deserve – and I am almost sorry to take the cheque' (fols 7–8). Accepting Grove's advice 'to crow on [his] own dung-hill', Morley ran the article in the periodical that he himself was then editing, the *Fortnightly Review*, in March 1877.
4. See, for example, Morley's *Recollections* 1: 85–91; Hirst 1: 63–87; and John Gross, *The Rise and Fall of the Man of Letters* (London: Weidenfeld and Nicolson, 1969) 99–102.

5. Morgan 101–18. Hirst is even less informative about Morley's editorship of *Macmillan's* (2: 178–81).

6. 'John Morley', *American Scholar* 51 (Summer 1982): 403. Also see R.G. Cox, 'The Reviews and Magazines', *From Dickens to Hardy*, ed. Boris Ford (Harmondsworth: Penguin, 1958) 192–3.

7. *John Morley: Liberal Intellectual in Politics* (Oxford: Clarendon Press, 1968) 123.

8. *The Personal Papers of Lord Rendel*, ed. F.E. Hamer (London: Benn, 1931) 222.

9. In a sense, this feature harked back literally to the beginning of *Macmillan's Magazine*: its first number, in November 1859, had led off with a comprehensive account of 'Politics of the Present, Foreign and Domestic', by David Masson, but there were no immediate successors to Masson's article.

10. 49 (1884): 312–13.

11. 50 (1884): 391.

12. 51 (1885): 392.

13. 52 (1885): 240.

14. 51 (1885): 447.

15. 18 (1868): 237.

16. 51 (1885): 242, 250.

17. Quoted in Janet Penrose Trevelyan, *The Life of Mrs. Humphry Ward* (London: Constable, 1923) 42.

18. Macmillan and Co. also brought out Ward's first novel for adults, *Miss Bretherton*, three years later. John Sutherland discusses the genesis of *Miss Bretherton* and its acceptance by Macmillan and Co. as a book (Morley apparently deemed it unsuitable for serialization in the *Magazine*), as well as its connections with Vernon Lee's *Miss Brown* and Henry James's *The Tragic Muse*, in 'Miss Bretherton, Miss Brown, and Miss Rooth', *Victorian Fiction: Writers, Publishers, Readers* (New York: St Martin's Press, 1995) 133–50. Ward's next novel, *Robert Elsmere* (1888), which unlike its two predecessors was a great popular success, was published by Smith, Elder, rather than by Macmillan and Co., under complicated circumstances succinctly described by Sutherland in 'Macmillans and *Robert Elsmere*', *Notes and Queries* ns 34 (1987): 47–48.

19. Ward's two-volume translation of Amiel's *Journal* was published by Macmillan and Co. in 1885, the year after her review of the French edition had appeared in the *Magazine*; it was praised by her Uncle Matthew in *Macmillan's* in September 1887 – a unique instance of such literary incest in this periodical. A regular reader of, as well as a frequent contributor to, the *Magazine*, Arnold not unnaturally kept an avuncular eye on her work. About her first *Macmillan's* piece, 'The Poem of the Cid' (October 1871), he was quite candid, writing to Grove that the 'paper was clever and well informed, but too *smart*: a common fault with young writers at present' (*The Letters of Matthew Arnold* 4, ed. Cecil Y. Lang [Charlottesville: University Press of Virginia, 2000] 61); he asked his brother Thomas, her father, to '[t]ell her from me, an old and jaded man of letters, that her style showed too much of a determination *de se faire vif*; one should never *try* to be vif, but leave it to the subject to animate the style in the proper places' (70).

20. 52 (1885): 134.

21. 52 (1885): 17.
22. The average number of poems per issue was much higher under Masson (1.8) and Grove (1.2). See my article 'Poetry in *Macmillan's Magazine*: A Preliminary Report', *VPR* 23 (1990): 56–60.
23. Add MSS 55417, fols 1113 and 1156; Add MSS 55418, fols 1085 and 1138.
24. Add MSS 55418, fols 984 and 960; Add MSS 55419, fol. 1182.
25. Add MSS 55415, fols 1371 and 1369.
26. In December of the following year, Fawcett was the subject of Leslie Stephen's sole contribution to *Macmillan's* while Morley served as editor, the obituary article 'Henry Fawcett: In Memoriam'.
27. Add MSS 55416, fols 881, 1006, 663 and 83.
28. Regular readers of *Macmillan's* would have encountered Turgenev in the *Magazine* before Morley became editor: Charles Edward Turner's translation of 'Sketches and Reminiscences by Ivan Turgenieff' appeared there, in August 1881, as did an article by Turner, 'Tourgenieff's Novels as Interpreting the Political Movement in Russia', in April 1882. Shortly after Morley's time, in May 1886, the *Magazine* ran Turgenev's 'A Fire at Sea'; the *Wellesley Index* identifies the translator of that sketch as Oscar Wilde (1: 625). Yet *Macmillan's* was hardly a pioneer in bringing Turgenev to the attention of monolingual British readers: *Fraser's Magazine* and *Household Words* had printed pieces by him as early as the mid-1850s, followed by *Temple Bar*, *London Society* and *All the Year Round* in the 1860s and 1870s; several book-length translations of Turgenev were published in Edinburgh and London between 1855 and 1878. See Royal A. Gettmann, *Turgenev in England and America*. Illinois Studies in Language and Literature 27, 2 (Urbana: University of Illinois Press, 1941) 187.
29. Add MSS 55418, fols 920 and 921; Add MSS 55419, fol. 722.
30. Dale Kramer has done the most thorough job conceivable of studying the complicated evolution of Hardy's text. See his two-part 'Revisions and Vision: Thomas Hardy's *The Woodlanders*', *Bulletin of the New York Public Library* 75 (1971): 195–230 and 248–82; and his critical edition of the novel (Oxford: Clarendon Press, 1981). Also see Philip Gaskell, *From Writer to Reader: Studies in Editorial Method* (Oxford: Clarendon Press, 1978) 196–212.
31. Kramer 'Revisions' 201.
32. *The Woodlanders*, ed. Kramer 428.
33. Letter in the Dorset County Museum, quoted in Kramer 'Revisions' 207. In the same letter, Morris implied that no one had as yet complained about any 'offence against morality' in *The Woodlanders*, but by April 1887 he did hear from at least one upset female reader, speaking for herself and 'other mothers', who felt strongly that Hardy's story was 'certainly not fit to be printed in a high-toned periodical and to be put into the hands of pure-minded English girls' (quoted in Nowell-Smith 130 and 131).
34. Kramer 'Revisions' 213 and 230.
35. Dorset County Museum; quoted in Michael Millgate, *Thomas Hardy: His Career as a Novelist* (New York: St Martin's Press, 1994) 284–6.
36. See *Thomas Hardy: The Critical Heritage*, ed. R.G. Cox (London: Routledge and Kegan Paul, 1970) xxvii–xxxii, 178–221.

37. *Quarterly Review* 174 (April 1892): 319–26.
38. Morris's earliest, anonymous, published comment on Hardy had appeared a decade and a half earlier. Reviewing some 'Christmas Books' in the *Times* of 22 December 1875, he devoted a paragraph to *Under the Greenwood Tree*, presumably inspired by a new edition of that 1872 novel. Morris did call it 'a pretty little story' but could not resist engaging in some characteristically feline sarcasm over Hardy's subtitle, 'A Rural Painting of the Dutch School' (6).
39. 61 (1890): 316, 317, 318.
40. A similar question about Morris's qualifications as a reader for Macmillan and Co. was raised by Charles Morgan. Alluding to his 'anti-realistic bias', Morgan mentioned 'opinions by Mowbray Morris written with a violence that men do not use except subconsciously in defence of a closed mind' (144–445). On the other hand, Frederick Macmillan told A.V. Baillie 'that during all the years he had read for the firm they had never published a book on his recommendation which had failed, nor published one against his advice which had succeeded' (Albert Victor Baillie, *My First Eighty Years* [London: John Murray, 1951] 53).
41. I borrow the word 'buck' from a younger contributor to *Macmillan's*, Stephen Gwynn, who called Morris that in his *Experiences of a Literary Man* (London: Thornton Butterworth, 1926) 152.
42. Charles Whibley, 'Musings without Method', *Blackwood's Edinburgh Magazine* 190 (August 1911): 276. A.V. Baillie called Morris's clothing 'reminiscent of the days of the dandies'; Morris's 'tall hat', Baillie added, 'had the curl of the brim that one sees in the hats worn by D'Orsay and his friends; he had whiskers, a moustache and an imperial, also in the same earlier fashion' (Baillie 52).
43. Whibley 275.
44. See *The History of 'The Times': The Tradition Established: 1841–1884* (London: *Times*, 1939) 497 and 500.
45. Some of this work for the *Times* appeared in book form: *Essays in Dramatic Criticism* (London: Remington, 1882).
46. Add MSS 55843, fols 97, 166, 343, 362 and 411; Add MSS 55844, fol. 587; Add MSS 55445, fol. 1095; Add MSS 55450, fol. 1251; Add MSS 55451, fol. 2514; Add MSS 55454, fol. 1001; Add MSS 55462, fol. 1701; Add MSS 55468, fol. 298; Add MSS 55844, fols 643–44; Add MSS 55473, fol. 1806.
47. *Social and Diplomatic Memories: 1884–1893* (London: Edwin Arnold, 1922) 16.
48. Whibley 275.
49. *Something of Myself and Other Autobiographical Writings*, ed. Thomas Pinney (Cambridge: Cambridge University Press, 1990) 48.
50. 'A Ballad of the King's Mercy' (November 1889), 'The Incarnation of Krishna Mulvaney' (December 1889), 'A Ballad of East and West' (December 1889), 'The Head of the District' (January 1890), 'The Ballad of the Last Suttee' (January 1890), 'The Ballad of the King's Jest' (February 1890), 'The Courting of Dinah Shadd' (March 1890), 'The Man Who Was' (April 1890), 'Without Benefit of Clergy' (June 1890), 'On Greenhow Hill' (September 1890), 'His Private Honour' (October 1891) and 'My Lord the Elephant' (January 1893). Kipling was paid £80, a considerably higher fee than the *Magazine*'s going rate, for the last of these stories

(Add MSS 55464, fol. 516). It is probable that he published no more work in *Macmillan's* because the *Magazine* in its increasingly straitened circumstances could no longer afford him.

51. *Rudyard Kipling: His Life and Work*. Revised edition (London: Macmillan, 1978) 179. Noting that the text of the 'Ballad' as printed in *Macmillan's* was different from later published versions of the poem, Brian Gasser wondered if it had been 'edited by Mowbray Morris before publication' in the *Magazine* ('Rudyard Kipling's "Ballad of East and West"', *Notes and Queries* ns 26 [1979]: 322–3).

52. See John William Fortescue's *Author and Curator* (Edinburgh: Blackwood, 1933) 83–4.

53. In his 'Mowbray Morris: A Late Victorian Man of Letters' (*A Biographer's Notebook* [New York: Macmillan, 1950] 162–205), Hector Bolitho gives only Baillie's initials, A.V.B., but Baillie's *My First Eighty Years*, in which he speaks warmly of his friendship with Morris, leaves no doubt about the identification. (A briefer version of Bolitho's essay, 'A Late Victorian Man of Letters', appeared in *Blackwood's Magazine* in January 1950.) Baillie told Bolitho that his first meeting with Morris took place when Morris came to Cambridge to see a student production of the *Eumenides* of Aeschylus 'in my fourth year – yes, it was 1886' (166). In view of the fact that Morris's review of that production appeared in *Macmillan's* in January 1886, this visit to Cambridge must have occurred late in 1885 rather than in 1886.

54. Bolitho gives no year for this letter but implies that it dates from 1887. This must be wrong: not only did Kipling's poem appear in *Macmillan's* in the later year, but Morris also mentions John Morley's *Walpole* as a new book in the same letter, and it too was published in 1889.

55. Quoted in Bolitho, *Biographer's Notebook* 204. (All future references to Bolitho in these endnotes will be to this text.) More of Morris's condemnation of Burne-Jones is quoted on 178–9; other letters to Baillie contain sardonic comments on such eminent Victorians as George Eliot, Disraeli, Longfellow, 'that wild and whirling ASS Gladstone' (180), John Singer Sargent and Tennyson. Morris's dismay at nineteenth-century 'progress' is evident throughout this fascinating correspondence, never more so than in his appalled reaction to the installation of electricity in the Temple Church: 'The electric light in a church built seven hundred years ago! There is no people but the English could have done such a thing' (195).

56. Bolitho 175.

57. Bolitho 204.

58. During the Morris years James contributed two major review-essays: on Emerson (December 1887), occasioned by the 1887 publication by Macmillan and Co. of James Elliot Cabot's *A Memoir of the Life of Ralph Waldo Emerson*, and on Flaubert (March 1893), which took as its point of departure the appearance of the fourth volume of the Frenchman's *Correspondance*, edited by Caroline Commanville (Paris: Corbeil, 1893); as well as two novellas: *The Reverberator* (February to July 1888) and *Lord Beauprey* (April to June 1892).

59. See Moore *passim*.

60. Moore 122–3.

61. Laurel Brake has seen a connection between the appearance of Harry Quilter's September 1880 attack on aestheticism in *Macmillan's* and Pater's

non-appearance in its pages during the next five years but does call the *Magazine* his 'principal place of publication in the 1880s' (*Walter Pater* [London: Northcote, 1994] 32). Seiler traces the relations between Pater and Macmillan and Co. (and *Macmillan's Magazine*); on this evidence, Morris seems not to have played much of a role in Pater's transactions with the firm. Quilter's article and its consequences are discussed by Lorna Mosk Packer in 'William Michael Rossetti and the Quilter Controversy: "The Gospel of Intensity"' *VS* 7 (1963): 170–83.

62. Bolitho 183.

63. The one exception was Pater's review of Jules Lemaître's *Sérénus: Histoire d'un martyr: Contes d'autrefois et d'aujourdhui* (Paris: Lamerre, 1886) in the November 1887 number.

64. It was joined in *Appreciations* by another *Macmillan's Magazine* essay, 'On Love's Labours Lost' (December 1885). Pater's 'M. Feullet's "La Morte"' (December 1886) was first collected in the second edition of *Appreciations* (1890). Other *Macmillan's* papers by Pater were reprinted in *Imaginary Portraits* (1887), *Plato and Platonism* (1893) and *Greek Studies* (1895): 'Sebastian Van Storck' (March 1886), 'Denys L'Auxerrois' (October 1886) and 'Duke Carl of Rosenmold' (May 1887) in the first of these; 'A Chapter on Plato' (May 1892) in the second; and 'The "Bacchanals" of Euripides' (May 1889) and 'Hippolytus Veiled: A Study from Euripides' (August 1890) in the third. For a discussion of the possible significance of what material Pater chose to include in and exclude from the first edition of *Appreciations* see Brake 1994, 72–8.

65. This edition of *Gaston* was prepared for the press by Charles L. Shadwell. It consisted of seven chapters, the first five from *Macmillan's*, the sixth from Pater's manuscript, and the seventh revised by Pater himself from his 'Giordano Bruno', originally published in the August 1889 *Fortnightly Review*. Also see *Gaston de Latour: The Revised Text*, ed. Gerald Monsman (Greensboro, NC: ELT Press, 1995).

66. Dorothy Richardson Jones, *'King of Critics': George Saintsbury, 1845–1933, Critic, Journalist, Historian, Professor* (Ann Arbor: University of Michigan Press, 1992) 44, 131.

67. Birrell sent Morris his 'The Office of Literature' in January 1886. Calling it 'a charming little essay', Morris wrote to Baillie on the 18th that 'I have only had time to glance at it, but a delightful allusion at the end to our great Sir Walter [Scott, a special favorite of Morris's] caught my eye and my heart at once' (Bolitho 169). It came out in the March number, the first of a half-dozen pieces by Birrell to be published in *Macmillan's* during the next four years.

68. *R.D. Blackmore* (Boston: Twayne, 1979) 4.

69. *Perlycross* was published in book form by Sampson Low, Marston in 1894. The Macmillan Archive contains some acrimonious letters from Frederick Macmillan to Morris and 'that confounded fellow Marston' about the timing of this three-volume edition, which Macmillan and Morris did not want to come out until the serial finished its run in the *Magazine* (Add MSS 55493, fols 741, 742, 765, 816, 1042, 1148 and 1153). The firm's correspondence about *Perlycross* with Blackmore himself was considerably more restrained (Add MSS 54965, fols 88–9; Add MSS 55443, fols 871–2). Blackmore, incidentally, received £600 'for the serial use of the story' (Add MSS 55443, fol. 816).

70. Add MSS 55262, fol. 124. Also see Add MSS 55457, fols 2501 and 2576; Add MSS 55458, fols 141 and 335; Add MSS 554896, fol. 7; Add MSS 55262, fol. 65; and Add MSS 55459, fol. 1697. For further epistolary documentation, see Randolph S. Churchill, *Winston S. Churchill: Companion Volume 1. Part 2: 1896–1900* (Boston: Houghton Mifflin, 1967) *passim*. The book version of *Savrola* was published by Longmans, Green in 1900. Keith Aldritt provides a succinct account of the composition, reception and significance of *Savrola* in his *Churchill the Writer* (London: Hutchinson, 1992) 27–32. Macmillan and Co. published Winston Churchill's life of his father, *Lord Randolph Churchill*, in 1906 and issued several of his later books in the 1940s; see Nowell-Smith 256–60.
71. Add MSS 55467, fol. 1142.
72. Macmillan and Co. became Tennyson's publisher in 1884 and issued five volumes of Meredith's poetry during the 1880s and early 1890s.
73. Add MSS 55420, fols 787, 788 and 790; Add MSS 55424, fols 1064–5.
74. *The Letters of George Meredith*, ed. C.L. Cline (Oxford: Clarendon Press, 1970) 2: 1057.
75. Bolitho 198.
76. William S. Peterson, *Victorian Heretic: Mrs. Humphry Ward's* Robert Elsmere (Leicester: Leicester University Press, 1976) 90.
77. His own *Tales of the Spanish Main* was published by Macmillan and Co. in 1901.
78. 53 (1886): 278.
79. Add MSS 55456, fol. 1588.
80. Add MSS 55456, fols 124–5.
81. 59 (1889): 243.
82. *The American Negro* was first published by the American Macmillan Co. For a fascinating treatment of its path to publication and the hostile reception it was given in the United States, see John David Smith, *Black Judas: William Hannibal Thomas and* The American Negro (Athens, GA: University of Georgia Press, 2000).
83. George Macmillan wrote Morris on 5 March 1906 that there had been two complaints about Hyatt's article and suggested that, in response, 'perhaps you may care to consider whether you would be prepared to insert a moderate statement from the missionary point of view, provided of course that it met with your approval when written' (Add MSS 55482, fol. 674). A second letter from Macmillan to Morris written four days later makes it clear that Morris did not care to do so (Add MSS 55482, fol. 837).
84. To be sure, other *Macmillan's* articles dealing with women during this period did not advance the feminist agenda that had characterized the *Magazine* a generation earlier. H.R. Tottenham's 'A Mixed University' (April 1888) argued against granting female students at Cambridge the right to qualify for degrees. E.P. Wylde's 'Can Women Combine?' (June 1890) opposed the unionization of female workers. And Emily C. Cook's rather innocuous 'On the Education of Girls' (May 1893) had to do with child-rearing in the home rather than formal schooling.
85. 53 (1886): 264.
86. 74 (1896): 449.
87. Among those who have been interested in this remarkable woman in the very different circumstances of the twentieth century Hannah Arendt was

by all odds the most distinguished. Her *Rahel Varnhagen: Lebensgeschichte einer deutschen Jüdin* was virtually complete when Hitler came to power in 1933 but not published until 1959 (Munich: Piper). A translation of Arendt's book by Richard and Clara Winston, *Rahel Varnhagen, The Life of a Jewish Woman*, appeared in 1974 (New York: Harcourt Brace Jovanovich), and the 'first complete edition', edited by Liliane Weissberg, came out in 1997 (Baltimore: Johns Hopkins University Press). Neither Arendt nor her editor includes Quekett in her bibliography.

88. 64 (1892): 76.
89. A different kind of elegiac note was struck in *Macmillan's* by W.P. James's 'A New Pipe-Plot' (October 1894), his last-ditch defense of the disappearing three-volume novel, a form which had been intimately connected during its mid-Victorian heyday with both the *Magazine* and Macmillan and Co. For an illuminating discussion of James's article and its context see Guinevere L. Griest's *Mudie's Circulating Library and the Victorian Novel* (Bloomington: Indiana University Press, 1970) 197–8.
90. Add MSS 55454, fol. 1618.
91. These calculations are to be found in the *Magazine*'s Pay Sheets: Add MSS 55999, fol. 212.
92. See, for example, Add MSS 54794, fols 57–8; Add MSS 55456, fol. 197; Add MSS 55460, fol. 1790; Add MSS 55472, fols 172, 193 and 207; and Add MSS 55478, fols 740, 953 and 964.
93. See, for example, Add MSS 55475, fols 66, 332, 422 and 460.
94. *Longman's Magazine* 46 (1905): 578. Patricia Anderson has traced the rise of Victorian illustrated periodicals, which accelerated during the last two decades of the nineteenth century 'as techniques for creating halftone prints became more sophisticated' (130), in her chapter on 'Illustration' in *Victorian Periodicals and Victorian Society*, ed. J. Don Vann and Rosemary T. VanArsdel (Toronto: University of Toronto Press, 1994) 127–42. Ironically, Macmillan and Co.'s *English Illustrated Magazine* had played a prominent role in undermining the position of print-only periodicals like *Longman's* – and *Macmillan's*. See Simon Houfe, *Fin de Siècle: The Illustrators of the 'Nineties* (London: Barrie & Jenkins, 1992) 10; and David Reed, *The Popular Magazine in Britain and the United States 1880–1960* (Toronto: University of Toronto Press, 1997) 95.
95. Add MSS 54794, fol. 92.
96. Add MSS 54794, fol. 88.
97. Add MSS 54794, fols 135 and 139; Add MSS 55488, fol. 139.
98. Francis 142.

Index

For Product Safety Concerns and Information please contact our EU
representative GPSR@taylorandfrancis.com
Taylor & Francis Verlag GmbH, Kaufingerstraße 24, 80331 München, Germany

www.ingramcontent.com/pod-product-compliance
Ingram Content Group UK Ltd.
Pitfield, Milton Keynes, MK11 3LW, UK
UKHW021439080625
459435UK00011B/313